The
Language
of Silence

The
Language
of Silence

On the Unspoken and the Unspeakable in Modern Drama

Leslie Kane

Rutherford • Madison • Teaneck
Fairleigh Dickinson University Press
London and Toronto: Associated University Presses

Associated University Presses
440 Forsgate Drive
Cranbury, N. J. 08512

Associated University Presses
25 Sicilian Avenue
London WC1A 2QH, England

Associated University Presses
2133 Royal Windsor Drive
Unit 1
Mississauga, Ontario
Canada L5J 1K5

Library of Congress Cataloging in Publication Data

Kane, Leslie, 1945–
  The language of silence.

  Bibliography: p.
  Includes index.
  1. Drama—20th century—History and criticism.
2. Silence in literature. I. Title.
PN1861.K33   1984   809.2'9353   82-49321
ISBN 0-8386-3187-8

Printed in the United States of America

Contents

To Pamela and David

Acknowledgments

I wish to thank those who gave generously of their time and advice: Tom Bishop, Professor of French at New York University, for his encouragement and the benefit of his expertise; Anna Balakian, Professor of Comparative Literature at New York University, for her careful reading of an early draft; Ben Nelson, Professor of English at Fairleigh Dickinson University, for his inspiring enthusiasm and invaluable criticism.

To George Steiner I acknowledge a special debt: his lucid analysis of the retreat from the word in twentieth century literature has profoundly influenced my thoughts on the function of a language of silence in modern drama. In addition, I am indebted to New York University for a Penfield Research Fellowship.

I am especially grateful to my children, Pamela and David, for their unqualified support, their continuing patience and their marvelous backrubs. Finally, I wish to thank my husband, Stu, for freeing me from domestic burdens to devote time to writing, for sharing problems as well as progress, and for sustaining me with a love that encourages me to grow.

I wish to thank the following publishers for having given me permission to quote from published works:

Coward, McCann & Geoghegan, Inc. for permission to quote from *The Zoo Story* by Edward Albee. Copyright © 1959 by Edward Albee. Reprinted by permission of Coward, McCann and Geoghegan, Inc.

From *The American Dream* by Edward Albee. Copyright © 1960 and 1961 by Edward Albee. Reprinted by permission of Coward, McCann and Geoghegan, Inc.

Editions Minuit, from *En attendant Godot* by Samuel Beckett, copyright © 1952.

Grove Press for permission to quote from *The Caretaker and The Dumb Waiter* by Harold Pinter. Reprinted by permission of Grove Press, Inc. *The Caretaker* copyright © by Theatre Promotions Ltd.; *The Dumb Waiter* copyright © 1960 by Harold Pinter.

Introduction

Originating in oratory, Western drama has attempted to come to terms with the world's mysteries and multiplicities through dialogue. Traditionally the dominant element in drama, dialogue spoken by highly articulate characters conveys the content: the motivations of characters, antecedents of the plot, and thematic concerns of the playwright.

Within the last eighty years several dramatists, merging form and content, have increasingly employed silence in the dramatic spectacle. In a conscious retreat from the word, considered by many to be an inferior, limited, devalued, and prostituted mode of communication, these playwrights have chosen to communicate through the multidimensional, nonverbal expression of silence. Thus speech, the characterizing signature of humanity, has been superseded by silence to communicate unspoken experience beyond the limitations of human consciousness, such as fear, longing, and death, as well as unspeakable experience beyond the comprehension of humanity such as the dehumanizing or bestial.

The seeds for this altered vision of the drama are to be found in the shifting ground of the late nineteenth century—the nihilism, uncertainty, alienation, and despair which emanated from the world of scientific, political, and social upheaval. Mallarmé's exquisite sensitivity to the dichotomy between the word and the world is reflected in the drama of Maurice Maeterlinck and Anton Chekhov, where turbulence, doubt, and helplessness are conveyed through oblique dialogue and silence employed as thematic, structural, and dramatic statement.

The uncertainty which pervaded the fin de siècle has been intensified in the twentieth century by psychology, scientific technology, and global conflagration. Ours is an age of great contradiction. Psychology has both freed our passions and relentlessly tied us to the irrational, scientific technology has immeasurably improved the quality of our lives and extended our terrestrial boundaries while implementing the means of our total annihilation, and global conflagrations have made the world safe for freedom but revealed to us the terrible face of our bestiality.

Joseph Wood Krutch contends that to be modern is to be different from anyone who lived before by perceiving the irrational as the dominant mode of life.[1] Man's confrontation with himself, his limitations, his inhumanity, and the threat of his annihilation, all are reflected in modern art which Ortega y Gasset terms "dehumanized," divorced from traditional art and value systems.[2] One of the most fundamental of these traditional art systems assumes that literature is housed in language.[3] But for a significant number of contemporary playwrights, the house has become a prison constraining the artist's efforts to convey the quintessence of human experience: uncertainty, incompleteness, inadequacy, impermanence. Preferring the freedom of silence, these artists seem to concur with Ionesco, for whom, though not everything is unsayable in words, "ce qui est à dire, ce qui est existence et non chose, c'est seulement cela qui ne veut pas être dit. L'essentiel."[4]

Linguistic devaluation and dehumanization, according to George Steiner, have directly contributed to the political inhumanity of the twentieth century. He argues that the disasters of world wars, the barbarism and lunacy of 1914–18 and the Nazi holocaust, can be neither adequately grasped nor described in words: these unspeakable events quite literally exceed the boundaries of language because, inhuman, they defy verbal expression.[5] Jean-Jacques Bernard, whose "Theatre of Silence" follows World War I, and Beckett, Pinter, and Albee, whose post–World War II dramas are distinguished by their shocking retreat from the word, yield to the temptation and authority of silence to express the unspoken and the unspeakable.

This is not to suggest that the majority of modern playwrights are characterized by their reliance upon nonverbal communication to convey uncertainty, incompleteness, and existential fear. Indeed, the opposite is true. But silent response, which emerged in the 1890s as a viable dramatic technique, exists to a lesser or greater extent in the body of work of several of the most important modern dramatists.

Reflecting a climate of incertitude, the theatre of Maeterlinck, Chekhov, Jean-Jacques Bernard, Beckett, Pinter, and Albee is distinctive in its repression of explicit expression and continuous, conceptual dialogue and the elevated status it gives silence. Intimating that words do not adequately express feelings, effect action, or authentically communicate personal and global disintegration, these dramatists convey ineffable and inexplicable experience through elliptical, disjunctive speech and evocative silences.

Whereas ambiguity, indistinctness, and opacity are generally considered liabilities of discursive symbolism, impeding communication, they are the assets that render nonverbal symbolism a perfect medium for revealing the multiplicity of human responses antithetic to time, place, and clarity. Suzanne Langer explains that verbal symbolism has a distinct form which requires us to string out our ideas; only thoughts arranged in this manner can be articulated. "An idea," she says, "which does not lend itself to this 'projection' is ineffable, incommunicable by means of words."[6] The fluidity of silence allows the artist to journey to the depths of the psyche, to exteriorize, dramatize, and emphasize what the Symbolists termed *l'état d'âme*. The dumb silence of apathy, the sober silence of solemnity, the fertile silence of awareness, the active silence of perception, the baffled silence of confusion, the uneasy silence of impasse, the muzzled silence of outrage, the expectant silence of waiting, the reproachful silence of censure, the tacit silence of approval, the vituperative silence of accusation, the eloquent silence of awe, the unnerving silence of menace, the peaceful silence of communion, and the irrevocable silence of death illustrate by their unspoken response to speech that experiences exist for which we lack the word.

For the playwrights considered here silence, indicated by ellipses, pauses, and wordless responses, is an intrinsic and indispensable component of the text. I shall examine their disjunctive expression with the intention of showing the multiplicity of silent responses to verbal symbolism, but I shall not limit my study to the absence of language. The retreat from the word encompasses not only nonverbal symbolism, but also many forms of connotative, indirect dramatic expression such as innuendo, intimation, hesitation, reticence, and bivalent speech that implicitly conveys more than it states. To adhere strictly to the commonly accepted, narrow definition of *silence* as the absence of speech would eliminate these diverse forms of implicit expression as elements of a language of silence: truly indicative of an altered dramatic vision and the repression of certain types of communication which we expect in traditional theatre, they would be classified inaccurately as speech. Therefore, for this study I have expanded the definition of silence beyond its familiar limitations in order to include not only the absence of speech as indicated by ellipses, pauses, and silences but various forms of connotative, indirect expression. When I refer to *silence*, I am employing the term in its broadest sense, encompassing both the absence of speech and implicit expression.

My purpose is to study silence as a multidimensional mode of expression intentionally chosen by Maeterlinck, Chekhov, Jean-Jacques Bernard, Beckett, Pinter, and Albee to convey both structure and statement, because although the oeuvre of individual playwrights has received extensive criticism, the development of a language of silence has been largely ignored. Adopting a chronological and comparative approach to the work of these dramatists should make it possible to ascertain the nature and idiosyncratic function of the unspoken and the unspeakable as distinctive artistic expression; to compare techniques as they are developed, refined, and employed to achieve similar or different effects; and finally to underscore the scope and extensive use of a language of silence which directly, dramatically, and implicitly reflects doubt and disjunction.

My method will be to examine one representative text by each author in order to isolate pauses incorporated into duologues or silences surrounding them to determine the qualitative nature of these silences and their thematic content. I also will pay attention to ellipses, pauses, and silences, as well as to the role of the inarticulate and/or mute. Essentially this study will reflect Jean-Paul Sartre's definition of silence:

> Le silence même se définit par rapport aux mots, comme la pause, en mu-
> ·sique, reçoit son sens de groupes de notes qui l'entournent. Ce silence est un

moment du language; se taire ce n'est pas être muet, c'est refuser de parler, donc parler encore.[7]

If, as Sartre suggests, "on n'est pas écrivain pour avoir choisi de dire certaines choses mais pour avoir choisi de les dire d'une certain façon," then when a writer chooses to remain silent on an aspect of the world, the reader and audience have the right, indeed the pressing need, to question why.[8] In this age of relative truth, I do not presume to know the answer. Neither do I presume to illuminate the mysterious nor define the ineffable that characterizes silent response. Rather, it is my intention to focus attention upon the increasing tendency of the drama, the most social and communal of the arts, to refuse to speak about man's relationship to himself, his world, and his God.

NOTES

1. Joseph Wood Krutch, *"Modernism" in Modern Drama* (New York: Russell and Russell, 1953), 5.
2. José Ortega y Gasset, "La deshumanización del arte," in *La deshumanización del arte e ideas sobre la Novela* (Madrid: Revista de Occidente, 1925).
3. George Steiner, *After Babel: Aspects of Language and Translation* (New York: Oxford University Press, 1975), 176.
4. Eugène Ionesco, *Journal en miettes* (Paris: Mercure de France, 1967), 123.
5. For an extensive study of the interrelationship of political inhumanity and the retreat from the word, see George Steiner, "Silence and the Poet" and "The Hollow Miracle," in *Language and Silence: Essays on Language, Literature and the Inhuman* (New York: Antheneum, 1976), 36–54, 95–109.
6. Suzanne Langer, *Philosophy in a New Key: A Study in the Symbolism of Reason, Rite and Art*, 3d ed. (Cambridge, Mass.: Harvard University Press, 1942), 93. See chap. 4, "Discursive Forms and Presentational Forms," 79–102, for an analysis of discursive and nondiscursive symbolism.
7. Jean-Paul Sartre, *Qu'est-ce que la littérature?* (Paris: Editions Gallimard, 1948), 32.
8. Ibid.

1
Speech and Silence

Ludwig Wittgenstein concludes *Tractatus* with the now-famous proposition: "What we cannot speak about we must pass over in silence."[1] For the playwrights under consideration all that is consigned to silence informs by its consonant or contrapuntal relationship to the text. In her classic study *Feeling and Form*, Langer points out that in drama "we do not have to find out what is significant; the selection has been made—whatever is there is significant, and it is not too much to be surveyed *in toto*."[2] We must assume that the silent response of the characters and the playwrights in modern theatre has specific meaning and purpose that in concert with the text is the content.

Despite its essential presence in these plays, indefinite, enigmatic silence continues to elude and baffle critics who fail to recognize its necessity and its nature. In his study of Harold Pinter's plays, Austin Quigley confronts what he terms "the Pinter problem," but it is a problem shared by all dramatists who employ silence as an integral element in the dramatic spectacle. Quigley maintains that literary critics continue to view dialogue as a contrast between language and "something else," and that unable to pin down this elusive something else, they confound the linguistic dilemma by assuming that that which is hidden is more profound, unanalyzed because it is unanalyzable.[3] Basic to my analysis of silent response in modern theatre is the assumption that silence is not absent from the text, neutral within the text, nor more profound than the text. In the play, as in life, silence is a moment in language.

Wittgenstein, more than anyone else in the twentieth century, has called our attention to the fact that speech is a social game involving mutual intelligibility.[4] According to him, it is through "language games" continually revised by a complicated network of relationships overlapping and crisscrossing that we accomplish the activities of giving orders, describing objects, reporting events, speculating and formulating hypotheses, fabricating stories, asking, thanking, cursing, and praying. Of central importance is Wittgenstein's "thread spinning" theory, in which he suggests that words, as well as sentences, have neither normal, fixed functions nor a defined range of application and meaning. Language is characterized by its multiplicity of responses and inherent plurality.[5]

Peter Farb, in *Word Play: What Happens When People Talk*, suggests that language games require a minimum of two players, well-defined rules with a goal at stake for both participants, and a social and/or psychological setting which determines both meaning and word choice.[6] He maintains that when two people who are known to each other approach, a duel immediately takes place to determine who will speak first. And when the participants are unknown to each other, one may initiate "sounding" by hurling a direct insult at the opponent to see if he will "play," or engage in a verbal strategy employed to determine social strata and linguistic prowess.[7] Soundings, or "brain battles" as Strindberg termed them, are potentially manipulative. Since speech is characteristically assertive, the more proficient participant commands authority. It is on this basis that Quigley rests his argument that verbal relationships are subject to "verbal negociation" and "verbal imposition."[8]

In social situations we are coerced into response that may take the form of active participation, speech, or passive participation ranging from active listening to silence.[9] Once the respondent chooses speech, he is committing himself not only to a human relationship with the person spoken to but to the existence of the thing spoken about and to a temporal reality in which speech occurs.

Thus language, fixed by syntactical and grammatical relationships, largely composes and segments time. Every speech act, observes Steiner, takes time and occurs *in* time.[10] In addition, speech shares with time the characteristic of irreversibility; the spoken word cannot be retracted. The time-factor of language is crucial. As Stuart Chase explains, Western languages, in particular, using the verb *to be* establish linear temporal equations and space/time relationships *(he was, he is, he will be)* which foster a two-valued linguistic system. The only way to neutralize a spoken word is by denial or contradiction *(this is white; this is not black)*, but denials and contradictions also constitute forward movement in time. The linear temporal equations and the verb *to be*, moreover, encourage clear, denotative and defining structures that establish identity.[11] A respondent may avoid clarity and accomplish circularity in speech, however, by offering alternatives to the thing spoken about by deliberate concealment, misstatement, polysemy, falsehood, or misinformation.[12]

The active listener, like the active speaker, participates in the interrelational language game by forcing the speaker to redefine and refocus his speech. In fact, argues Chase, if more than two people play, the pressure on the speaker increases in an increasing ratio to the number of listeners.[13] We see an example of this in Beckett's *En attendant Godot* when the orator Pozzo recites for his active listeners (distracted would be a more accurate description) Lucky, Didi, and Gogo. When their attention strays, Pozzo demands that they play their roles properly: "Mais soyez donc un peu plus attentifs sinon nous n'arriverons jamais à rien."[14] Completing his monologue on the nature of the twilight, the ham actor once again requests the active participation of his listeners in the language game; and craving acclamation as much as he does "society," as he terms it, Pozzo inquires of his audience, "Comment m'avez-vous trouvé? Bon? Moyen? Passable? Quelconque? Franchement mauvais?" (*Godot*, 52–53). The request for critical evaluation draws blank expressions and silence from Didi, Gogo and, we presume, Lucky.

Silent response to speech, most obvious in the passivity of the reticent or mute observer, characterizes in good part the disjunctive dialogue of the plays under consideration. According to Harold Pinter, one of our most accomplished practitioners of the silent mode, it is in the quiet places that characters are hidden and simultaneously exposed.[15] The grandfather in Maeterlinck's *L'Intruse*, Andrey in Chekhov's *The Three Sisters*, Martine in Bernard's play of the same name, Lucky in Beckett's *En attendant Godot*, Peter in Albee's *The Zoo Story*, and Aston in Pinter's *The Caretaker* are only a few characters in modern drama who are taciturn and inarticulate. Closer scrutiny of the plays reveals that these characters stand outside; their nonparticipation in the speech act symbolizes withdrawal from temporal, spatial, or social reality.

To comprehend their withdrawal and passivity, we must understand the role of silence in language games. Let us turn again to Wittgenstein's linguistic philosophy:

> One might say that the concept "game" is a concept with blurred edges.—But is a blurred concept a concept at all?—"Is an indistinct photograph a picture of a person at all?"—Is it even always an advantage to replace an indistinct picture by a sharp one? Isn't the indistinct one often exactly what we need?[16]

If indistinctness were by nature obscure and silence by nature inexpressive, attempts to define the ineffable would be an exercise in futility. Yet we may learn much by comparing silence to its obverse, speech. Through language—structured, sequential, human, linked to time configuration—man seeks to humanize, define, and control the chaos of phenomenal and psychological reality. Explicit and denotative, language, as noted is interrelational and manipulative whereas silence, neither bound to nor fragmented by time, is ambiguous and suggestive, implicit and connotative. This does not mean that denotative discursive symbolism is typified by its specificity. Conceptual in nature, speech is schematic and general; and hardened into impersonal, fossilized clichés, it proves itself imprecise, obtuse, and obscure, more a hindrance than an aid to genuine communication, more a distortion than a revelation of the complexity of the language of the self. Language, rather than breaking down the walls of isolation, rather than binding man in common understanding, often serves to perpetuate barriers of misunderstanding. Our deepest emotions—our fears, our anxieties, our loneliness, our disillusionment—lie buried beneath layers of repetitious, mundane, routinized, and essentially vacuous trivia.

Whether we concur with Eugène Ionesco that the opacity of speech makes communication nearly impossible in that medium or with George Steiner that the ambiguity in language is its genius, its regenerative potential, or even with Harold Pinter that "speech is a constant strategem to cover nakedness" (and whether we believe that obscurity in speech is the fault of the mode or of man), we cannot avoid the fact that, linguistical by nature, we are frustrated when words that we had assumed conveyed information lose their efficacy and mean-ing.[17] When, for example, Hamm in Beckett's *Fin de partie* questions the mean-ing of the words which Clov employs, the latter violently retorts, "J'emploie les mots que tu m'as appris. S'ils ne veulent plus rien dire apprends-m'en d'autres. Ou laisse-moi me taire."[18]

Silence is repeatedly the response of character and playwright in this century, as it was in the fin de siècle. But of crucial importance in passive language games is that silence, like speech, is interrelational and manipulative. Nonparticipation in the speech act does not constitute nonparticipation in the social act; on the contrary, as Quigley observes, one chooses to remain silent or avoid silence, to control or be controlled.[19] In discursive language games characterized by sound-ing, or verbal dueling, one can go for the jugular, as the following excerpt from Chekhov's *The Sea Gull* illustrates. Madame Arkadin and her son Treplev engage in a verbal battle which rages only until she has obliterated her opponent:

Mme. Arkadin: Decadent!
Treplev: Get away to your charming theatre and act there in your paltry, stupid plays!
Mme. Arkadin: I have never acted in such plays. Let me alone! You are not even capable of writing even a wretched burlesque! You are nothing but a Kiev shopman! living on other people!
Treplev: You miser!
Mme. Arkadin: You ragged beggar! *(Treplev sits down and weeps quietly)* Nonen-tity![20]

A crushed Treplev desists under seige.

Similarly, in Edward Albee's *Who's Afraid of Virginia Woolf?* the Strindberg-ian battle of the sexes is underscored by verbal dueling. Martha jabs at George with "You getting angry, baby?" and "You getting angrier?" but it is George who parries and thrusts with words and ultimately destroys Martha with a poisonous lunge to the quick. Having informed Martha that their son will not be coming home for his birthday, George concludes their verbal confrontation with a controlled and controlling explanation: "Now listen, Martha; listen care-fully. We got a telegram; there was a car accident, and he's dead. POUF! Just like that! Now, how do you like it?"[21] Martha's destruction is reflected in a howl of pain which weakens into a moan of lament for herself and for her imaginary son.

In language games where silence plays a predominant role, on the other hand, the shift of power from one character to another, communicated wordlessly, nearly evanescent, is often exquisitely subtle. In Chekhov's *The Cherry Orchard*, for example, the expectation builds throughout the play that Lopahin will propose marriage to Varya. Varya is expectant, Mme. Ranevsky is expectant, and the audience is expectant. Finally alone together, the couple does not speak of love; Varya speaks about an item she has misplaced and Lopahin chats about business. On the subject of marriage he is silent and Chekhov is silent. Mme.

Ranevsky, camped outside the door, later finds a wilted and weeping Varya and, significantly, mother and daughter are also silent on the subject of marriage (114–15). Similarly, silence in *En attendant Godot* reveals relationship and manipulation. Didi and Gogo discover that Godot's continual nonappearance and silence keep them tied to a place, to each other and to Godot. In a drastically different context, silence is not only manipulative but also maddening in Albee's *The Zoo Story*. Jerry, lacking meaningful human communication, is driven wild by a dog's noninvolvement with him:

> I was so hoping for the dog to be waiting for me. I was . . . well, how would you put it . . . enticed? . . . fascinated? . . . no, I don't think so . . . heart-shatteringly anxious, that's it; I was heart-shatteringly anxious to confront my friend.[22]

But various attempts to appease the beast and encourage response result in "sadness, suspicion and solitary, but free passage" for Jerry, which, as he notes, is much more a loss than a gain.

In silent language games, moreover, the opponent is frequently unnamed and unnameable. Like Davies in Pinter's *The Caretaker*, who literally shadowboxes in the dark with Mick, or Maeterlinck's pilgrims in *Les Aveugles*, who figuratively strike out against Death, we are puppets in the hands of the silent one. The threat of human and cosmic menace and manipulation typically elicits the silent responses of helplessness, complicity, and paralytic fear.

Essentially we may conclude that communication takes place between two or more participants in the language game, whether verbal or nonverbal. Employing silent language games, the playwright may intimate or insinuate interrelation and manipulation without specifically delineating the nature of the relationship or the threat.

Hermetic traditions such as Zen, Taoism, mysticism, and Hasidism have always placed a premium on silent communication, regarding the act of speech as human intervention, presumption, assertion, vulgarization, indeed, blasphemy.[23] Words, bound to temporal configuration, are viewed as the fetters binding man to human reality and restricting his attainment of perfect unification with the One. Because the mystic believes that ultimate Truth lies beyond the fragmentation of time and the frontier of language, meditative silence, intimations, and intuitions are the primary conduits for the transmission of knowledge to the initiate—knowledge which would be distorted or completely destroyed if not shrouded in wordlessness. Ineffability is the quintessence of the mystical experience and its sole expression.[24]

It is ineffability—suggestive, ephemeral, hermetic—which the French Symbolists, most of whom were mystics, adapted to artistic advantage in an orphic poetry signaling a retreat from the word and marking a principal division in the history of Western literature.[25] The clearly traceable pattern of the retreat from the word is, in Steiner's opinion, toward progressive untranslatability because of an unbridgeable chasm between scientific and psychological reality and poetic statement. Darwin, Nietzsche, Freud, Einstein, the Industrial Revolution, and the improved technology which it precipitated, challenged every established view of God, human nature, social organization, and the physical universe. Steiner sees the most decisive challenge to Western intellectual life with its humanistic authority in the submission of successively larger areas of knowledge to the modes and procedures of mathematics.[26] Specifically, "the space-time continuum, the atomic structure of all matter, the wave-particle state of energy"—all illustrate that "in cardinal respects reality now begins *outside* verbal language."[27]

The retreat from the word is startling and disconcerting in late nineteenth-century art—painting, poetry, and drama—all of which rebelled against verbal equivalence and concordance. Rejecting realistic portraiture as inauthentic, impressionism opted for a fleeting, muted, "unfinished" picture of reality, while post-impressionism (anticipating surrealistic "inscapes") preferred to view the objective world through subjective lenses.

The symbolist poet, like their counterparts in the plastic arts, valued subjectivity over objectivity, fluidity over fixity. The ambiguity of indirect communication, the centrality of silence, an affiliation with music, and a prevailing decadent spirit characterize the Symbolists' rejection of language and preference for intimation, correspondence, synesthesia, and suggestion.[28] Whereas Mallarmé orchestrated oracular and enigmatic utterances, indefinite modifiers, and a profusion of negatives to evoke the mysterious and obscure inner reality of nothingness and void, Verlaine created a symphony in gray through simple words and muted tones to suggest the melancholic and contemplative mood of loss and reverie. Recalling Wagner, for whom music was the "language of the senses," Verlaine's "De la musique avant toute chose" was a clarion call to wring the neck of rhetoric and adopt the tonal over the conceptual.[29] Essentially, many felt that the fluid structure of music, with its natural caesura, was the efficacious medium for the communication of ineffable experience.

Of central importance to a discussion of the uses of silence in the dramatic arts is consideration of the effect of symbolist techniques and thematic preoccupations on fin de siècle theatre. So essential is the shaping influence of symbolism and its use of elliptical expression that Maurice Valency maintains in *The Flower and the Castle* that we must credit its orphic poets with the recognition that the irrational is a crucial creative element in art.[30] Ibsen, who Valency believes was a "symbolist before the Symbolists," employed elements of the symbolist school: symbolist imagery, correspondence, dramatic metaphor, cabalistic background, mystery, and hypnotism.[31] His retreat from the word, moreover, was reflected in an innovative dramatic language that was dualistic, simultaneously revealing and concealing character.

Like the author of *The Master Builder*, Strindberg was interested in presenting inner reality characterized by its fluidity and flux. In his famous preface to *Miss Julie* he rejects the fixed concept of character as inauthentic. In an age of transi-

tion, his characters, like the historical period in which they live, will be "vacillating, disintegrated, a blend of old and new." And dialogue, the linguistic
means by which they convey this new blend, will no longer be the "symmetri-
cal, mathematical construction of French dialogue," but a more accurate fac-
simile of the inner ramblings of the mind.[32] The associative structure of this
disjunctive dialogue, like the poetry of Mallarmé, will resemble that of a musical
composition.

Inexplicitness, oblique dialogue fragmented by pauses, and the evocation of
l'état d'âme characterize the drama of Maeterlinck and Chekhov, for whom the
rejection of continuous, conceptual speech is integral to meaning and structure.
Chekhov's and Maeterlinck's contributions to modern drama and their idiosyncratic use of silence will receive attention in chapters devoted to their theatre.
Presently we note that the central role of silence in their fin de siècle drama
reflects an altered perspective on the nature and function of dialogue and dramatic silence. These dramatists do not wish to clarify phenomenal experience,
but rather to dramatize the unintelligibility of that experience.

Krutch reminds us that the late nineteenth century was faced, as no prior
time had been, with experience it could not comprehend. The assertion of
Truth was replaced by Doubt.[33] Hebbel's prototypical hero, Anton, who cries
out in despair and confusion at the conclusion of *Maria Magdelena*, "I don't
understand the world any more," prefigures Mrs. Alving in *Ghosts*, the lost
pilgrims in Maeterlinck's *Les Aveugles*, and Julie in *Miss Julie*, all questors seeking
a direct road to knowledge who are faced with the lamentable fact that they are
wandering in a world they do not recognize and cannot know. In what Una-
muno termed "the tragic sense of life," man finds himself victim to invisible
silent forces which overpower him. Denied absolute certainty or absolute
doubt, he hovers in a gray purgatory of unspoken silence between the extremes.

Thus the drama of the fin de siècle turned more and more to the mode of
silence to convey that which was not understood and could not be articulated:
the invisible, the inexpressible, the unintelligible. Later, even more challenging
to postwar playwrights in our century was how to speak about the unspeakable—that which cannot be verbalized because the experience it would illuminate exceeds the defining act of human consciousness which is speech.
Unspeakable silence is inarticulate witness to and collaborator in inhumanity.

The tendency to incorporate silence increasingly in the dramatic spectacle,
however, is not a phenomenon of the fin de siècle, nor even a reaction to
twentieth-century global hostility. We can go to the well and trace the use of
silence to Greek drama. Aeschylus's taciturn characters Pylades and Cassandra
are significant in their nonverbal presence: an unspoken silence communicates
Pylades' love and support for Orestes, while Cassandra's wall of silence contains
and is ultimately shattered by her unspeakable apocalyptic vision. Sophocles'
masterful application of nonverbal response can be illustrated in *Oedipus Rex* and
Electra. In the former, Jocasta's refusal to respond and remain witness to the
arrival of the old man communicates terror to the expectant chorus; in the latter,

Electra's silent response of assent and communion at the conclusion of the play stands in stark contrast to her loquacity throughout the drama. In Euripides' *Electra* we note the inarticulate response to uncertainty. The disconcerting silence of the poet on the issue of justice wordlessly communicates the playwright's thematic concern.[34]

Similarly, we observe that inarticulate characters, dramatic pauses, and silence play an important role in Shakespearean drama. Cordelia infuriates Lear and King Hamlet's ghost frustrates the prince by refusing, despite coercion and encouragement, to express themselves more fully. The dramatic pause, according to A. C. Bradley in *Shakespearean Tragedy*, was employed to increase and release tension, in good part because Shakespearean drama lacked scenery changes to vary tension and tempo.[35] Pregnant pauses, as in "To be or not to be," keep us hanging in the balance of every word.[36] Of particular relevance to consideration of speech and silence in the dramatic spectacle is Shakespeare's innovative and extensive use of soliloquy. In acts I–IV of *Hamlet*, for example, Prince Hamlet's contemplative, melancholic state, his expectations, his anticipations, his paralyzing doubt, while voiced to the audience, remain unspoken even to his closest associates. In the fifth act, however, soliloquy is notable in its absence. Hamlet's ruminations are consigned to silence; the nonverbal response of reconciliation and recognition finally dignify Hamlet the Dane.

Historically, then, silence has been employed by playwrights to evaluate, censure, or support an act, to indicate manipulative relationships, to increase or release dramatic tension, to make words more significant by their contrast with silent response, to reveal interior states of being, and to make thematic statement. In addition to these traditional functions of nonverbal symbolism, the modern playwright, reducing the role of speech and increasing that of silence, has employed the latter as a metaphor for evanescence and entrapment. He conveys evanescence nonverbally by the contraction of time; the time of life is, then it is not. In what Robert Brustein terms "double time," alternatingly swift and tedious, the playwright contrasts the protracted duration of stasis to the rapid movement of evanescence.[37] In plays of inaction, when nonprogression in language and nonprogression in time, combined with confined settings, underscore the sensation of entrapment, silent response and muteness reinforce the portrait of man as not merely estranged from his world, but entrapped in the hell of the self. As a metaphor of solitary confinement, silence confirms man's inability or unwillingness to relate to others and his concomitant torture by exclusion. Illustrations from *The Cherry Orchard* and *En attendant Godot* suggest that the torture of isolation need not be a direct result of the social situation, but of the human condition. Speech is inadequate to express our deepest emotions, and even the confidences it would impart are rejected. In *The Cherry Orchard* Gaev discourses on nature, but the younger members of the household would prefer, for his benefit and for theirs, that instead of expressing his emotions he were "cannoning off the red" (Chekhov, 88). Similarly, in *En attendant Godot*

Gogo repeatedly attempts to share his nightmare with Didi, but his efforts are to no avail:

> *Gogo:* J'ai fait un rêve.
> *Didi:* Ne le raconte pas!
> *Gogo:* Je rêvais que . . .
> *Didi:* NE LE RACONTE PAS!

(Godot, 19)

The nightmare can and must be suppressed. The unspeakable vision must be silenced, maintaining isolation.

The individual, isolated and imprisoned in a corporeal state and a material world from which he desires escape, was well known to the Symbolists, whose influence is apparent in the drama of Maurice Maeterlinck. The next chapter is concerned with his early static plays, which unleash the fetters of human language and chronicity to reveal the silent night journey of the initiate seeking mystical knowledge and unity beyond the fragmentation of speech.

NOTES

1. Ludwig Wittgenstein, *Tractatus logico-philosophicus*, trans. D. F. Pears and B. F. McGuiness (London: Routledge, 1961), 151.

2. Suzanne Langer, *Feeling and Form* (New York: Charles Scribner's Sons, 1953), 310.

3. See Austin Quigley, *The Pinter Problem* (Princeton, N.J.: Princeton University Press, 1975), for a sensitive study of Pinter's work and for compelling insights on the interrelationships between dialogue and silence. Concerning the issue of criticism of silence, see particularly 14–29.

4. Ludwig Wittgenstein, *Philosophical Investigations*, trans. G. E. M. Anscombe (New York: Macmillan, 1953), 11.

5. Ibid., 31e, 11e.

6. Peter Farb, *Word Play: What Happens When People Talk* (New York: Knopf, 1973), 6.

7. Ibid., 94.

8. Quigley, *The Pinter Problem*, 49.

9. Farb, *Word Play*, 6.

10. George Steiner, *After Babel: Aspects of Language and Translation* (New York: Oxford University Press, 1975), 130.

11. Stuart Chase with Marian Tyler Chase, *Power of Words* (New York: Harcourt, Brace, 1953), 1.

12. Steiner, *After Babel*, 130.

13. Chase and Chase, *Power of Words*, 194.

14. Samuel Beckett, *En attendant Godot* (Paris: Editions de Minuit, 1952), 51 (references hereafter will be to this edition unless otherwise indicated).

15. Harold Pinter, "Between the Lines," speech to the Seventh National Student Drama Festival in Bristol, *Sunday Times* (London), 4 March 1962, 25.

16. Wittgenstein, *Philosophical Investigations*, 34.

17. See the following sources for provocative, divergent views on the nature and function of speech/silence: Eugène Ionesco, *Journal en miettes* (Paris: Mercure de France, 1967), 101; Steiner, *After Babel*, 221–35; Pinter, "Between the Lines," 25.

18. Samuel Beckett, *"Fin de partie" et "Actes sans paroles"* (Paris: Editions de Minuit, 1957), 62 (references hereafter will be to this edition).

19. Quigley, *The Pinter Problem*, 47.

20. Anton Chekhov, *Four Great Plays: The Sea Gull, The Cherry Orchard, The Three Sisters, Uncle Vanya*, trans. Constance Garnett (New York: Modern Library, 1930), 37 (references hereafter will be to this edition unless otherwise indicated).

21. Edward Albee, *Who's Afraid of Virginia Woolf?* (New York: Pocket Books, 1964), 233 (references hereafter will be to this edition unless otherwise indicated).

22. Edward Albee, *"The American Dream" and "The Zoo Story"* (New York: New American Library, 1961), 33–34 (references hereafter will be to this edition unless otherwise indicated).

23. Concerning the prestige accorded silence in Eastern mysticism, see D. T. Suzuki, *Zen Buddhism*, ed. William Barrett (Garden City, N.Y.: Anchor-Doubleday, 1956); Lin Yutang, ed., *The Wisdom of China and India* (New York: Modern Library, 1942), "Laotse, the Book of Tao," 583–624.

24. Alice Borchard Greene, *The Philosophy of Silence* (New York: Richard R. Smith, 1940), 185.

25. For insights into the interrelationship of symbolism and mysticism, as well as the techniques of the Symbolists, see Anna Balakian, *The Symbolist Movement: A Critical Appraisal* (New York: Random House, 1967); Arthur Symons, *The Symbolist Movement in Literature*, rev. ed. (1913; reprint, New York: E. P. Dutton, 1958).

26. George Steiner, *Language and Silence: Essays on Language, Literature and the Inhuman* (New York: Antheneum, 1976), "The Retreat from the Word," 12–35. No summary of his argument does justice to this important essay.

27. Ibid., 17.

28. Balakian, *The Symbolist Movement*, 101.

29. See Richard Wagner, *On Music and Drama: A Compendium of Richard Wagner's Prose Works*, trans. H. Ashton Ellis, ed. Albert Goldman and Evert Sprinchorn (New York: E. P. Dutton, 1964).

30. Maurice Valency, *The Flower and the Castle: An Introduction to Modern Drama* (New York: Macmillan, 1963), 396. Valency argues that the three trends—naturalism, impressionism, and symbolism—which shaped the art of Ibsen and Strindberg, plus Strindberg's expressionism, have shaped the drama of the last fifty years.

31. Ibid., 204.

32. August Strindberg, Preface, *Six Plays of Strindberg*, trans. Elizabeth Sprigge (Garden City, N.Y.: Anchor-Doubleday, 1955), 65.

33. Joseph Wood Krutch, *"Modernism" in Modern Drama* (New York: Russell and Russell, 1953), 12.

34. For an examination of the use of nonverbal symbolism in Greek drama, see H. D. F. Kitto, *Greek Tragedy*, 2d ed. (1939; reprint, Garden City, N.Y.: Anchor-Doubleday, 1950).

35. A. C. Bradley, *Shakespearean Tragedy* (1904; reprint, Greenwich, Conn.: Fawcett, n.d.), 48.

36. Despite the obvious and important use of silence in the drama, it is only in the nineteenth century that specific indications for ellipses and silence were included in the text (see James Kolb, "Language, Sounds and Silence in Modern Theatre" [Ph.D. diss., New York University, 1974], 11).

37. Robert Brustein, *The Theatre of Revolt: An Approach to Modern Drama* (Boston: Little, Brown, 1962), 27–30.

2
Maeterlinck

In her important study, *The French Drama of the Unspoken*, May Daniels suggests that it is not until we come to Maeterlinck that the unexpressed—the eloquent use of silence and unprententious dialogue implying more than it superficially communicates—"constitutes the main preoccupation of the dramatist."[1] Maeterlinck conceives of life as essentially mysterious; the invisible, inexpressible, and unintelligible color his mystical thought and art. His world is characterized by ambiguity—the polarities of youth and old age, vision and blindness, light and dark, exteriority and interiority, time and timelessness, intellect and intuition, life and death—and he finds language and silence integral to the enigma of life and its dramatization.

Describing Maeterlinck as a mystic, Arthur Symons maintains that the mystic "conceives of life, not indeed, so much as a road on which one walks, very much at one's discretion, but as a blown and wandering ship, surrounded by a sea from which there is no glimpse of land."[2] Intuitively the mystic trusts himself to the currents, allowing forces he cannot see nor comprehend to direct his hand upon the rudder. In this metaphor Symons has not only capsulated Maeterlinck's philosophy of life, but also illuminated his philosophy of drama exemplified in the characterization, thematic concerns, and dramatic and linguistic structures of his early silent plays.[3]

Maeterlinck's archetypal pilgrims, young, vulnerable, old, and literally or figuratively blind and/or deaf, are buffeted by the forces of love and fear and death. Characteristically lamenting "ne pas savoir où l'on est, ne pas savoir où l'on va, ne plus distinguer midi de minuit, ni l'été de l'hiver . . . et toujours ces ténèbres . . . ," these exposed and isolated wanderers are adrift on a sea of doubt, their vision obscured by the mist and their progress controlled by currents that keep them becalmed or propel them at will.[4] Threatened always with crashing into the rocks or capsizing into the dark abyss, they seek terra firma, a direct, discernible road, a definable goal, shelter from the elements, knowledge about self and cosmos.

By his use of archetypes, Maeterlinck underscores the universality and continuum of human experience. Through what Northrop Frye terms the "analogy of innocence," which includes the comic, idyllic, romantic, idealized, and magical modes, Maeterlinck attempts to present "the desirable in human, familiar, attainable and morally allowable terms."[5] Frye defines the innocent world as "neither totally alive . . . nor mostly dead, like ours: it is an animistic world, full of elemental spirits" in which nature is characterized by the "inaudible harmony of the music of the spheres."[6] In prefatory remarks to his collected plays, Maeterlinck confirms that it is indeed his intention to evoke these spirits: "J'ai essayé d'expliquer ces choses qui dorment, sans doute, au fond de notre instinct et qu'il est bien difficile de réveiller complètement."[7]

The archetypal child, not only empirically but linguistically innocent, relates directly to the elemental and instinctive of which Maeterlinck speaks because, as Suzanne Langer explains, childhood is the period of greatest synthesia in which sounds, colors, temperatures, forms, and feelings coalesce. And there is a strong tendency on the part of the child to formulate associations among senses not fixed by words, as well as to demonstrate "over-active feelings" which most often find their outlet in fear.[8] Ignorant of both themselves and the world, the young grope for words with which to verbalize and exteriorize their emotions. The infant, the most innocent and vulnerable of Maeterlinck's children, is a pivotal character in many of the silent dramas: a nonverbal cry echoes through the concluding scene of *L'Intruse*, *Pelléas et Mélisande* and *Les Aveugles*, announcing not only the presence and passage of death but also the continuation of life. The analogy of innocence, moreover, accounts for the wise old man linked to childhood by his vulnerability and his babbling, stammering, disjunctive speech, but distinctive in his empirical experience and intuitively perceived knowledge which as "secret teller" he may communicate to the innocent.

Maeterlinck's archetypal characters, the personification of his thematic concerns, are inextricably bound to his dramatic structure and linguistic techniques. His dramas of the unspoken, often considered static or non-dramatic because they lack dramatic crisis, exploit the non-directional structure of waiting: waiting for nuns to arrive, for an opportunity to escape, for a priest to lead the lost blind, for the arrival of the chivalric hero who will save the damsel in distress.[9] Stasis is reinforced by the unity of setting—in the realistic plays one room in *L'Intruse*, one island in *Les Aveugles*, one vantage point from which to observe the family in *Intérieur*—and in the legendary plays, such as *Pelléas et Mélisande*, *Alladine et Palomides*, and *Les sept princesses*, one setting of garden, forest, and castle.

One may suggest that these plays are inappropriately termed "static." Marcel Postic argues that Maeterlinck's dramas reflect a continually intensifying cycle, a distinct progression "d'une incertitude à un pressentiment à une inquiètude, d'un inquiètude à une effrante et précise conviction."[10] Daniels similarly maintains that instead of immutability the plays show a threefold "silent dramatic dynamism" based on the advance of invisible fatalities, the growth of fear, and the active imagination of the spectator.[11] *Les Aveugles* illustrates a dynamic progression which begins in a state of relative inertia and builds silently and inexorably into a frightening confrontation with the abyss. We witness what Bettina

Knapp terms "the decay and disintegration of the dying complex."[12] The silence of foreboding spreads contagiously through the circle of the blind, so oppressive and suffocating and ultimately insupportable that the pilgrims break rather than bend under the pressure. Terror alone grips the hearts and minds of the abandoned souls whose initial condition of ignorance has been irrevocably replaced with frightening certitude: the death of hope. The young blind woman's inquiry, "Qui êtes-vous?" receives the silent response of affirmation (1 : 342).

In each of these plays, of course, the initial situation differs markedly from the concluding one. In each an innocent dies. In *La Princesse Maleine* Maleine dies, in *L'Intruse* the young mother dies, in *Alladine et Palomides* and *Pelléas et Mélisande* the lovers die, in *Les sept princesses* the princesses die, in *Intérieur* the young daughter dies, and in *La Mort de Tintagiles* it is Tintagiles who dies. Rilke suggested that these plays be termed *drames de la mort* because of their obvious preoccupation with death, but the paradigm of the presence of an infant in several of them suggests that Maeterlinck is concerned not only with the decadent theme of the daily intrusion of death into life, but more importantly with its mysterious intrusion as a universal and timeless experience connected to and reflecting the continuum of life.[13] Besides treating the imaginative cycle of waking and dreaming life, Maeterlinck parallels the cyclical pattern of death and rebirth in the cyclical rhythms of the solar cycle of light and darkness and in the literal and figurative descent downward or inward (or cessation of movement), balanced by a movement upward and outward toward life-renewal.[14] Examination of the plays reveals extensive use of such archetypal symbols as caverns, grottoes, towers, and corridors in which characters are trapped and from which they mysteriously escape, or to which they descend and from which they miraculously return. We note that the conclusion of *L'Intruse* calls for a ray of light and the conclusion of *Pelléas and Mélisande* the removal of the newborn from death's chamber. The archetypal characters and dramatic structure, both apparently quiescent, are only superficially so; cyclical flux and nondirectional progression inform both.

Most essential to a study of the unspoken in Maeterlinck's *théâtre de l'inexprimé* is the relationship of mystical philosophy, characters symbolic of the analogy of innocence, cyclical fluctuation, and nondirectional structure to this playwright's linguistic innovations. Avant-garde in his own age, Maeterlinck fused thought with technique. Balakian notes that he employed technical aspects of the symbolist theatre, primarily the repetition of words, echoes from one character to another, pauses, and enigmatic speech.[15] Including her classifications, the typifying elements of Maeterlinck's methodology may be summarized as these:

1. repetitions
2. disjunctive, enigmatic utterances
3. questions marked by obsessions
4. long pause between question and response

  5. numerical symbolism
  6. quotidian dialogue implicitly conveying more than it explicitly com-
     municates
  7. silence as a metaphor for absence
  8. silence as a conduit for mystical knowledge
  9. mute protagonist and/or antagonist
 10. silence of the playwright

Short responses, disjunctive phrases, distracted association of ideas, and repetitive utterances have earned Maeterlinck's characters the derogatory criticism of being inarticulate.[16] One must recall that during the 1880s *Scribisme*,
with its artifically contrived plots and its precision of expression—dialogue
which characterized the speaker, provided expository information, and pro-
pelled the action—was firmly entrenched in the French theatre.[17] In stark contrast to carefully articulated motivations and intentions, Maeterlinck offered
dialogue which failed to provide this information and, more importantly, was
intentionally indistinct, imprecise, and apparently static. How are we to understand this iconoclastic linguistic methodology? I suggest that Maeterlinck's intentions were threefold: to dramatize imperceptible flux, to achieve
psychological realism in speech and action, and to convey mystical knowledge
through the contrast of unpretentious dialogue with silent response.

Daniels has defended Maeterlinck's techniques by explaining that disjunctive
speech struck a blow at Scribean artificiality while simultaneously achieving
psychological realism.[18] Our paradigm of deceptive stasis concealing fluctuation
in character and structure also can be seen to operate in repetitious dialogue that
appears to be nondirectional and disjunctive phrases that are apparently discontinuous. By what is termed *le langage indirect* characters reveal by their halting or
compulsive speech patterns and by their hesitation to find a word to express
what they wish to communicate, or for that matter what they wish to leave
unspoken, the irrational, subconscious choice and arrangement of words, rather
than rational, conscious progression. Significantly, repetitions simulate circular, obsessive thought processes and disjunctions, the separation between
thinker and his thought, thought and its completion. Space becomes a dynamic
component of the dramatic art, just as it was to become integral to the plastic
arts, and it is against the backdrop of interior space that Maeterlinck bounces his
words, now halting, now compulsive, so that the fluctuation between interior
and exterior experience, between impasse and free-flowing speech is dramatically realized. Through an abundance of *points de suspension* Maeterlinck
invites the actor to make a regular pause in order to allow the words to resonate
and expand in the silence.[19] We witness the fluctuation and trembling—to use
symbolist terminology—of *l'état d'âme* and follow the emotion, most often fear
in the early plays, through increasing spirals of intensity.

Our interest in the reticent, indistinct speech patterns of Maeterlinck's
characters, suggests Daniels, lies in their similarity to our own.[20] A desire for

greater realism in dialogue explains Maeterlinck's use of the speech one naturally associates with the very young and the very old: babbling and stammering.
What is apparently incoherent can be interpreted as mystically oracular and
enigmatic or, on the other hand, dismissed as the nonsensical "baby-talk" of the
child or prattle of the senile. Similarly, Maeterlinck simulates emotional and
psychological stress and trauma by discontinuous, incompleted phrases and
incoherent phrases marked by prolonged silences. As the members of the family
in *L'Intruse* illustrate, sluggish speech that mirrors physical and emotional exhaustion can be accepted on this realistic level. But disjunctive speech need not
be limited to emotional stress. One sees in these plays the use of discontinuous
speech patterns which realistically reflect conversation in which one voice naturally drifts off and the other, responding to what has been said, or left unsaid,
picks up the dropped line of thought.

Some selections from these silent plays will more clearly focus what Maeterlinck has intentionally left indistinct and suggest the specific functions of imprecision in the dramas. The realistic stammering of the child marks an emotional
exchange between Yniold and Mélisande in *Pelléas et Mélisande*, when in tears he
tries to make himself understood:

> *Mélisande:* Qu'y a-t-il, Yniold? Qu'y a-t-il? . . . pourquoi pleures-tu tout à
> coup?
> *Yniold* *(sanglotant):* Parce que . . . Oh! oh! parce que . . .
> *Mélisande:* Pourquoi? . . . Pourquoi? dis-le moi . . .
> *Yniold:* Petite-mère . . . petite-mère . . . vous allez partir . . .
> *Mélisande:* Mais qu'est-ce qui te prend, Yniold? . . . Je n'ai jamais songé à
> partir . . .
> *Yniold:* Si, si; petit-père est parti . . . petit-père ne revient pas, et vous
> allez partir aussi . . . Je l'ai vu . . . je l'ai vu . . .[21]

Yniold's hesitations reflect his efforts to find the words to express his disappointment and his fear that once again in his young life he will lose a loved one.
On the other hand, we note that Mélisande's stammering and disjunctive speech
is a function of her surprise and her efforts to conceal rather than reveal her
emotions. How does this child know? How much does he know? How can she
convince him of the falsity of his perceptions? These questions move through
her mind as she fluctuates from a state of imposed calm and mothering concern
for Yniold to hysteric fear that she will reveal too much. The obsessive quality
of his repetitious speech reveals the extent of his trauma, just as the obsessive
quality of her repeated pauses reveals the impasse in which she is trapped.

A disjunctive, repetitive pattern can similarly be illustrated by King Hjal-
mar's outburst at the death of Maleine in the final scene of *La Princesse Maleine*:

> C'est elle! c'est elle! Et moi! moi! moi! j'y étais aussi! . . . Elle l'a étranglée!
> Ainsi! Ainsi! Voyez! voyez! voyez! On frappait aux fenêtres! Ah! ah! ah!
> ah! . . . (1:189)

Although *La Princesse Maleine* is a pre-symbolist play that relies heavily on language, Maeterlinck is already experimenting with a "broken record" effect to convey *l'état d'âme* experiencing stress and trauma.

Repeated phrases, moreover, need not follow directly to weave a pattern of compulsiveness and to imply stressful, growing fear. As Maeterlinck illustrates in *Alladine et Palomides*, the repetition of the phrase "Où sommes-nous?" does not produce an atmosphere of spiralling hysteria, but rather one of sedated somnambulism. When Alladine first inquires, "Où sommes-nous?" Palomides responds, "Où êtes-vous?" After efforts to reach one another are unsuccessful, Alladine once again calls out, "Où êtes-vous?" The space between them, which they are endeavoring to close, seems to grow with each repetition. Palomides continues his search, "Vous êtes là?" Even after touching one another Alladine repeatedly asks her lover, "Où sommes-nous . . . où sommes-nous?" to which he replies, "Nous sommes dans des grottes que je n'ai jamais vues. . . ." (2:198–206). Although Palomides provides her with an answer, the pause concluding his unfinished thought reveals the paralyzing doubt and fear which grips this young man. On the literal level we accept the superficial explanation, but we understand that figuratively we are in the grottoes of the mind that no one has seen or ever will see. Like the trapped initiates, we take a night journey into the depths of the psyche and wonder, Who now? Where now?

Maeterlinck's disjunctive structure, while respondent to stressful and disorienting situations, is similarly appropriate to the rhythmic pattern of quotidian conversation. This illustration from *Intérieur* reflects the fluctuation within the speaker who, in choosing his words, emphasizes the space between what is said and what is left unsaid, as well as the distance between two speakers who share a common subject but bring to it personal and psychological differences:

> *L'Etranger:* En ce moment, ils sourient en silence dans la chambre . . .
> *Le Vieillard:* Ils sont tranquilles . . . Ils ne l'attendaient pas ce soir . . .
> *L'Etranger:* Ils sourient sans bouger . . . mais voici que le père met un doigt sur les lèvres . . .
> *Le Vieillard:* Il désigne l'enfant endormi sur le coeur de la mère . . .
> *L'Etranger:* Elle n'ose pas lever les yeux, de peur de troubler son sommeil . . .
> *Le Vieillard:* Elles ne travaillent plus . . . Il règne un grand silence.
> *L'Etranger:* Elles ont laissé tomber l'écheveau de soie blanche . . .
> *Le Vieillard:* Ils regardent l'enfant . . .
> *L'Etranger:* Ils ne savent pas que d'autres les regardent . . .
> *Le Vieillard:* On nous regarde aussi. . . .[22]

(2:242–43)

One observes in this characteristic excerpt that the Maeterlinckien polarities of tranquility and flux, vision and blindness, childhood and old age, interiority and exteriority, sleep and wakefulness coalesce to weave a tapestry of terrestrial and mystical experience.

Maeterlinck's mystical philosophy, which underlies his use of nonverbal discursiveness, also informs his significant use of numbers, a linguistic technique often ignored or minimized by scholars. Sammie Jo Mullen, for example, maintains that integers substitute for words like *plusieurs* and *beaucoup* and, like colors, are properties to be felt.[23] On the contrary, I suggest that Maeterlinck's numerology may be viewed as a conscious retreat from the word that characterizes modern art and literature, just as it does modern science. No aspect of Maeterlinck's nonverbal art should be ignored, certainly not the conspicuous, recurrent use of the mystical numbers three, seven, and ten implicitly conveying mystical correspondence. Witness these examples:

La Princesse Maleine	7 nuns	
L'Intruse	3 men	
	3 young girls	7
	1 intruder	
Les Aveugles	6 blind men	
	6 blind women	13 (10 & 3)
	1 infant	
Alladine et Palomides	3 sisters	
Pelléas et Mélisande	10 servant mourners	
La Mort de Tintagiles	3 sisters	

Langer illuminates the use of integers instead of words by explaining that numbers say nothing about the existence or efficacy of things. Rather, they suggest insubstantial relationships,[24] being still another nonverbal expression to convey insubstantial, ineffable, mystical conceptions.

It is through dialogue characterized by simplicity and superficiality to conceal its profundity, however, that Maeterlinck revitalized the drama and laid the foundation for the theatre of the unspoken. It is minimal, colloquial dialogue which carries the action, itself reduced to the barest minimum, and operates simultaneously on objective and subjective levels that typifies Maeterlinck's plays and the plays of Chekhov, Jean-Jacques Bernard, Beckett, Pinter, Albee, and other contemporary dramatists. In his dramaturgical essays *Le Trésor des humbles*, written after his composition of the silent plays, Maeterlinck explains his intentions and defends his use of bivalent dialogue:

> Il n'y a guère que les paroles qui semblent d'abord inutiles qui comptent dans une oeuvre. C'est en elles que se trouve son âme. A côté du dialogue indispensable, il y a presque toujours un autre dialogue qui semble superflu. Examinez attentivement et vous verrez que c'est le seul que l'âme écoute profondément, parce que c'est en cet endroit seulement qu'on lui parle. Vous reconnaître aussi que c'est la qualité et l'étendue de ce dialogue inutile qui détermine la qualité et la portée ineffable de l'oeuvre.[25]

This "hidden dialogue," only apparently superfluous, in conjunction with silent response, both informs Maeterlinck's iconoclastic concept of drama and denotes his modernity. As Jean-Marie Andrieu confirms in her recent critique of Maeterlinckien theatre, "Ce théâtre parle également deux langages: celui du balbutient par lequel les êtres laissent chanter leur coeur . . . celui des souffles suspendus dans les vibrations des pressentiment et des nuances." True dialogue is to be found "non dans les répliques échangées, mais entre les mots et les silences, l'anecdotique et l'imperceptible."[26]

The following exchange between the father and the uncle in *L'Intruse* illustrates the realistic superficiality of the dialogue and the underlying profundity of words that, in their ignorance of mystical and metaphysical truth, the speakers fail to perceive. Indeed, one notes that their remarks underestimate the value of the words of the old man they discuss, rendering ironic comment on their own:

> *Le Père:* Il a eu bien des inquiètudes.
> *L'Oncle:* Il s'inquiète toujours outre mesure. Il y a des moments où il ne veut
> pas entendre raison.
> *Le Père:* C'est assez excusable á son âge.
> *L'Oncle:* Dieu sait où nous en serons à son age!
> *Le Père:* Il a près de quatre-vingts ans.
> *L'Oncle:* Alors, on a le droit d'étre étrange.
> *Le Père:* Il est comme tous les aveugles.
> *L'Oncle:* Ils réfléchissent un peu trop.
> *Le Père:* Ils ont trop de temps à perdre.
> *L'Oncle:* Ils n'ont pas autre chose à faire.
> *Le Père:* Et puis, ils n'ont aucune distraction.
>
> (1:216–17)

The father and uncle suggest that the old man, senile and babbling, too often has strange ideas and moreover, "il dit absolument tout ce qu'il pense." The old man, however, does not say absolutely everything that he thinks, specifically because his "strange ideas," incomprehensible to the others, remain inexpressible. What he does verbalize, most often his disquietude, merely indicates all that remains unspoken.

In addition to his use of dialogue as "thematic communication," Maeterlinck's treatment of the unspoken includes silent response, most characteristically for impasse, solemnity, confusion, expectation, and menace—silence which evokes *l'état d'âme* and silence as a metaphor for absence, specifically, Death.[27] His uses of the unspoken reveal direct correspondence among mysticism, silence, and timelessness. It must be remembered that language is structured and sequential human action linked to time, man's terra firma. Through language man seeks to humanize, define, and control the chaos of external and internal experience and with its essential correlative, time, to order and measure directional progression. Thus, if one extends Symons's metaphor of a ship adrift from which there is no sight of land, lacking the use of both compass and rudder, we postulate that the rudder represents linguistic control, the compass temporal measurement. Lacking both, man floats free on a sea of silence.

For this playwright, silence is the ideal medium for the transmission of spiritual knowledge, and his theories of the unexpressed can be linked directly to his concept of cosmic subconscious and soul-to-soul communication. Maeterlinck elaborates on the special, wordless communication among souls in his important essay "Le Silence":

> Et dans le domaine où nous sommes, ceux-là mêmes qui savent parler le plus profondément sentent le mieux que le mots n'expriment jamais les relations réelles et spéciales qu'il y a entre deux êtres. Si je vous parle en ce moment des choses les plus graves, de l'amour, de la mort ou de la destinée, je n'atteins pas la mort, l'amour ou le destin, et malgré mes efforts, il restera toujours entre nous une vérité qui n'est pas dite, qu'on n'a même pas l'idée de dire, et cependant cette vérité qui n'a pas en de voix aura seule vécu un instant entre nous, et nous n'avons pas pu songer à autre chose. Cette vérité, c'est *notre vérité* sur la mort, le destin ou l'amour; et nous n'avons pu l'entre-voir qu'en silence.[28]

Essentially, he asserts that we cannot approach elusive and ineffable concepts through speech. Despite our efforts to verbally communicate, there remains between souls a unstated truth, a truth "qu'on n'a même pas l'idée de dire." Communicated in silence, it remains "notre vérité," private, personal, and inviolate. This crucial medium for the communion of souls Maeterlinck terms "active" silence, whereas silence that reflects sleep, death, or inexistence is "passive."[29]

In prefatory remarks to his collected volume of silent plays published in 1896, Maeterlinck states that the greatest efforts of the artist must be directed toward the creation of "une vie supérieure, une vie plus proche de notre âme," but human presence interferes and destroys the fragility of this dramatic symbol. One can postulate that man, intruding with his physical presence, intrudes, moreover, with his linguistic presence and threatens to destroy art, which in Maeterlinck's words employs "toujours d'un détour et n'agit pas directement."[30] The "détour" to which Maeterlinck refers is around conceptual dialogue; his insistence upon indirect dialogue is central to his dramaturgy. Whereas language traps the initiate in superficiality, conceals him from the profundity of life's mysteries, and fragments the unity of mystical knowledge, silence, characteristically fluid, conveys the ineffable, the unintelligible, the untranslatable spiritual experience. Silence functions in this iconoclastic theatre as the inextricable link between the outer framework of metaphysical concerns and the inner, instinctive comprehension of them. Maeterlinck's *théâtre de l'inexprimé* is constructed of polarities which elicit and evoke the ambiguous and the enigmatic while simultaneously subjecting the individual to universal elements. And it is in the individual's silent response, the wordless evocation of *l'état d'âme* or, as Guy Donneux suggests, "une succession d'états" wherein "chaque tableau n'est

qu'un cadre de toile de fond sur laquelle ils projettent leur paysage intérieur"
that we see the coalescence of Maeterlinckien symbolism and his innovative
drama of the unspoken.[31]

One of the most important applications of silence in Maeterlinck's theatre is
to be found in the muteness of the protagonist on whom our attention is fixed
but whom we neither see nor hear, as well as in the muteness of some antago-
nists—if it indeed be appropriate to term *antagonist* Maeterlinck's helpless victims of silent forces.[32] Death predominates in *L'Intruse*, *Les Aveugles*, and *La Mort
de Tintagiles* and creeps silently through *Pelléas et Mélisande*, *Intérieur*, *Alladine et
Palomides* and *Les sept princesses*. Taking his cue from Aeschylean mute characters,
Maeterlinck improves upon the technique of presenting the silent character by
coloring it with his mystical philosophy. Thus in his theatre human characters
play a reduced role, while invisible, silent forces which move the universe take
center stage. In an interesting juxtaposition of the focus of our attention,
Maeterlinck creates and maintains interest in the dying mother whom we
neither see nor hear in *L'Intruse*, in the seven dying princesses whom we see but
never hear in *Les sept princesses*, in a priest who remains unseen not only by the
audience, but also by the pilgrims who search for him in *Les Aveugles*, and in a
family who remain within our grasp but elude our ability to hear what is
exchanged within the privacy of their home in *Intérieur*.

Inarticulateness informs Maeterlinck's characters and similarly informs the
playwright himself. In one of the most important contributions to the theatre of
the unexpressed, we observe the taciturn posture of the author. Unlike his
characters who say more than they know, Maeterlinck insists on saying less
than he knows: What has delayed the Sister of Mercy in *L'Intruse?* What was
Mélisande about to reveal when she died? Who calls the ten servants to mourn
for her? Why is Tintagiles summoned home to die? How do Alladine and
Palomides survive the tortures of the crypts and drowning? Events of this kind
are neither fully described nor explained, and prosaic connection between an
actor's intention and action is significant in its absence. Through this technique
the playwright intensifies the mystification and confusion of the audience, who
must question and wait with Maeterlinckien characters. However, more importantly, in abandoning the elevated vantage point and position of control of the
artist, Maeterlinck acknowledges the human limitations of the artist who suf-
fers, as do his pilgrims, the agony of doubt and the certainty of death. Thus one
notes that Maeterlinck's reliance upon silent expression and suspension of linear
chronological progression are functions of his mystical philosophy from which,
as secret teller, he is not exempt. On the contrary, he must endeavor to reveal
spiritual knowledge without destroying the enigma which shrouds and protects
it.

These modern conceptions of the role of the artist and the interrelationship of
speech, silence, and time to the dramatic spectacle evolved in Maeterlinck's
thought and art as a result of his formative exposure to the Symbolist cénacle
and his own experimentation in poetry, both of which antedate his dramatic

career and directly influenced its development. Arriving in Paris in 1886, he found his mystical philosophy and artistic attitudes compatible with those of the fin de siècle symbolists, particularly Mallarmé and Villiers de l'Isle-Adam.[33]

Mallarmé, whose philosophy of art is reflected in the famous injunction *"Nommer* un objet, c'est supprimer les trois quarts de la jouissance du poëme qui est faite de deviner peu à peu: le *suggérer*, voilà le rêve," profoundly affected the direction and development of symbolist poetry by his example and inspiration.[34] In his critical study, *Mallarmé and the Symbolist Drama*, Haskell Block summarizes the pivotal aspects of Mallarméan aesthetics: to evoke mood through ambiguity and indirect statement, to elicit mystery and absence.[35] Cognizant of the need for a symbolist theatre which would effectively transform the Parisian theatre of the 1880's, Mallarmé envisioned a theatre which would replace vaudeville, thesis drama, and naturalism with mystery, raise "un coin de voile" to reveal the shrouded *l'état d'âme*, and dramatize "l'antagonisme de rêve chez l'homme avec les fatalités à son existence." Citing *Hamlet* as the prototypical drama of internalization, Mallarmé extended his concept of linguistic suggestiveness and connotation to the dramatic arts.[36] Unable to accomplish, to his satisfaction, the dramatization of "Hérodiade" and "L'Après-midi d'un faune," he focused his genius on dramatic criticism and theory, and in the opinion of Haskell Block, was responsible for the stimulus, growth, and development of the symbolist theatre.[37]

Maeterlinck's theatre of silence was inspired not only by Mallarmé, but also by Villiers de l'Isle-Adam, who encouraged him to shun romanticism and adopt symbolic techniques in his art.[38] In Villiers's *Axel* one notes the evocation of mood, the mystical flight from material reality, and the use of silence. Sara's reaction to Axel's request for their joint suicide in lieu of union in marriage is an excellent illustration of the playwright's utilization of nonverbal techniques. The stage directions call for a "silence profond," a dramatic silence of the traditional type which creates anticipation and dramatic tension, and then Sara replies, "Je tremble . . . si tu persistes, je t'obéirai!" Significantly, it is in the pause which follows "Je tremble" that Sara's silent response reveals surprise, confusion, fear, and resignation.[39] Daniels, who believes that the efforts of Villiers to achieve the theatre of the unexpressed are at best "elementary," suggests that his use of long static scenes, the inarticulateness of Sara, and the utilization of nonverbal response to convey the enigma of life and absence from it find refined, concentrated, and sophisticated form in Maeterlinck's drama.[40]

In addition to the external sources of inspiration and encouragement, such as Mallarmé, Villiers de l'Isle-Adam, and his Belgian friend Charles Van Lerberghe, one finds the seeds of Maeterlinck's drama within his own garden: *Serres chaudes*. Mullen observes that the symbolic emblems of door and window, which nonverbally imply free passage between interior and exterior, between concrete reality and interior mood, figure importantly in *Serres chaudes* and *Les Chansons*, written concurrently with the silent dramas.[41] These multivalent symbols of access and egress are unpredictable, threatening, and generally restrictive: windows refuse to stay closed, doors mysteriously open or stubbornly remain firmly locked. Grottoes and labyrinthine caves also metaphorically suggest literal entrapment in the bowels of castles, psychological entrapment in the mind, linguistic entrapment in language. In *La Princesse Maleine*, for example, the literally isolated maiden trapped within the confines of her dimly lit room is figuratively trapped in her paralyzed and paralyzing fear. As the fear intensifies, a storm breaks into her room and within her mind. Similarly, in *L'Intruse* the family, expecting one visitor, receives another: invisible and invincible death forces open a locked door and violates the security of their interior space to steal the life of the sick mother. And in *Les Aveugles*, where there are neither doors nor windows, circular imagery informs thematically and nonverbally. The blind, trapped in their blindness, form a circle to protect themselves; but their circle, mirrored in the circle of water isolating them on the island and entrapping them as prisoners of the forest, of ignorance, and of death, is violated by the intruder, death, who enters and silently takes control of the circle.

For Maeterlinck the most divisive barriers separating man from himself and from knowledge of the cosmos are not doors, windows, or water barriers. Daniels observes that, though materialistic man perceives silence as a "baffling, impenetrable barrier," for this playwright language itself locks man in intellectual isolation chambers.[42] Thus in his early dramas Maeterlinck eludes the confines of language and dramatizes the unexpressed, both in plays which Guy Donneux terms *théâtre de l'éffroi*, that have their basis in realistic subject, setting, and characterization, such as *L'Intruse, Intérieur*, and *Les Aveugles*, and in *théâtre de la tristesse*, in which subject matter, setting, and characterization find origin in fairy tale such as *Pelléas et Mélisande, Alladine et Palomides*, and *Les sept princesses*.[43] It is in the *théâtre de l'éffroi* that Maeterlinck makes the most dramatic use of silence and achieves a "slice of interior life" that draws heavily on realistic, quotidian dialogue and setting.[44]

I intend to confine my in-depth examination of Maeterlinck's idiosyncratic use of speech and silence to *L'Intruse*, the first of his plays to exhibit the full range of his iconoclastic linguistic techniques and the one, I believe, most successful in merging realistic foundation with mystical philosophy. Completed in December 1890 and produced for the first time by Paul Fort of the Théâtre d'Art on 20 May 1891, *L'Intruse* has been called "the jewel of the symbolist theatre" by Anna Balakian.[45] In its own time, however, it attracted cries of plagiarism, not praise: as Hanse explains in "La genèse de *L'Intruse*," Maeterlinck's plagiarism of Charles Van Lerberghe's *Les Flaireurs* was charged, as was Van Lerberghe's supposed plagiarism of *L'Intruse*.[46] The subject of death's visiting a young woman is common to both. In *Les Flaireurs* death is expected, resistance is offered to its visible personification, and violent action and noise inform the dramatic and linguistic structure, whereas exegesis of *L'Intruse* reveals that death is not expected, does not take visible form, and encounters no resistance. Originally entitled "L'Approche," *L'Intruse*, as Balakian observes, suggestively elicits the advance, presence, and passing of death merely by its effects upon natural objects and human victims.[47]

In this one-act drama (the tightness of which, in my view, is responsible for its success, as tightness contributes to the success of *Les Aveugles* and *Intérieur*), anxiety communicated through mini-conversations electrifies the atmosphere and grips the family in a frenzy that dissipates only after death has passed. Unified by a single setting, the duologues are linked in series by such recurring motifs as interiority/exteriority, security/danger, tranquility/anxiety, vision/ blindness, light/shadow, sounds/silence, and the constant presence of the Old Man, who is spoken about even when he does not contribute to the conversation. The dynamics of Maeterlinck's deceptively static dramatic and linguistic structure is revealed in the fluctuating rhythm within and between conversational units.

The initial conversation of *L'Intruse* introduces a blind man, his three granddaughters, their father, and their uncle. The question of whether to remain within the room in which they find themselves, comfortably under the light of the lamp or go outside on the terrace to enjoy the night air leads to the subject of the daughter-mother's failing health. Fluctuating in his decision, the grandfather chooses to remain within the room—a decision based neither on an intellectual estimation of his sick daughter's condition nor on assurance of the doctor, but rather on instinct. "Je crois qu'elle ne vas bien. . . ," he admits. Unable to verbalize the source of his disquietude and unwilling to continue this line of thought, he breaks off his speech and his uneasy words drift into silence. The father, seeking to assuage the Old Man's fears, assures him that "les medécins affirment que nous pouvons êtres tranquilles . . . ," but his own incompleted sentence belies his tranquility, intimating that the father is not convinced of his wife's improvement. The mood is implicitly underscored by repetition of the word "inquiétude" throughout the play. Speaking directly to the father and attempting to ease the tension which he has not explicitly expressed but implied in his repeated denials and unfinished thought, the uncle criticizes the grandfather: "Vous savez bien que votre beau-père aime à nous inquiéter inutilement." This connotative remark is not explained, however, and in the absence of specific information we are encouraged to wonder when the grandfather has disquieted the group previously and if his present concerns are unfounded. Responding to the uncle, the grandfather suggests, "Je n'y vois pas comme vous." This quotidian exchange implicitly conveys more than it explicitly and superficially communicates, but the profundity of the grandfather's remarks is missed by the uncle, who accepts them at face value. "Il faut vous en rapporter alors à ceux qui voient," the uncle informs him, attempting to short-circuit further discussion. What remains unexpressed, of course, is that those who are sighted lack insight and must inevitably turn to the blind to lead them to spiritual light.[48] In accord with Maeterlinck's mystical philosophy, the Old Man will be the "mystical seer" and "mystical teller." But rather than pursue conversation with the uncle or incur criticism for his verbalized fears, he re-treats into a contemplative silence. The initial conversational unit has in-troduced a recurring motif through thematic dialogue and elicited the unexpressed through silent response, a silent protagonist, bivalent dialogue, and silence as the medium of communion between souls (1:201–3).

The father and the uncle express their desire to relax and enjoy the serenity of the evening, but the grandfather's intrusion into the discussion initiates a new turn in the dialogue. Maeterlinck utilizes this paradigm repeatedly throughout the play: flux and fluidity between conversations is directly attributable to the Old Man. "Pourquoi n'ai-je pu voir ma pauvre fille aujourd'hui?" he inquires, leaving unexpressed the disquietude that the missed visit has caused him. The uncle, always realistic and practical, reminds the Old Man that the doctor has forbidden it, and adds, "Il est inutile de vous alarmer. . . ." Repetition of the word "inutile," however, and his unfinished, disjunctive speech clearly express that the uncle is already alarmed. The motifs of illness, anxiety, and sounds link this duologue with the next, which concerns itself with the physical state of the young infant, mute since birth, and that of the mother, whose illness is obvi-ously, though implicitly conveyed, the result of childbirth. Concern for the sick daughter elicits concern for the sick infant. "Je crois qu'il sera sourd, et peut-être muet . . . ," observes the grandfather, whose disappointment at the child's inability to speak (cry) leaves him momentarily speechless. Hesitating, he makes an elliptical reference to the fact that such conditions issue from a blood mar-riage, his voice drifting off, the thought left incomplete. It is not only his words, but the implications of the unfinished sentence, reinforced by a "silence réprobateur," that make condemnatory statement (1:203–5).

Mention of the marriage returns the conversation to the subject of the ailing mother, the play's main concern, who is awaiting the arrival of the Sister of Mercy. This is the first explicit mention of waiting; but a mood of expectation and a silence of anticipation has been operative since the child was born and the mother fell ill. The silence of anticipation informs this silent play and many dramas of the unspoken under consideration in this study. And most natural, as well as linguistically imperative, is the subject of time and how it passes. It is established that it is already nine o'clock, but what is left unsaid is that at nine o'clock in the evening it is no longer safe for a nun to be travelling to the chateau. As it grows later and later in the evening, the likelihood of her arriving, or arriving safely, is greatly diminished; and in her persisting absence, the anxiety linked to the sick woman that had flowed first to the child now flows to the absent nun. The Old Man asks, "Vous n'avez plus d'inquiétudes?" to which the uncle responds, "Pourquoi donc aurions-nous des inquiétudes?" Why in-deed? The uncle provides us with rational and logical explanations, but his growing anxiety remains unexpressed verbally. The motifs of sound and si-lence, tranquility and anxiety recur, and while the father and uncle refuse to verbalize intensifying concern and disquietude, the Old Man anxiously de-clares, "Je voudrais que cette soirée fût passée!" (1:207).

The three girls who have ventured into the infant's room return, and once again the subject is focused by the uncle: "Qu'allons-nous faire en attendant?"[49] The young girls fill the time and divert attention from the cause of concern by reporting on the state of the garden and the events which transpire within it. The motifs of interiority/exteriority, clarity/opacity, and sounds/silence which have characterized previous duologues unite this one to the others. The father, anxious about the nun, asks his daugher, "Tu ne vois rien venir, Ursule?" and to the repeated question, "tu ne vois personne?" the girls respond negatively. This seems inconsonant, however, with the fact that the swans have swum to the other part of the lake in apparent fear: what can be explained intellectually, that the unseen sister must be in the garden, stubbornly refuses to be defined and verified. This is an excellent illustration of the effectiveness of the muteness of both protagonist and playwright. Through Maeterlinck's silence we remain uninformed about the whereabouts of the sister and the specific nature of the invisible intruder. Mystery is not only evoked, but encouraged and emphasized. The approach of death, anticipated by the Old Man in his initial disquietude, has now been intensified. So quiet is the garden that the father exclaims, "Il y a un silence de mort." In this typically indirect, bivalent dialogue, the speaker says more than he comprehends (1:208–11).

The overt subject of the conversation is again altered by the intrusion of the grandfather, who has been silent during discussion of the garden. "Toutes les fenêtres sont-elles ouvertes?" he inquires of Ursula (1:212). Mention of the window links it to her response that the door is open, and essentially it is the door to the garden which remains ajar—the repeated efforts to close it are ineffective—and brings the wind, specifically the breath of death, into the room. Rational explanations of the insubstantial are beginning to give way to silence. Thus, when the grandfather hears a sound and shudders, the startled uncle demands, "Qu'est-ce que c'est?" His question receives a feeble response from the young girl, who suggests that it may be the gardener. The father, concealing his concern by expanding upon his daughter's suggestion, observes, "C'est le jardier qui va faucher." The uncle is incredulous and apparently unconvinced by the explanation: "Il fauche pendant la nuit?" (1:214).

The tension in the room dissipates when the others note with relief that the Old Man, exhausted from three nights of anxious worry, has finally fallen asleep. During his silence, the father and the uncle discuss the Old Man's infirmities: the motifs of infirmity, light, repose, and blindness echo in their repartée. Employing to full advantage his technique of dualistic dialogue, Maeterlinck allows the idle chatter to operate simultaneously on a superficial and a mystical level: explicitly relating the Old Man's condition, the two are implicitly revealing their own. In the oft-quoted passage referred to earlier in this chapter, the uncle muses that he would rather be dead than live, like the blind octogenarian, in the shadows of existence. It appears that repeatedly the speaker says more than he knows; but in this reflective passage phrases are broken by disjunctive pauses to communicate implicitly the uneasiness of the speaker and his doubt. Faced with his verbalized anxiety, the uncle hesitates, a final pause affording him the opportunity to avoid the subject and the serious tone. "Est-ce que c'est absolument incurable . . . absolument aveugle?" he inquires of the father, to receive the simultaneously reasonable and mystical response, "Il distingue les grandes clartés" (1:216–18).

The grandfather, awakened by the chiming of the clock, rejoins the conversation with an anxious question: "Suis-je tourné vers la porte vitrée?" Receiving no response and disquieted by an unfamiliar presence that he intuitively senses, he persists and repeats his inquiry. Then, remembering that someone has been expected, the Old Man reintroduces the motif of expectation and intensifying disquietude by asking, "Et votre soeur n'est pas venue?" The uncle abruptly dismisses the question with "Il est trop tard," an attempt to short-circuit the discussion; but the father admits, "Elle commence à m'inquiéter." This understatement, designed to assure the others and himself, conceals the unspoken; rather than just now becoming worried, he is exceedingly concerned by the lateness of the hour and the persistent absence of the sister. A sound indicative of a presence within the house receives an enthusiastic response from the uncle, one which reveals the depth of the anxiety he has tried to mask: "Elle est là! avez-vous entendu?" As the father, uncle, and grandfather trace the footfalls they believe to be the sister's on the steps, their reasonable dialogue, informing bivalently, yields to the pressure of doubt:

> *Le Père:* Elle est entrée très doucement.
> *L'Oncle:* Elle sait qu'il y a un malade.
> *L'Aieul:* Je n'entends plus rien maintenant.
> *L'Oncle:* Elle montera immédiatement, on lui dira que nous sommes ici.
> *Le Père:* Je suis heureux qu'elle soit venue.
> *L'Oncle:* J'étais sûr qu'elle viendrait ce soir.
> *L'Aieul:* Elle tarde bien à monter.
> *L'Oncle:* Il faut cependant que ce soit elle.
> *Le Père:* Nous n'attendons pas d'autres visites.
> *L'Aieul:* Je n'entends aucun bruit dans les souterrains.
> *Le Père:* Je vais appeler la servante; nous saurons à quoi nous en tenir.
> (1:220–21)

Anxiety escalates when the servant, summoned to assure them and reduce their disquietude, produces the opposite effect. The uneasiness thus revealed travels from person to person in the room and from moderate, manageable levels to intense, uncontrollable ones. The grandfather's persistent questions—such as "Votre soeur est à la porte?" "Qui est-ce qui soupire ainsi?" and "Est-ce qu'elle pleure?"—resist logical response and intensify the mood of uneasiness. An extensive exchange with the maid about the opening and closing of the front door linguistically exposes the state of anxiety in which we find the father, long insistent on tranquility, now yielding to stress. The maid's reiterated "je ne sais pas" to the series of questions which the father initiates, reflects the uncertainty of all gathered. Disoriented by her denials, which directly conflict with what he has heard and sensed, the father dismisses the servant: "Et s'il veneait quel-qu'un, dites que nous n'y sommes pas" (1:219–25). This absurd instruction, with which the uncle immediately concurs, functions as a pause, allowing the two the breathing space in which to recover their senses and control.

The grandfather, taking the movements of the servant as his cue, reverses the attention focused on the outside of the room, specifically the front door, to focus attention inside the room. The rapid-fire exchange between the father, uncle, and grandfather conceals the anxiety, which only the Old Man will specifically delineate and verbalize, that has now become a palpable presence:

> *L'Aïeul:* Elle est entrée?
> *Le Père:* Qui donc?
> *L'Aïeul:* La servante?
> *Le Père:* Mais non, elle est descendue.
> *L'Aïeul:* Je croyais qu'elle s'était assise à la table.
> *L'Oncle:* La servante?
> *L'Aïeul:* Oui.
> *L'Oncle:* Il ne manquerait plus que cela!
> *L'Aïeul:* Personne n'est entré dans la chambre?
> *Le Père:* Mais non, personne n'est entré.
> *L'Aïeul:* Et votre soeur n'est pas ici?
> *L'Oncle:* Notre soeur n'est pas venue.
> *L'Aïeul:* Vous voulez me tromper!

> (1:226–27)

The Old Man, persistent in his line of questioning, reveals by his obsessive repetitions the recurrent motifs of interior and exterior space, literal and figurative blindness, and a new variation for the old song of truth and deception. Echoing the questions asked earlier in the evening concerning the noises in the garden, the grandfather endeavors to express what the others leave unspoken. What is ineffable and invisible refuses linguistic definition. Whose truth is the truth? Who is the seventh at the table? What do they all leave unspoken? The Old Man, spiritual leader of this group, "calls the roll" to convince himself that what he knows intuitively is not empirically verifiable.

When the oil lamp flickers, foreshadowing the death of the sick woman, what becomes clear in the darkened room is that it is very late and all are exhausted by the strain of waiting and worrying. In a long, emotional outburst, broken by pauses which reveal his concern, fear, grief, frustration, and ignorance, the Old Man harangues his audience only to realize that their silence is deafening. "Mais pourquoi ne parlez-vous plus?" he demands. Their muteness gives him the long-overdue opportunity to vent his hitherto unspoken observation: "Il s'est passé quelque chose dans la maison. . . . Il y a des moments où je suis moins aveugle que vous, vous savez? . . ." After a long pause in which the Old Man gathers his strength and his wits, he informs those gathered in the room, "Je n'ose pas dire ce que je sais ce soir . . . Mais je saurai la vérité . . . J'attendrai que vous disiez la vérité" (1:236). It is in the pauses between emotional outbursts that the grandfather exposes the depth of his torment and his sense of victimization at the hands of his family and the hands of the unseen intruder. Though he strikes out verbally against his loved ones, what remains unspoken is the utter frustration of shadowboxing with death.

So unnerved is the father that he suggests changing the tone and topic of conversation by physically moving from the room to that of the sick woman in order to verify her condition. The grandfather's probing questions and intimations about a presence in the room have succeeded in disorienting not only the father and uncle, but also his granddaughters, who intermittently break their silence and cry in unison: "Grand-père! grand-père! qu'avez donc, grand-père?" The grandfather, hesitant and reluctant to enter his daughter's room, declines the invitation of the father to clear up the misunderstanding about the events of the evening. "Non; non, pas maintenant . . . ," he replies, respecting a mystical sense of timing which supersedes his own. Qualifying his denial, "pas encore . . . ," the Old Man's voice drifts off, the enigmatic thought left incomplete. What remains unspoken is that he will enter his daughter's room after death departs (1:237).

Still another duologue concerning physical, intellectual, and spiritual illumination is suggested by the flickering lamp. The noise it makes elicits the Old Man's observation, "Il me semble qu'elle est bien inquiète . . . bien inquiète . . . ," but this comment, while realistic and verifiable, intimates the uneasiness which has reigned and reigns in the room. Repetition of the term "inquiète," so often echoed through the play in conjunction with the pause which surrounds and emphasizes the word, reinforces and affirms the circularity, indeed obsessiveness, of the grandfather's thoughts.

Movement, which has not been mentioned since someone was thought to be in the garden earlier in the evening, recalls the motifs of interior and exterior and physical as opposed to chronological progression. Like a caged animal, the uncle cannot sit still but has taken to pacing expectantly about the room. His groping speech, punctuated by pauses and a final silence of disorientation, mirrors his efforts to relax the tension which grips him:

C'est moi, c'est moi, n'ayez pas peur. J'éprouve le besoin de marcher un peu. *(Silence)* —Mais je vais me rasseoir; —je ne vois pas où je vais. *(Silence)*
                                                                                              (1:241)

Lacking physical and linguistic control of the situation, the uncle's pacing only serves to obliterate any thread of assurance or security he still holds. In stark contrast to the immobility of the initiates, Death, which Maeterlinck terms "la présence infinie, ténébreuse, hypocritement active," moves through the room announcing its arrival in the imperceptible fall of dead leaves (1:iv).

Darkness finally descends upon the room and so does silence. The family, no longer relying upon language to separate them from their fear, each other, or the truth of the situation which they can no longer pretend to control, yield to the power of silence, preferring its truth to the artificiality they had sought to impose on the chaos of their minds. In her critique of *L'Intruse*, Daniels observes that "when the material object of fear" is close, the characters maintain "a kind of paralyzed silence" broken only by a repetitive, somnambulistic dialogue of half-thoughts echoing and dying.[50] The following passage from the concluding moments of the drama is illustrative:

> *L'Oncle:* Il me semble qu'elles sont bien pâles, ce soir.
> *(Silence)*
> *L'Aieul:* Qu'est que j'entends encore?
> *La Fille:* Rien, grand-père; ce sonts mes mains que j'ai jointes.
> *(Silence)*
> *L'Aieul:* Et ceci? . . .
> *La Fille:* Je ne sais pas, grand-père . . . peut-être mes soeurs qui tremblent un peu?

When a ray of light penetrates the darkness, the clock chimes to announce midnight and the sound of someone rising is heard in the room. The climactic moment is underscored by the Old Man's insistent, recurring question, "Qui est-ce qui s'est levé?" Despite the granddaughters' echoing, stichomythic denials, "Moi non plus!" he insists, "Quelqu'un s'est levé de table!" (1:243–44). The intruder has approached, entered, and passed through, and Maeterlinck's stage instructions call for "un vagissement d'épouvante" which continues "avec des gradations de terreur, jusqu'à la fin de la scène." The child's cry is heard, and the Sister of Mercy appears to silently announce, by the sign of the cross, the death of the mother. After a pause during which members of the family grasp the full meaning of the silent message, their reactions implicitly convey that for each the loss of the loved one—depending upon his or her relationship, age, and psychological preparedness—is a distinctly different experience. Through silence, Maeterlinck elicits not only the invisible and ineffable, but also the unexpressed and inexpressible reactions to the forces which determine our existence.

The Old Man, left alone in the shadows, calls to the others: "Où allez-vous? —Où allez-vous?" (1:245), but their silent response confirms what he has known throughout the evening, and probably what he has known since his daughter first gave birth to the mute child. In all of his attempts to alert the others to impending danger, he has stubbornly refrained from expressing an unspeakable truth, that his daughter would succumb to death. Maeterlinck has focused his art of indirect language and silent response on the unspoken, rather than the unspeakable, but in the face of death unspoken responses are not merely inexpressible, they are unspeakable.

In this multidimensional drama our attention is focused on stasis: the immobility of the sick mother, the immobility and impassivity of the six around the table, and the immobility of death. Yet juxtaposed with this fixity is emotional progression in accord with accurately recorded chronological progression. The dialogue, in conjunction with time, performs bilaterally. On the quotidian level, it carries realistic action in time: we wait, we justify the natural noises we hear while waiting, we respond to the passing of time. But on the mystical level silent communication takes place between denuded souls in an enclosed detention center who anticipate menace, experience it and respond to the menace which invisibly separates them and unites them in disaster. Time, mirrored in ellipses, pauses, and silences—all of which Maeterlinck differentiates—and indirect, nonprogressional dialogue appear to be static. In the absence of speech the natural, timeless flux of life and death is imaginatively reenacted and implicitly communicated.

We must note the striking and irrevocable silence of the character on whom the attention of the audience has been fixed. The physical and linguistic nonparticipation of the young mother in the play's tight social unit contrasts sharply with the fact that she is a constant topic of conversation. We concern ourselves with her welfare and her destiny and anticipate her demise; but this woman, whose postnatal illness has precipitated the weariness and worry of the family, the call to the doctor, the journey of the Sister of Mercy, and the all-night vigil, is dramatically dead to us from the inception of the play. And similarly in *Les Aveugles* the priest, who is the cause of worry and anxiety, is dead initially; the blind simply do not know this and thus keep him "alive" through their anxious verbal and physical peregrinations. The technique of speaking about the mute as if he or she were there is an essential contribution to the theatre of the unexpressed that has also been employed in twentieth-century drama.[51]

One of the most striking silences in *L'Intruse* is that of the playwright, who chooses not to employ dialogue as a vehicle for his mystical philosophy. Knowing that silence is the most suitable medium for his message, Maeterlinck makes the confrontations among the grandfather, the father, and the uncle as natural and as strained as they would realistically be, considering the differences in ages, personality, and reactions to crisis, as well as the clearly important but only implicitly suggested problem of blood marriage. Maeterlinck does not ask us to believe that the Old Man is right, the others wrong; but by leaving his point of view unexpressed, he allows his audience and readers to evaluate the unidentifiable noises in the garden, the cold draughts, and other phenomena which refuse to be delimited. The approach, intrusion, and departure of the seventh from our midsts—ours because we, too, are inextricably drawn by the intensity of the emotion simultaneously expressed and unexpressed—is a universal as well as a daily experience. In choosing to locate the "action" in the family and its quotidian setting, in choosing the illness of the mother, a newborn child, and the visit of death as his subject, Maeterlinck has placed his mystical philosophy within a naturalistic situation, merging thought with technique. In a letter to Albert Mockel before he wrote *L'Intruse*, Maeterlinck confided, "Ce que nous considerons comme des instruments de découverte et d'échange, la vision, la parole, ce sont au contraire, les marques de notre infirmité: l'oeil nous empêche de voir; le mot nous empêche de nous comprendre. Le seul clairvoyant est donc ici l'aveugle!"[52] Accordingly, not only in his linguistic techniques and his mute characterizations, but also in his silent posture, Maeterlinck implicitly emphasizes that he does not have the word—the right one or the last one. Rather, he encourages a silent theatre that communicates emotional and metaphysical truth through silent response.

Maeterlinck was to be occupied with the silent communication of philosophical truth until the completion of *La Mort de Tintagiles* in 1894, but he did not again achieve the unity of purpose and design that he accomplished in *L'Intruse*. He is most effective in this play because he communicates not the spiritual, empirical, or metaphysical truth, but the intensity of feeling produced by the truth.

In his study of the Symbolist movement, Arthur Symons suggests that Maeterlinck's symbolical theatre was itself a symbol; but for the theatre-going public of the 1890s it was not a symbol they cared to decipher.[53] Lacking demonstrable crises, consequential dialogue, play of emotions, and the exchange of ideas, as Balakian explains, it was deemed nondramatic for failing to entertain or instruct.[54] By eliminating the intellect and concentrating on a narrow field of pure emotion, Maeterlinck limited himself to a few variations on a theme which quickly exhausted themselves.

Although his static theatre was soon considered dead as a literary experiment, in this century new attention has been paid to it—and to Maeterlinck as a linguistically innovative precursor of both Jean-Jacques Bernard's theatre of silence and the theatre of the absurd.[55] As Marcel Postic notes, Maeterlinck's early dramas are worthy of our consideration as "les premiers temoinages de l'expression tragique de l'angoisse contemporaine."[56]

The drama of Chekhov exhibits sophistication of the indirect dialogue and silent response with which Maeterlinck experimented and which he employed to satisfy his mystical preoccupations. In Chekhov's hands subtlety and the silence of the unexpressed become the tools of an infinitely talented and humane artist.

NOTES

1. May Daniels, *The French Drama of the Unspoken*, Language and Literature, no. 3 (Edinburgh: Edinburgh University Press, 1953), 16. This is a perceptive landmark study in the *théâtre de l'inexprimé*; see particularly the chapters on Maeterlinck and Bernard.

2. See Arthur Symons, *The Symbolist Movement in Literature*, "Maeterlinck as a Mystic," 84–93.

3. It is important to note that this reference (and all future reference to Maeterlinckian drama in this book) refers to his early dramas, 1889–94, *La Princesse Maleine* to *La Mort de Tintagiles* inclusive, where the unexpressed is inextricably linked to thought and technique.

4. Maurice Maeterlinck, *Théâtre* (Brussels: P. Lacomblez, 1903), 1:217 (references hereafter will be to this edition unless otherwise indicated).

5. On the "analogy of innocence" see Northrop Frye, *Anatomy of Criticism: Four Essays* (Princeton, N.J.: Princeton University Press, 1957), 151–59.

6. Ibid., 153.
7. Maurice Maeterlinck, Preface, *Plays of Maurice Maeterlinck*, 2d ser., trans. Richard Hovey (1896; reprint, Great Neck, N.Y.: Core Collection Books, 1977), ix.
8. Suzanne Langer, *Philosophy in a New Key: A Study in the Symbolism of Reason, Rite and Art*, 3d ed., (Cambridge, Mass.: Harvard University Press, 1942), 123.
9. See Guy Michaud, *Message poétique du symbolisme* (Paris: Nizet, 1947), for a discussion of *théâtre de l'attente*. Regarding the issue of stasis in this theatre, Balakian suggests, in *The Symbolist Movement*, "If there is an impression of an absence of crisis in these plays, it is because the crisis is in truth ever-present, and that continuous presence must be conveyed by a high pitch of sensitivity rather than action" (125–26).
10. Marcel Postic, *Maeterlinck et le symbolisme* (Paris: Editions Nizet, 1970), 48.
11. Daniels, *French Drama of the Unspoken*, 54.
12. Bettina Knapp, *Maurice Maeterlinck* (Boston: Twayne, 1975), 59.
13. Rainer-Marie Rilke, quoted in Roger Bodart, *Maurice Maeterlinck* (Paris: Editions Pierre Seghers, 1962), 86.
14. See Frye, *Anatomy of Criticism*, 159; Maud Bodkin, *Archetypal Patterns in Poetry* (1934; reprint, London: Oxford University Press, 1963), 52–53, (a trenchant discussion of poetical cyclical structures).
15. Anna Balakian, *The Symbolist Movement: A Critical Appraisal* (New York: Random House, 1967), 136–37.
16. See, for example, T. S. Eliot, "'Rhetoric' and Poetic Drama," *Selected Essays* (1932; reprint, New York: Harcourt, Brace, 1950), 29. Eliot suggests that Maeterlinck's inarticulated emotions are not worthy of articulation.
17. Regarding the Parisian theatre of this period, see Daniels, *French Drama of the Unspoken*, chap. 2, "The French Theatre after 1870," 17–45, for an excellent survey of the Scribean influence, the attempts to counter this artificiality in the drama, and the importance of the *animateurs*, particularly Antoine, Paul Fort, and Lugné Poë, to emerging modern drama.
18. Ibid., 12–13.
19. Sammie Jo Mullen, "The Poetic Techniques of Maurice Maeterlinck" (Ph.D. diss., New York University, 1974), 135.
20. Daniels, *French Drama of the Unspoken*, 43.
21. Maurice Maeterlinck, *Théâtre* (Paris: Bibliothèque Charpentier, 1929), 2:58 (references hereafter will be to this edition).
22. It is interesting to note that the preoccupation with observation by an unseen being and/or his abandonment is of primary importance in the theatre of silence in the twentieth century. See in particular the role of menace in Pinter and that of isolation in Beckett. Note that Vladimir's observation in *En attendant Godot*—"Moi aussi, un autre me regarde, en se disant, Il dort, il ne sait pas, qu'il dorme"—echoes the Old Man's prophetic words.
23. Mullen, "Poetic Techniques of Maurice Maeterlinck," 135.
24. Suzanne Langer, *Philosophy in a New Key*, 19.
25. Maurice Maeterlinck, *Le Trésor des humbles* (Paris: Mercure de France, 1896), 173–74.
26. Jean-Marie Andrieu, *Maeterlinck* (Paris: Editions Universitaires, 1962), 51.
27. With regard to Maeterlinck's use of dialogue as "thematic communication" rather than "consequential dialogue," see Balakian, *The Symbolist Movement*, 155.
28. Maeterlinck, *Le Trésor des humbles*, 22. The essays "Le Silence" and "Le tragique quotidien" contain Maeterlinck's dramatic theories of the unexpressed and are essential to an understanding of his mysticism and methodology.
29. Ibid., 13.
30. Maeterlinck, Preface, *Plays*, ix.
31. Guy Donneux, *Maurice Maeterlinck: Une poésie, une sagesse, un homme* (Brussels: Palais des Académies, 1961), 80.
32. Daniels, *French Drama of the Unspoken*, 56.
33. Jethro Bithel, *Life and Writings of Maurice Maeterlinck* (London: Walter Scott, 1913), 12.
34. Stéphane Mallarmé, *Oeuvres complètes*, ed. Henri Mondor and G. Jean-Aubry (Paris: Editions Gallimard, 1945), 869. See particularly Mallarmé's dramatic criticism included in this edition, "Crayonné au théâtre," 293–351.
35. Haskell Block, *Mallarmé and the Symbolist Drama* (Detroit, Mich.: Wayne State University Press, 1963), 34. See 85–103 for an informative précis on Mallarmé's concept of the theatre, the influence of Wagner, and the importance of ritual and Catholic mass.

36. Mallarmé, *Oeuvres complètes*, 300.

37. Block, *Mallarmé and Symbolist Drama*, 34.

38. In Jules Hurêt, *Enquête sur l'évolution littéraire* (Paris: Fasquelle, 1891), 128, Maeterlinck acknowledges his debt to Villiers.

39. Jean-Marie Villiers de l'Isle-Adam, *Oeuvres complètes*, vol. 4 (Geneva: Slatkine Reprints, 1970), 265.

40. Daniels notes that *Axel* was not produced until 1894, but that Maeterlinck was obviously familiar with the text (see Daniels, *French Drama of the Unspoken*, 35–40).

41. Mullen, "Poetic Technique of Maurice Maeterlinck," 78.

42. Daniels, *French Drama of the Unspoken*, 45.

43. Donneux, *Maurice Maeterlinck*, 86. Concerning the role of the fairy tale see Knapp's trenchant study, *Maurice Maeterlinck*.

44. Daniels, *French Drama of the Unspoken*, 43.

45. Balakian, *The Symbolist Movement*, 132.

46. For an informative précis of the history, publication, stage production, and the various stimuli responsible for the subject and style of *L'Intruse*, see Joseph M. Hanse, "La genèse de *L'Intruse*," in *Le Centenaire de Maurice Maeterlinck, 1862–1962*, comp. Académie Royale de Langue et de Littérature Française (Brussels: Palais des Académies, 1964), 177–202.

47. Balakian, *The Symbolist Movement*, 132.

48. The blindness theme, which appears in other Maeterlinckien plays (most obviously *Les Aveugles*), has its origin here.

49. Beckett's bums who while away the hours waiting are reminiscent of Maeterlinck's characters who pass the time by commenting on the exterior environment.

50. Daniels, *French Drama of the Unspoken*, 57.

51. It is interesting to note that the mute, both offstage and on, is an important personage in the *théâtre de l'inexprimé*. We will see him also in Beckett, Pinter, and Albee.

52. Maeterlinck to Albert Mockel, 15 February 1890, quoted in Postic, *Maeterlinck et le symbolisme*, 61.

53. Regarding the reception of these plays, see W. D. Halls, *Maurice Maeterlinck: A Study of His Life and Thought* (Oxford: Clarendon Press, 1960), 40.

54. Balakian, *The Symbolist Movement*, 145–46.

55. Concerning reevaluation of Maeterlinckian theatre, see ibid., 131–55; Postic, *Maeterlinck et le symbolisme*, 157–59; Joseph Chiari, *Landmarks of Contemporary Drama* (London: Herbert Jenkins, 1965), 67–70.

56. Postic, *Maeterlinck et le symbolisme*, 159.

3
Chekhov

Anton Chekhov, respected for the concision, objectivity, sensitivity, and humanity of his short stories, began writing for the theatre in the 1880s. He was, in the opinion of Robert Corrigan, "the first playwright who sought to create in his plays a situation which would reveal the private drama that each man has inside himself and which is enacted everyday in the random, apparently meaningless and undramatic events of our common routine."[1] *The Sea Gull*, *Uncle Vanya*, *The Three Sisters*, and *The Cherry Orchard*, written at the end of the nineteenth century and the beginning of the twentieth, represent perfection of the Chekhovian dramatic form: the subtle, complex interplay of expression and suggestion.

Chekhov achieves the coalescence of phenomenal and psychological experience by fusing thought and technique.[2] His experimentation with dramatic form, content, and linguistic methodology results from his intention to present the complexity, universality, and essential mutability of life. Therefore, examination of Chekhov's symbolist and naturalist techniques, his use of the quotidian, and his apparently static structure can lay the foundation for an estimation of this playwright's distinctive use of the unspoken.

In *The Breaking String* Maurice Valency suggests that the dominant literary trend of the fin de siècle was symbolism and that Chekhov, responsive to literary experimentation, came very much under its influence.[3] Affinity to symbolism is apparent in Chekhov's lyrical interpretation of experience, concern for the transitory nature of beauty, evocation of mood, literary reference, and use of nuance, intimation, and suggestion, as well as his exploitation of symbols and emphasis on imprecision. Indeed, it is the dramatist's reliance on introspection and the synthesis of concrete reality with interior mood that most clearly align Chekhov to symbolist techniques.

A skeptic living in an age characterized by doubt and unrest, Chekhov did not share the symbolist's mysticism but nevertheless maintained that there is discrepancy between what man has and what he strives for. Central to his mature work is a spiritual unrest, rooted in awareness of life's mysteries and incompleteness coupled with the expectation of something better.

It would be a mistake, however, to label Chekhov a symbolist, just as it would be erroneous to label him a naturalist or social critic.[4] Chekhov wears all these hats and is defined by none. "Life as it is"—the barren facts of substantial reality and private, half-conscious perceptions, illusions, suspicions, and reveries of insubstantial experience—provide the content for this artist's drama; he provides the artistic form to realize and imaginatively distill its essence. Emphasizing the importance of artistic objectivity, Chekhov writes:

> In life people do not shoot themselves or hang themselves, or fall in love or deliver themselves of clever sayings every minute. They spend most of their time eating, drinking, running after women or men, talking nonsense. It is therefore necessary that this be shown on the stage. A play ought to be written in which people should come and go, dine, talk of the weather or play cards not because the author wants it that way but because that is what happens in real life.[5]

Taking his cue from the authenticity of Chekhov's portrait of reality and the dramatist's insistence on objectivity, John Lahr stresses the impact of Zola's naturalism on the naturalistic character of Chekhov's dramas.[6] And Robert Brustein concurs that the seemingly "arbitrary landscape, character details, aimless dialogue, silences, shifting rhythms and poetic mood" which typify Chekhovian drama constitute the most convincing attempt at dramatic verisimilitude of the modern theater.[7] However, we are admonished, by Chekhov's own correspondence, to distinguish between scientific accuracy and creative artifice. "I may note incidently," he writes to Grigori Rossolimo, "that artistic considerations do not always allow me to write in complete harmony with scientific data; on stage you cannot show death by poisoning as it actually occurs."[8]

Clearly, Chekhov is neither a symbolist nor a naturalist, but an astute artist who employs techniques peculiar to both schools of thought to create an "artifice of reality," to use Bernard Beckerman's term, which subtly balances subjectivity and objectivity, interiority and exteriority, vague intimations and clearly delimited detail, psychological time and anthropocentric chronicity in order to achieve emotional realism.[9] The seemingly formless Chekhovian form is a meticulously constructed dramatic composition stripped bare of the lines of construction to convey naturally the desired effect of fluidity and fixity. Lacking in intrigue, complication, climax, and denouement, the mature plays are a sequence of scenes wherein spatial arrangement supplants linear arrangement and unity of mood supplants unity of action.[10]

Both Valency and F. L. Lucas have noted the importance of Maeterlinckien static drama to the development of Chekhov's methodology.[11] Chekhov's plays employ the substitution of the effects of an event for the event itself, the use of nuance and suggestion to evoke mood, the use of quotidian dialogue, family gatherings in restricted areas, and an apparently quiescent structure that belies cyclical and chronological fluctuation.[12] But Chekhov's is the more gentle, subdued, and deeply analytic art. Maeterlinck's static drama evokes an atmosphere of spiralling anxiety, but Chekhov's drama elicits sustained *nastroenie;* Maeterlinck's gatherings are excruciating and funereal, Chekhov's characteristically ceremonious, social occasions such as name day celebrations, summer reunions, and farewell gatherings. The focus of Maeterlinck's static plays is the silent progression, intrusion, oppression, and finality of death, but death is displaced in Chekhovian drama by the agonizing, progressively debilitating process of dying. Ossifying in their rural surroundings, Chekhov's characters eventually wither and waste away, witness to and participant in the destruction of themselves, their environment, their social order.[13] Characteristically, in addition, Chekhov eschews the archetypes of young and old, preferring to reflect emotional, material, spiritual, and temporal dispossession through varying states of decrepitude. In *Uncle Vanya*, for example, Vanya and Sonya are threatened with the loss of their estate; in *The Three Sisters* and *The Cherry Orchard* eviction and dispossession are an accomplished fact. Spiritual deterioration is illustrated in these plays by Andrey's loss of hope, Nina's loss of innocence, Mme. Ranevsky's loss of beauty, Masha's loss of Vershinin. For all, the loss of time is the most shocking and the most difficult to accept. Vanya's reaction is typical:

> *Vanya:* Day and night the thought that my life has been hopelessly wasted
> weighs on me like a nightmare. I have no past, it has been stupidly
> wasted on trifles, and the present is awful in its senselessness.
>
> (205)

Significantly, epiphanic awareness comes to Chekhov's characters when it is too late to reverse their ossification and deterioration. They are, and remain, helpless and passive in the face of social and cosmic forces which determine their lives.

Like Maeterlinck's pilgrims, Chekhov's characters wait, but for the anxious wait for Sisters of Mercy, priests, news of death, and escape from entrapment the Russian static dramas substitute the less terrifying, but no less anxious, tiresome, and debilitating wait for trains, for carnival people, for auctions, for lovers, for duels, for the release from boredom, for the realization of dreams—and, always, for tea.

Unlike nineteenth-century playwrights for whom the quotidian either depicted customary manners and morals or was overshadowed by events, Chekhov moved events to the periphery, as if they were details, and brought the ordinary, constant and recurring to center stage. Like Maeterlinck, he exploited the daily flow of the customary and habitual, not as setting but as subject of his art. To support his artistic representation of "life as it is" and to dramatize continuity and perpetuity, Chekhov employed the four-act structure, preferring the elongated form to the Maeterlinckien one-act structure and the naturalistic *quart d'heure.*[14] Emphasizing progression in time, rather than in action, Chekhov provides us with great specificity of detail: intricate arrival/departure patterns, pertinent "acts of God," the exact season, date, and age of the characters.[15]

Nature figures importantly in the Chekhovian tapestry, providing a beautiful background for the drab foreground and graphically showing the cyclical and degenerative pattern of life. For example, in the first acts of *The Three Sisters* and *The Cherry Orchard* the reunion coincides with the springtime; the mood is expectant and exultant. In Act 4, on the other hand, the mournful farewell is set against the autumn sky and the imminent destruction of the trees; the mood is one of distress and disillusionment. Similarly, in Act 1 of *The Sea Gull* the heat of the summer season mirrors the burning passion of the lovers Treplev and Nina who are united in the birth of their artistic creation; but by Act 4 we learn that Nina has carried, delivered, and buried Trigorin's baby. His career aborted and his love for Nina unrequited, a despondent Treplev takes his own life on a night when the wind howls through the chimney and windows are shuttered against the draft.

Simultaneous with chronological progression, Chekhov focuses attention on the changing state of consciousness of each character. By particularizing temporal details, the playwright fashions a fragment of time in which everything, or more accurately, nothing, takes place. And by subordinating plot to characterization and event to stasis, he diverts attention from process to motive, from phenomenal reality to psychological.[16] The pervading effect, as William Gerhardi observes, is "at once static and transitory," indeed "static in its absolute transitoriness."[17]

However, the seemingly quiescent surface belies fluidity. The conclusion of each play (superficially similar to the beginning, but strikingly different in its lack of hope) confirms the swift passage of time which has gone unnoticed. Loss displaces promise; weariness displaces vitality; waste displaces beauty; resignation displaces hope.

Chekhov, cognizant of the iconoclastic nature of his structure and content, wrote to Alexei Suvorin in 1895, "I sin frightfully against the conventions of the stage . . . lots of talk on literature, little action and tons of love."[18] Significantly, the playwright fails to note that love in his dramas is either painfully or perpetually unsatisfied and unsatisfying or, if satisfied, painfully transitory. Beckerman suggests that the number of transitory and unfulfilled love affairs, with the central position they occupy in Chekhov's plays, is notable when seen against the background of the decay of aristocratic society.[19] But the number is crucial, less for its social relevance than for the multivalent human responses associated with it. Chekhov chose as central a universal emotion, ambivalent and evanescent in nature, which defies the limitation of time, place, and verbal expression. Unlike Maeterlinck's silent plays which primarily evoke the condition of fear, his drama elicits the vacillating, prismatic, confounding emotion of love tempered by joy, expectation, hope, disillusionment, and the searing pain of loss and rejection. Put differently, Chekhov's treatment of love is a function of his treatment of time: at once static and transitory, at once empirically verifiable and psychologically imprecise, at once measured and illimitable.

Because Chekhov's drama is a forum of emotion, not idea, the universal, evanescent, insubstantial, and undefinable emotions of loneliness and loss take their place with love in the broad spectrum of life experience that the dramatist impressionistically presents. Typically, Chekhov draws his content from life as it is; but the well he taps is deep and dark, and the emotions he evokes are inextricably linked to his use of the unspoken.

Chekhovian dialogue performs a great number of essential dramatic functions: revealing character, furthering the action (more particularly, inaction), uncovering theme, and arousing in the spectator a mood similar to that of the character.[20] However, this playwright fulfills these dramatic necessities in an innovative way: by simulating aimless, fluid speech and thought. So convincing is the Chekhovian linguistic artifice that it may appear to be an irrational choice and accidental arrangement of words. But Chekhov is a consummate craftsman; what appears alternatingly fluid and fixed is in fact achieved by the intricate counterpointing of speech and silent response. Crucial to a study of Chekhov's use of the unspoken is the relationship of symbolist and naturalist techniques, deceptive stasis, cyclical flux, and the quotidian to this dramatist's linguistic innovations. The distinctive elements of his methodology may be considered under these topics:

1. disjunctive, indirect speech
2. colloquial dialogue
3. negation
4. repetition and echoing
5. pauses
6. counterpointing through overstatement and understatement
7. silent scenes
8. mute characters
9. silence as a metaphor for isolation
10. silence as a metaphor for evanescence
11. silence of the playwright

Oblique disjunctive speech elicits imperceptible fluctuation both within the mind of the speaker and between speakers. Repetitions, recurring motifs, and pauses reinforce the apparent stasis suggested by the eventless drama, and the continued use of negations (which have the effect of nullifying the statement just made) effectively slow or reverse the progression of time. Overstatement and understatement, moreover, report, by their exaggeration, both the emotional condition of the speaker and the quotient of attention and reception his comments receive from the listener. Kahn observes that through antiphonal counterpointing the dramatist achieves the impact of ironic statement that has the "special effect of not actually being stated."[21]

Unlike his predecessor in the symbolist theatre, the Russian playwright did not wish to accentuate the distance between speech and silence, the quotidian and the profound, the human and the mystical. Demonstrating grace and artistry of concision, Chekhov softens the harsh lines of Maeterlinck's polarized portrait through resonance, achieving in language the indistinctness and imprecision which typify all of his art.[22] The resonances produced by choral speaking, negative statement, understatement and overstatement, and the repetitive use of pauses narrow the gap between speech and silence while simultaneously revealing the distance between thought and meaning, between illusion and reality, between a person's conception of himself and the conceptions of his companions, and between speaker and listener. Indeed, Chekhov manifests his modernity by his awareness of man's essential fragmentation and isolation. Chekhovian characters escape to the relative security of memory or the relative promise of philosophy in order to forge a link in time and meaning. But as Corrigan observes, Chekhov, more than any other dramatist of the late nineteenth and early twentieth century, was very conscious of the existential loneliness of the human condition. In order for him to portray life as it is, Chekhov had to define his characters by their "solitude and estrangement from life" and not by their participation in it.[23] Chekhov employs restricted settings to underscore the fact that his characters are always in close physical contact, but rarely, if ever, in emotional contact. Efforts to break out of the imprisonment of isolation are foiled or gently mocked: confidences are ignored, confessions fall on deaf ears.

Aware that speech, like time, is an anthropocentric effort to limit, control, and elucidate the chaos of experience, Chekhov relies on the unspoken to expose and examine the elusive and the enigmatic both within and beyond man. Disjunctive, indirect speech is particularly well suited to the dramatization of exterior and interior experience. Citations from the mature plays clearly illustrate the discontinuity in conversation when one voice drifts off and another picks up the dropped line, in situations of physical or emotional stress or exhaustion, in the reversal or corrected direction of a thought. In the arrival scene of *The Cherry Orchard*, for example, the thoughts of Mme. Ranevsky, Gaev, Charlotta, Pishtchik, Dunyasha, and Varya overlap and cut across one another. What the dialogue lacks in continuity, it gains in authenticity. Mme. Ranevsky, exhausted from the long trip and the trauma of returning from Paris nearly destitute, is nevertheless exhilarated by the sight of her beloved nursery. Memories of her childhood flood her mind and fill the moment. Time and speech momentarily stop for her, and then through tears she remembers the presence of her own daughter, Varya. "Varya's just the same as ever," she notes, but for Gaev, who has been impatiently waiting two hours for her delayed train, time did not stand still. Grumbling about the delay and the ineptitude of the rail system, Gaev demands, "What do you think of that," but he might as well be talking to himself. At the same moment, Charlotta informs Pishtchik that her dog "eats nuts, too." In all the confusion, both literal and linguistic, Pishtchik replies, "Fancy that," but one hardly knows whether this remark is to answer Mme. Ranevsky, Gaev, or Charlotta—or in fact all three (64).

Through the use of quotidian expressions and situations, this dramatist reveals disjunction not only between participants in a conversation, but also
between the thoughts of one speaker. In the last act of *The Cherry Orchard*
Pishtchik arrives in time to say farewell to the departing family; but in his effort
to cover all the subjects on his mind he jumps from one to another without
apparent logic or continuity:

> *Pishtchik:* What! *(in agitation)* Why to the town? Oh, I see the furniture . . .
> the boxes. No matter . . . *(through his tears)* . . . no matter . . . men
> of enormous intellect . . . these Englishmen. . . . Never mind be
> happy. God will succour you . . . no matter . . . everything in this
> world must have an end *(kisses Lyubov Andreyevna's hand)*. If the
> rumour reaches you that my end has come, think of this old horse,
> and say: "There was once such a man in the world . . . Semyonov-
> Pishtchik . . . the Kingdom of Heaven be his!" . . . most extraordi-
> nary weather . . . yes. *(Goes out in violent agitation, but at once returns
> and says in the doorway)* Dashenka wishes to be remembered to you
> *(goes out)*.

(110)

The passage shows that disjunctive speech is often broken by negative statements which have the effect of linguistically erasing not only what has been
said, but also the progression in thought and time that speech implies. Thus
Chekhov dramatizes the flux between statement and counterstatement and the
stasis achieved by nonprogressional verbal action.

Although indicative of stress and discarded thought, negation also implies an
imposition of silence on a subject that the speaker refuses to participate in and
continue. An excellent illustration of this technique can be found in the beginning of act 4 of *The Three Sisters* when Tchebutykin is approached by Irina,
Kuligin, Andrey, and Masha for information about the impending duel between Tusenbach and Solyony. To each who wants to continue the topic the
doctor offers a variation of this negative statement: "What happened? Nothing.
Nothing much *(reads the paper)*. It doesn't matter!" (172–75). The newspaper
provides escape for the doctor, but it is negation that short-circuits conversation.

In addition to the use of negatives to evoke the impression of stasis, Chekhov
expands and sophisticates the technique of repetition, which had been used
extensively, and obviously, by Maeterlinck to intensify mood and to reinforce
fixity. Chekhovian repetitions, while admittedly tedious, do not intensify
mood; rather, they elicit and continually perpetuate a condition such as entrapment, monotony, frustration, loneliness, despair. In these plays of "come and
go" (structured around intricate arrival/departure paradigms), motifs, phrases,
and pauses repetitively come and go. Significantly, repetition, like other aspects
of Chekhovian drama, works simultaneously on the realistic and psychological
levels and, more importantly, is cumulatively effective. The speaker who reiter-

ates a particular emotion or illusion reveals a compulsive pattern of behavior from which he is unwilling or unable to extricate himself. Thus Kuligin is "content, content, content," or at least he will steadfastly hold to that illusion, while Masha is "bored, bored, bored" with Kuligin. Olga and Irina are typified by their chant "to Moscow," its continued repetition gaining the impact of prayer. With each repetition, however, the disparity between the first expression and those which succeed it, as well as the emotional, spiritual, and linguistic deterioration of the speaker, is progressively laid bare.

The words repeated, moreover, are of less importance than the mental baggage which the reiteration conveys. This is illustrated by the central role that memory plays in the dramas. In memory images are neither recorded nor recalled in strict chronological or spatial order, but rather according to emotional impact and stimulus. Chekhov dramatizes the ability of broken shards of reverie to break through consciousness and find verbal form. A characteristic citation from *The Three Sisters* illustrates the cumulative effect of fragments intermittently reiterated: Masha, who continually recalls phrases from Pushkin's *Ruslan and Lyudmila*, tries to calm herself after Vershinin's departure by reciting the lines. The confusion of her words, however, reflects emotional chaos, signifying to her that she is not in control of her life. "What does 'strand' mean? Why do these words haunt me?" she mourns, seemingly aware for the first time of her entrapment (183). That the words lack meaning does not mean she will be freed from the grip they have on her mind.

Repetitions, however, need not be compulsive. "Echoing," a nuanced, associational variation of the technique of repetition, is particularly effective in these plays of come and go in which reunion and separation of the family are experienced differently by each member. In echoing, the same words are subject to multiple interpretations comparable to the refraction of light by a prism or to a symphonic theme and variation. In the farewell scene of *Uncle Vanya*, for example, Sonya, Marya, Marina, Astrov, and Vanya take note of the departure of Yelena and Serebryakov. The phrase "They've gone" is repeated in turn by each, but the unspoken emotions of loss, relief, and anticipated loneliness inform their mood more accurately than the words they all share. Similarly, the technique is masterfully employed in *The Cherry Orchard*, where, in the opinion of Francis Fergusson, each of the characters, in his own way, gains insight into his or her situation and that of the doomed estate.[24] Essentially, Fergusson maintains by offering a multiplicity of nonverbal responses simultaneously with common expression, Chekhov evokes a condition or an emotion which precedes the emotionally charged attitude of the characters. Undoubtedly, the associational effect of this technique derives in good part from undefined, infinite silence.

The principal recurring motif in Chekhovian theatre is the pause. Static and nonprogressional, and comparable to the rest in musical composition, the pause is an essential and integral element of structure which effectively stalls the advancement of thought, action, and time. Moreover, nonverbal hesitation is

cumulatively effective and responsible in great part for the oppressive sense of
timelessness in Chekhov's world. This dramatist's treatment of the unspoken
includes the silence of impasse, anticipation, reflection, reverie, doubt, revelation and cover-up, helplessness, isolation, and complicity. Although interesting
studies have been written on the quantitative nature of the Chekhovian pause, a
simple count of pauses as they appear in stage directions constitutes a superficial
examination of this dramatist's extensive use of the unspoken.[25] Also to be
considered are his use of silent scenes, such as those of Irina left alone at the end
of act 2 of *The Three Sisters* and of Gaev and Mme. Ranevsky at the end of *The
Cherry Orchard*, his use of mute characters, his use of silence as a metaphor for
entrapment, evanescence, and isolation, and his own silence. These uses will
subsequently be examined more fully; now, however, it is necessary to reiterate
that nonverbal responses are inextricably linked to verbal techniques in Chekhovian drama, just as expression/suggestion informs all the elements of this dramatist's art. In these eventless plays attention must be focused both on all the
events that are not explicitly dramatized and on many responses that are not
explicitly communicated.

Crucial to an understanding of Chekhov's reliance on silent response is the
centrality of the motifs of love, loneliness, and loss—all emotions, essentially
untranslatable, which would be immeasurably reduced in significance, complexity, and verisimilitude if verbally defined and delimited. The following
characteristic passage from *Uncle Vanya* illustrates both the coalescence of verbal
and nonverbal discursiveness and the gamut of silent responses from revelation
to impasse, doubt, anticipation, and reflection. Yelena, who has approached
Astrov on Sonya's behalf, finds herself embroiled in a suggestive tête-à-tête with
the attractive doctor:

> *Yelena* (*perplexed*): Bird of prey! I don't understand.
> *Astrov*: A beautiful, fluffy weasel. . . . You must have a victim! Here I have
>   been doing nothing for a whole month. I have dropped everything. I
>   seek you greedily—and you are awfully pleased at it, awfully. . . .
>   Well, I am conquered; you knew that before your examination (*fold-
>   ing his arms and bowing his head*). I submit. Come and devour me!
> *Yelena*: You are mad!
> *Astrov* (*laughs through his teeth*): You—diffident . . .
> *Yelena*: Oh, I am not so bad and so mean as you think! I swear I'm not (*tries to
>   go out*).
> *Astrov* (*barring the way*): I am going away to-day. I won't come here again,
>   but . . . (*takes her hand and looks round*) where shall we see each other?
>   Tell me quickly, where? Someone may come in; tell me quickly . . .
>   (*Passionately*) How wonderful, how magnificent you are! One
>   kiss. . . . If I could only kiss your fragrant hair . . .
> *Yelena*: I assure you . . .
> *Astrov* (*preventing her from speaking*): Why assure me? There's no need. No
>   need of unnecessary words. . . .

                                                                  (221–22)

Notably, Yelena leaves unspoken her attraction to him, as she leaves unspoken her assurances that, happy in her marriage, she has no interest in pursuing their blossoming relationship. Moreover, the pause which breaks the doctor's speech elicits the chaos of emotions breaking in his heart and mind: the relief of revealing his passion, the exhilaration of seduction, the sexual excitement of Yelena's presence, the frustration of her reluctance to agree upon a meeting place.

Yelena's laconism illustrates one of the most important applications of silence in Chekhovian theatre. It is through their muteness that some of Chekhov's characters, like Masha, Andrey, and Varya, maintain the privacy of their thoughts. It must be remembered that speech shares with time the characteristic of irreversibility; thus, we postulate that characters who prefer the silence of isolation do so to separate themselves not only from the judgment and recrimination of others, but also from a confrontation with the truth within themselves. We note, moreover, that when these withdrawn and normally taciturn characters participate in dialogue, the psychic distance between them and their external reality is emphatically underscored, not necessarily by what they say, but rather by the fact that they speak at all. Corrigan maintains that the use of muteness reveals Chekhov's modernity: his most profound insight is knowing each man is alone and that he seeks to maintain his solitude, though he also knows that for each man solitude is unbearable.[26] Chekhov's characters alternatingly break out of entrapment in self to attempt to relate to others, only to comprehend once more the limitations of their ability to verbalize elusive emotions and the limitations of those who would hear, if they cared to. Thus, typically, Andrey holds his peace while Natasha torments him, questions him, emasculates him, bores him, and lectures him. His response, "I have nothing to say," is counterpointed by the conversation with Ferapont which immediately follows his passive conflict with Natasha (138–39). Significantly, duologue disintegrates into monologue, further emphasizing the solitariness of the individual and the willful or indifferent silent response of the other. Andrey's confession to Ferapont is met with the old man's reply, "I don't hear well" (140). In Chekhovian drama the silence of the mute, broken intermittently, is most often met with the silence of exclusion or incomprehension.

Inarticulateness informs Chekhov's characters and similarly informs the playwright himself. In a frequently quoted letter, Chekhov responds to Suvorin's criticism of his taciturnity, which the latter had equated with indifference and moral irresponsibility:

> You scold me for objectivity, calling it indifference to good and evil, lack of ideals and ideas. . . . Of course it would be nice to combine art with sermonizing, but that kind of thing I find extraordinarily difficult and well-nigh impossible because of technical considerations.[27]

Admittedly, Chekhov valued restraint and concision in art, and in fact he often chided fellow artists for their excessive verbalism.[28] Neither lack of space nor

other "technical considerations," however, prevented Chekhov's subjective intrusion into his material. It is not the form which precedes the artist, but the
artist who devises and controls the medium. Chekhov's style of compression,
which eschews subjectivity, can be explained by his perception of the artist's
role: distillation, not amplification of the complexity of life. He trusted the
reader of his short stories to supply subjective observation; similarly, we can
assume that he expected the audience attending the dramas to do likewise. But
Suvorin failed to realize that the absence of verbalized commentary did not
preclude nonverbal commentary. Unlike his stage characters who talk too much
or too little, Chekhov maintains his silence. Employing imprecision delicately
and evocatively to convey empirical and psychic experience, this playwright
refuses to limit his world by defining himself or his art, because he believes that
"the artist . . . must pass judgment *only on what he understands*."[29] Siegfried
Melchinger observes that Chekhov lived in a loquacious epoch, and his laconism
was thus interpreted as harshness, but it might just as easily have been accurately interpreted as skepticism.[30] The doubt which plagued Chekhov personally and clouded the historical period, shrouds his gray people and gray world.
Compassion replaces indifference.

Chekhov's attitudes about the role of the artist and the interrelationship of
speech, silence, and temporality can be traced directly to the professional and
personal life of the artist, the socio-political milieu of fin de siècle Russia, the
author's experimentation and expertise in the short-story form, and the literary
heritage of Russian theatre which he inherited.

Chekhov's debt to his training and career in medicine is immense; it provided
him with analytical methodology, subject matter, and firsthand exposure to
inexplicable and irremediable suffering.[31] Tuberculosis, which debilitated the
playwright and finally claimed his life in 1904, increased daily his awareness of
and sensitivity to man's vulnerability and ultimate mortality: in his mature
plays the alternatingly static and transitory condition dramatized is one of
suffering. Typically, Drs. Dorn, Astrov, and Tchebutykin lament their helplessness; Dorn cannot relieve Masha's pain, Astrov has no medication for
Vanya, and Tchebutykin, drinking to kill his own pain, can neither help the
wounded injured in the fire nor save the life of the Baron. Although Chekhov
does not explicitly exploit the shifting political scene and the social depression in
his Russia, the reality of the menacing and tedious situation provides the macro-
cosmic contrast for the unrelieved mental and physical suffering of his characters.

Valency maintains that Chekhov's drama profited most from his short-story
writing (his most prolific period immediately antedates *Uncle Vanya*), in which
he perfected the techniques of concision, portraiture, and imprecision, from the
tradition of Ostrovsky, Tolstoy, and Turgenev and from the theatrical reform
in 1882 which Ostrovsky initiated. Ostrovsky's emphasis on the quotidian and
Turgenev's on life as a process of self-realization figured importantly in
Chekhov's use of epiphanic structure and his portrayal of life as it is.[32]

Chekhov's success in the Russian theatre, however, cannot be directly attributed to his dramatic or linguistic versatility and innovativeness, but rather to the uneasy marriage of the avant-garde playwright with the fledgling Moscow Art Theatre in 1898. Nemirovitch-Dantchenko, noting in Chekhov's plays a release from antiquated stage clichés and a depth of psychological perception, encouraged the merger between Chekhov and Stanislavsky, who was less than enthusiastic about the playwright.[33] Everything we know of this union, from Chekhov's correspondence, the reminiscences of Nemirovitch-Dantchenko, and the prompt-book of Stanislavsky, suggests a difficult but rewarding symbiotic relationship between Chekhov and the M.A.T. In Chekhov the ensemble acting company found a native playwright to whom they could readily respond, and Chekhov found a group of accomplished actors who could sensitively bring to life the nuance, resonance, and complexity of his eventless, quiescent dramas. However, Stanislavsky's definition and dramatization of Chekhov's modern realism differed so sharply from that of the playwright that Chekhov complained that Stanislavsky was ruining his plays. The most obvious and most crucial excess for which Chekhov faulted Stanislavsky was the latter's insistence upon natural noises to fill the absence of sound created by the pauses. What the artist had intentionally left evocatively undefined, imprecise, and unexpressed, he would too often find filled not with silence, but with sound.[34]

It is *The Three Sisters*, produced by the M.A.T. on 31 January 1901, which we will subject to exegesis to illuminate Chekhov's idiosyncratic use of the unspoken as it evolves and develops within the text. Although this play contains the greatest number of specifically indicated pauses, it is not for this reason that we look at its text but because, as has been argued, Chekhov's subtle and sophisticated treatment of silence entails in it a coalescence of explicit expression and implicit suggestion, an integral interplay of indicated silences and vague intimations. In this four-act drama duologues are linked by the recurring motifs of love and loss, by references to past and future time, and by the central symbol, Moscow. In order to appreciate the intricate texture of what is only superficially formless, we will need to establish the significance of, and the content and fluctuation both within and between, conversational units.

The initial conversation in *The Three Sisters* typifies the contrasting and associational nature of Chekhovian dialogue. Olga's monologue immediately focuses upon the dissimilarity between Irina's name day and their father's funeral one year ago, and in the pause necessitated by the clock's chiming twelve times, Olga moves deeper into the sadness and loneliness of that time. But the thought of loss and the beauty of springtime elicit still another memory of loss: Moscow displaces both father's death and the gloomy mood. With all that the city implies in terms of culture, vitality, and education, Moscow evokes an enthusiastic expression of longing in Olga, but characteristically Chekhov undercuts her words by the technique of choral speaking. Tusenbach, chatting in another room, answers Tchebutykin's comment with "Of course it's nonsense"; and although this statement is not intended to reply to Olga's, it has the effect of rendering ironic comment on it. Reiterating the longing to escape from provincial morass, Olga's words drift off into reverie, and Irina, echoing the dream of return to Moscow, finishes the statement left incomplete by her sister's silence. Similarly her voice drifts off into silent reverie.

Unlike her younger sister, Olga's longings are not limited to the return to Moscow. This twenty-eight-year-old spinster schoolteacher muses, "If I were married and sitting at home all day, it would be better." Pausing to reflect on the contentment, serenity, and inner peace that married life would offer her, Olga adds, "I should be fond of my husband." Once again Tusenbach's response, directed now to Solyony, cuts across Olga's statement and mocks her wistful ruminations (120–21). Intimated but left unspoken is Olga's awareness that at her age and in their financial situation, her opportunities for marriage are indeed meagre.

This initial dialogue has introduced several important, recurring motifs: loss/promise, death/birth, longing/disillusionment, purpose/uselessness, interiority/exteriority, light/darkness, coming/going, escape/entrapment, and joy/sadness. The unspoken may be presented by silent response, overstatement undercut by negation, understatement, choral speaking, and silent protagonist. Significantly, Masha's refusal to join in the conversation of her two sisters or to respond to Olga's comments signals the lack of unanimity of the three sisters. The dream of Moscow is counterpointed by Masha's disillusionment, their joy by her sadness, their talk of escape by her entrapment in a marriage that yields none of the contentment about which Olga dreams, their faith in promise by her loss of innocence, their emphasis on memory by her forgetfulness. Masha's silent presence implicitly conveys that her sisters' expectations are illusory.

Typically, Chekhov juxtaposes the optimism of Olga and Irina with the cynicism of Tchebutykin, and the next conversational unit employs both fluctuation between one philosophical posture and another and within the mind of a single speaker. Tacitly, the motifs of promise, longing, escape, and purpose are juxtaposed to Tchebutykin's sense of loss, disillusionment, entrapment, and uselessness. One observes, moreover, that his disjunctive speech is continually punctuated by negative statements that have the effect of terminating discussion, rendering ironic comment, and providing figurative, if not literal, escape for the old doctor. The lethargy which typifies this character, however, is displaced by Irina's vitality. Overcome with her beauty and the depth of his love for the girl that might have been his daughter, Tchebutykin addresses Irina, "My white bird . . ." (p. 121). His voice drifts off, the emotions too diffuse to define. Their conversation is broken off by the doctor's departure to retrieve her name day present, and it is only after his exit that we understand that the old man has been impatiently and silently awaiting the arrival of the present. The silence of expectation and the paradigm of coming and going figure importantly in this act, as they inform the structural and linguistic methodology of the play. We await the arrival of Kuligin, Vershinin, and Natasha and the return of Tchebutykin, but while we wait, Masha, a nonparticipant in the conversation and the party mood, decides to go. Feeling the need to offer explanation to her sister Irina, she tries to explain that she is melancholy today, but in her disjunctive speech punctuated by pauses we understand that mourning, unexpressed and uncommunicated to the others, both for her father and for herself, prohibits her participation. Irina discontentedly remarks, "Oh, how tiresome you are. . . ," and Olga tearfully adds, "I understand you, Masha"; but what is clearly implied by the playwright is that neither sister conveys the disappointment she feels nor understands emotions that for Masha are elusive and enigmatic (124).

Masha repeatedly says, "I'll go," but she postpones her departure to make two observations; in stark contrast to her prior laconism, Masha fires a caustic retort to Solyony and renders negative judgment on Protopopov. Chekhov leaves unspoken any further comment on Protopopov, the intruder in this static drama who will menace both the family and the Prozorov homestead though he neither appears nor is heard in the play. This character, comparable to death in *L'Intruse*, makes his presence and power known through tangible and intangible effects on the other characters. Here, the casual and connotative mention of Protopopov in the conversational unit is particularly effective because it is delivered by Masha, who has so insistently kept her counsel, and because it is prophetic.

Attention returns to Tchebutykin, whose present, a samovar, is a most inappropriate gift for Irina. Each sister echoes reprimand and Tusenbach chimes in, "I warned you," but the doctor does not respond to their criticism. Rather he explains, "I am an old man, alone in the world, a useless old man. . . . There is nothing good in me except for my love for you, and if it were not for you, I should have been dead a long time ago . . ." (124–25). His voice drifts off, the thought left unfinished; confused, he has revealed his deep love for their dead mother, who obviously comes to his mind in an emotional moment eliciting birth and death, love and loss.

The awkwardness of the moment is displaced by the arrival of Vershinin, the new battery commander, known to General Prozorov and a regular visitor to the Prozorov home. He tries to place the women, whom he knew as three little girls, and simultaneously they try to place him in their memory. Once again memory links present and past, and once again the mention of Moscow subtly reiterates the motifs of joy and sadness, coming and going. Significantly, it is Olga and Irina who chat with him while Masha, silent and reflective, searches her mind. "Now I remember," she interrupts, but the picture her memory produces is one of a younger, more attractive man. Chekhov reintroduces the theme of love and loss as we learn that the "love-sick" major has not made a very happy match. The most essential and most elusive loss, that of time, to which Vershinin alludes, becomes the topic of a typical philosophical peroration. Tusenbach engages in conversation with Vershinin; but the conviviality of the moment is disrupted, as is their speech, by the intrusion of Solyony, whose "chook, chook, chook" is rude not only to Tusenbach, but also to Vershinin

(128). No further comment is made by Tusenbach or the others gathered, but the silence of the group excludes Solyony, who, like Protopopov, will continue to intrude upon the lives of this family to weave, repetitively and inexorably, a web of disaster.

The only member of the Prozorov family who has not made an appearance is Andrey; his music precedes him. In his absence, his sisters take the opportunity to praise his many talents. Indeed, there is a most awkward silent moment when Irina shows Vershinin the present her brother has made for her birthday; in stark contrast to his usual loquacity, the battery commander is speechless. "Yes . . . it is a thing . . ." is all he can reply (129), his dumb silence conveying how little he thinks of Andrey's handiwork. Rather than speak of craft, the two men speak of education in an exchange that reiterates the theme of promise and foreshadowed loss. The playwright offers no comment on Andrey, but his pessimism with regard to the value of education renders ironic comment on his professed career goals. Andrey's pessimistic attitude elicits Vershinin's famous "future" speech, but what is most pertinent about their conversation is not the political positions each takes, but rather the emotional posture each reveals. Masha, who has been vacillating in her decision to stay or go, simply says, "I'll stay to lunch." Her understatement is startling and suggestive. It is for Irina, young, impressionable, romantic, to sigh and say, "All that really ought to be written down . . ." (130). Her older sister, however, conveys in her silence of communion, if not awe, a deep attraction to Vershinin.

Vershinin continues to speak about possibilities and promise, punctuating with a pause his desire to live again in a house like the Prozorovs' and to live as a bachelor. When at this moment Masha's husband, Kuligin, enters the room and joins in the conversation, for Masha it is an intrusion. The conversation immediately turns to "going," but it is not a departure which Masha welcomes. Whereas earlier in the afternoon she searched for excuses to leave, now with Tusenbach and Tchebutykin she distractedly searches for an excuse to prevent her departure. Anguished, Masha breaks down, "Oh yes, don't go! . . . It's a damnable life, insufferable . . . ," but her incomplete sentence emphasizes the fact that her verbalized despair is only the tip of the iceberg (133).

Masha's outburst is covered by the noise of the crowd entering the dining room for lunch. In the silence, made more apparent by the noise which precedes it, Tusenbach pauses to brace himself for his declaration of love to Irina. Repeatedly he asks, "What are you thinking of?" but her silent response conveys that she does not share his love. She tries to change the direction of his thoughts from love to work, and as her voice drifts off, Natasha, muttering to herself, arrives to intrude upon their privacy. Significantly, the last conversational unit of the act is a reversed replay of this romantic exchange between Irina and Tusenbach. Natasha, who has run from the dining room, embarassed by the teasing of the others, has Andrey in hot pursuit, assuring her of his ardent love and the playful affection of his family. His disjointed speech conveys the excitement and passion that he feels, and unlike Tusenbach Andrey is rewarded by a kiss. Intrusion marks this passionate moment, as the unseeing lovers are observed by Roddey and Fedotik, two officers arriving late for the luncheon. Their silence of amazement passes ironic comment on the passionate lovers, for intimations have been made throughout the act that Natasha would marry Protopopov and that Andrey's affection for the provincial girl is only a ruse to tease his sisters.

The silent, passionate scene which concludes act 1 is strikingly counterpointed by the initial conversational unit of act 2. Chekhov subtly and evocatively links the two acts through a common setting markedly different in mood. Springtime is replaced by a blizzard and sunshine by darkness. The noisy conviviality of the party and the silent affection of the lovers is juxtaposed with the uneasy silence of anticipation and tension which permeates the room, Natasha's calculated and purposeful intrusion upon Andrey's privacy, and Andrey's insistent laconism. Approaching Andrey's room, Natasha appears distracted. "Reading?" she inquires of her husband. "Never mind, I only just asked . . ."; but obviously she has something more on her mind than the late arrival of her sisters-in-law. Continuing to babble about their son Bobik, the carnival people, and his obesity, Natasha suddenly realizes that Andrey has maintained his silence throughout her speech. Affectionately she asks, "Andryushantchik, why don't you speak?" Tacitly Chekhov conveys, by innuendo and mincing tones, vicious quips, and emasculating comments that explain in good part Andrey's reticent response to his wife, that time passing has affected their relationship. We note that her shy affection has metamorphosed into assertive verbiage; and though he says he has nothing to say, his silence of complicity implies that he has no say. Indeed, carefully picking her moment and feigning absentmindedness, Natasha wonders, "Yes . . . what was it I meant to tell you? . . . Oh, yes; Ferapont has come from the Rural Board, and is asking for you" (138–39). Obviously, Natasha has already said what she "meant" to tell him, that she intends to dispossess his sister Irina and put baby Bobik in her room, but her disjunctive speech not only exposes emotional realism but also reinforces the impression of distance and lack of verbal communication between Andrey and herself.[35]

It is only in the duologue between Andrey and Ferapont that we learn that Ferapont has been kept waiting for hours, because no one told Andrey that he was there. Once again the motif of waiting reappears and informs the characters and their responses. Whereas Natasha had been agitated and anxious, the long wait seems to have little effect on the old servant and for Andrey tediousness characterizes life. "It's dull at home . . . (*a pause*)," he notes, but his few words addressed to the old man are emphasized by his inability to continue speaking. Getting a grip on his emotions, he tells Ferapont that for amusement he reread his university lecture notes. "I laughed. . . . Good heavens!" What he does not say is that he laughed until he cried, that boring reality is blessedly relieved by his nightly dreams. Pathetically, Ferapont replies, "I can't say . . . I don't hear well . . . ," but we surmise that he could not say if he could hear well. Andrey, understanding that he has sought protection from ridicule and condemnation by confessing to a deaf man, is agonizingly aware that, although he is among family and friends, he is "a stranger—a stranger . . . A stranger, and lonely. . . ." Ferapont's "Eh?" is underscored by a pause. Andrey has hesitated to verbalize his thoughts, then hesitated to find the proper word to describe his anguish, then repeated and conveyed his obsession with alienation, and Ferapont's monosyllabic response implies a silence of bafflement. The brief conversational unit advances the motifs of promise and disillusionment, coming and going, light and shadow, memory and forgetfulness. Andrey's parting words, "Good-bye *(reading)*. Come to-morrow morning and take some papers here. . . . Go . . . *(a pause)*," significantly fall on deaf ears. Ferapont has already gone, leaving the distracted, disappointed young man alone with his pain (139–41).

After Andrey has again sequestered himself in his room, the audience hears a conversation between Masha and Vershinin obviously begun before their entry into the dining room. The formerly taciturn Masha is now loquacious. Relating her former respect for Kuligin, she continues, "And now it is not the same unfortunately. . . ." In the pause that follows, the absence of speech underscores the depth of her sadness at having to admit to Vershinin, and to herself, that "unfortunately" things are not what they once were. Compassionately and intuitively he replies, "Yes . . . I see. . . ," his voice drifting off to the picture she has wordlessly drawn of her marriage and wordlessly evoked of his (141). The motif of disappointment in love sounded by Masha is echoed by Vershinin, who speaks of his own marital relationship. Styan maintains that although Vershinin claims never to speak of it, he incessantly does and wins Masha by his confession: "Don't be angry with me. . . . Except for you I have no one—no one . . . *(a pause)*," maintaining, moreover, that this is a ploy to seduce Masha.[36] But there is a pitiful aspect to this character which Styan fails to accept. If it is only to Masha that Vershinin confesses, then his is indeed the reverse of Andrey's confession to Ferapont, for Masha thrives on Vershinin's anguish and loneliness and reaps the benefits of his protestations of love. Laughing softly, Masha pleads, "Please don't do it again . . . *(In an undertone)* You may say it though; I don't mind . . . *(covers her face with her hands)*, I don't mind. . . ." The pauses reveal that Masha's heart responds while her mind rejects; her contradictions reinforce her vacillation between reason and passion.

This private emotional scene is counterpointed by one with another couple, but they are unrequited lovers. The pause in Irina's speech reflects neither embarrassment nor infatuation, but rather exhaustion. Tusenbach's talk of joy is countered by her sadness and disillusionment with work. She attempts to explain that "It is work without poetry, without meaning. . . ," but weary in mind and spirit her voice drifts off. In the silence she hears the doctor's signal and entreats Tusenbach, "Do knock, dear . . . I can't . . . I am tired" (143). She is too tired to complete the sentence, too tired even to send a signal.

Tchebutykin joins them and quietly sits reading his paper while Masha and Irina lovingly tease him, but a silence settles over the group. In fact, it is so quiet that Irina inquires of normally talkative Vershinin, "Why are you so quiet?" He explains that he is longing for a cup of tea; what he leaves unspoken is that he is longing to be alone with Masha. Surrounded by family, Vershinin seeks to cover his emotions with silence, but this tactic becomes unbearable. Finally he suggests that Tusenbach and he discuss something, anything, while they wait for tea. Agreeably, Tusenbach concurs. "What shall we speak about?" he asks, but Vershinin answers his question with a question: "What?" "Let us dream . . . ," he suggests; and in the pause following the suggestion we are aware that this is what Vershinin has silently been doing while the others spoke. While the men philosophize about happiness, Masha counterpoints the seriousness of the topic with a joyful, private laugh. But her laugh turns to the silence of contemplation and metaphysical yearning when she intrudes upon the conversation to passionately assert, "One must know what one is living for or else it is all nonsense and waste." The pause which punctuates her protestation reveals the depth of her emotion and the need to believe what the words say rather than the truth she knows the silence suggests (143–47).

Fedotik, Natasha, and Anfisa join the group and the long-awaited tea arrives. Anfisa calls Masha to the table and to Vershinin she says, "Come, your honor . . . excuse me sir. I have forgotten your name." Anfisa hesitates, embarrassed by a lapse in memory that is realistically acceptable, but Chekhov pokes fun at Vershinin, who obviously has been a frequent visitor to the Prozoroz house for at least a year and a half. The mood has changed with the intrusion of the others, and Masha, reluctant to share Vershinin with the others, and unwilling to sit at the table with Natasha and Solyony, leaves her emotions unexpressed. Rather, she asks Anfisa to serve Vershinin and her separately; but alas, no sooner than Vershinin has said, "We have no happiness, and never do have, we only long for it," a letter arrives informing him that once again his wife has attempted suicide. Sadness silently intrudes upon joy, entrapment in marriage supplants escape in love affairs. Noting Vershinin's absence, Anfisa expresses her annoyance that she has just served him tea, but Masha is unwilling to verbalize the cause of her anguish. Instead, she viciously snipes at Anfisa and all around her, leaving herself open to their criticism. Typically, Masha's emotions remain undefined, her distress and disappointment at Vershinin's abandonment unexpressed to her family and friends. Once again we note the motifs of coming and going, purpose and usefulness, longing and disillusionment, superficial conviviality and essential loneliness (148–49).

The motif of expectation is revived at the conclusion of this act as we remember that the carnival people have been expected. But Natasha, whispering to Tchebutykin, leaves it to him to convey to the others that they are not welcome. Masha, who does not accept Bobik's poor health as a credible excuse for Natasha's rudeness, searches for words to describe her sister-in-law. The motifs of escape and entrapment, promise and loss, light and darkness inform the conclusion of the act as they did the initial scene. Andrey sneaks away with Tchebutykin to lose himself gambling, while Solyony sneaks in to surprise

Irina. When he inquires "Are you alone?" she responds "Yes," but quickly seeks to cut off conversation by an abrupt "Good-bye" (153). He professes his love as if he had not heard her response and speaks as if unaware of Natasha's intrusion into the room. The motif of coming and going characterizes the conclusion of this act, as the arrival of the carnival people, the arrival of Vershinin, Kuligin, Solyony, Roddey and Fedotik is counterbalanced by the departure of these, in addition to the departure of Andrey and Tchebutykin and the departure of Natasha for a sleigh ride with Protopopov. Primarily through counterpoint, disjunctive speech, and echoing Chekhov reinforces linguistically the physical oscillation and emotional fluctuation of his characters. Irina, left alone at the end of act 2, moans repetitively, "Oh, to go to Moscow, to Moscow!" Entombed in the desolate room now deserted by the others, she is walled in by loneliness.

Juxtaposed with the silent, empty scene which concludes Act 2 is the cluttered, crowded bedroom which Irina and Olga share that, in a state of disarray, is the initial scene of act 3.[37] In shifting the physical setting from the dining room to a more personal sanctum deeper within the house, Chekhov registers linguistically the literal and metaphoric disorder and disjunction. We observe that the act is composed of an intricate network of conversational units which overlap and cut across one another and essentially share the motif of confession and lack of comprehension. The initial conversational unit involves Anfisa, who has kept her deteriorating relationship with Natasha a secret. Succumbing to the mental and physical strain of the fire, she begs Olga to intercede on her behalf. Olga's disjunctive speech punctuated by pauses exposes the depth of her anguish at the physical deterioration of her beloved nurse and the linguistic barrage which Natasha fires at her. The motif of purpose and usefulness is reiterated as Natasha orders the "useless" Anfisa, whom Olga has had resting, out of the room. There is pause in which Natasha gathers her strength and arrogance: "Why do you keep that old woman, I can't understand!" Anfisa has just admitted to Olga that she is an old woman, Masha discourteously has called the nurse an old woman, and admittedly her visage reveals that she is an old woman; nonetheless, Natasha's use of the term shocks Olga. "Excuse me," Olga retorts, taking a moment to understand the full meaning of Natasha's intent, "I don't understand either. . . ." Understanding is epiphanic awareness; Olga sees as if for the first time Natasha's baseness and coldness, but her revulsion remains unspoken. Natasha characteristically pauses to change the subject and explain that as mistress of the house she must have order. She fails to explain the correlation between old age and disorder, except to imply that old can be defined as obsolete. Natasha maintains the flow of conversation while Olga, her mind spinning with the catastrophic events of the evening and the implication that she will be head mistress, finds herself unable to continue speaking with Natasha. Catching her breath with a drink of water, her words sticking in her throat, Olga responds to Natasha, "You were so rude to nurse now . . . Excuse me, I can't endure it . . . It makes me faint." She cannot endure callousness, she cannot endure Natasha, but her disgust will remain unspoken and her outburst unfinished. Natasha makes a feeble attempt at apology, and it is Masha's unverbalized disgust expressed through silent observation and then physical withdrawal that counterpoints Olga's complicitous silence. The duologue is concluded with the same note of lack of mutual comprehension on which it began. Olga observes, "This night has made me ten years older," but Natasha responds unhearing, "We must come to an understanding . . . that old witch shall clear out of the house tomorrow!" Obviously the old servant was the initial, superficial subject for this tête-à-tête between Olga and Natasha, but more was conveyed in the evocative, threatening, aggressive, and alternatingly placid moments which surround and inform the disjunctive speech (pp. 157–59). Natasha's dispossession of Anfisa anticipates and draws fire from the dispossession of Olga from her room, just as the dispossession of Irina in act 2 was prepared and adequately anticipated. Although she hesitates before changing her tone, Natasha intends to press on for full power of the upstairs management.

Natasha's departure and Kuligin's entrance reverse the tone and prepare for the drunken profundity of Tchebutykin. Significantly, the doctor's emotional confession is dismissed as drunken prattle, just as Gaev's perorations are dismissed as the gabble of a senile old man. Kuligin observes that Tchebutykin is a "bit fuddled," and this superficiality is typical of the comprehension of those gathered. The focus is empirical rather than psychological; Tusenbach is presently organizing a musical benefit for the fire victims. Similarly, Vershinin's comment that the brigade is being transferred goes almost unnoticed: what is intimated is characteristic of Chekhov's artistry. Vershinin's comment is not followed by any exclamation, but rather an evocative generalization. Tusenbach remarks wistfully, "The town will be a wilderness." A wilderness indeed. It is only in act 4 that we begin to perceive the consequences of this statement (159–61).

At this moment, as if to underscore the loss, disappointment, and despair all experience at the news of departure, but characteristically do not verbalize, Tchebutykin smashes the china clock. Returning to the same motif that he sounded earlier, the doctor affirms that negation is affirmation, but the others have been listening without hearing. Seeking to strike out at their deafness, he chants, "Natasha has got a little affair on with Protopopov, and you don't see it" (161). Offering Vershinin a date, Tchebutykin departs, having expressed for the first time a truth known by the others for some time though the silence of evasion afforded them comfortable escape from reality.

Reflecting on all that has transpired during the catastrophic blaze, Vershinin reiterates the motifs of promise and loss, joy and sadness, light and darkness, longing and disillusionment. Anxious and distraught over the proposed departure of the brigade, he speaks in order to control and to conceal his emotions. Masha, silent throughout the act, picks up her pillow and joins Vershinin, her silent response to his comments on the future implying support and compassion. Inspired, Vershinin continues, but knowing that his philosophizing is often annoying in its verbosity he apologizes: "I have such a desire to talk about the future. I am in the mood." The pause which follows underscores the depth of his despair, a despair he hopes to talk his way out of. Concluding his reverie, Vershinin notes, "I am in such a strange state of mind to-day. I have a fiendish longing for life . . . (sings)." No one, not even Tusenbach, answers Vershinin's proselytizing. All that remains unspoken in his speech is his fiendish love for Masha (162–63).

Although the others are present, this conversation appears to be understood only by Masha, for whom it is intended. Masha responds, "Tram-tam-tam!" to which Vershinin echoes, "Tam-tam!" In their special Morse love code, their unanimity is implicitly and nonverbally conveyed.

Solyony enters the room and the mood changes. He upsets Irina and awakens Tusenbach, who sleepily confesses to Irina all that Vershinin left unsaid when conversing with Masha. Unfortunately, his confession of love falls on deaf ears. It is Masha now who has something on her mind, and she encourages not only Tusenbach, but also her own husband, Kuligin, to go. Finally alone with her sisters, she blurts out her frustration at the injustice and waste of her brother's reckless gambling. She is obviously revolted by more than the loss of the family estate; her sense of injustice is related to the loss of her lover and her ultimate entrapment in the provinces with Kuligin. Masha's resentment is counterpointed by Irina's confused, disjunctive speech reflecting a literal and emotional world in disorder. Even her illusion of Moscow seems to slip away as she sobs, "Life is slipping away and will never come back, we shall never, never go to Moscow . . . I see that we shan't go. . . ." Irina had dreamed of meeting her Prince Charming in Moscow; now her repetitions of the word *nonsense* and her incomplete phrases suggest that she wishes that it were not "nonsense." But the repetitive use of negations reinforces the circularity of the thinking as well as the nonprogression of time. Natasha crosses through the room during this emotional scene, and Masha, silent during her sister's confession, interrupts to note that Natasha "walks about as though it were she had set fire to the town" (165–66). Natasha's culpability for the destruction of the Prozorov home, however, goes unverbalized; it is only Natasha's adultery which pricks Masha's mind at this moment and inspires her to confess her sin of adultery to her sisters.

Masha encounters isolating and censuring silence, just as Tchebutykin, Andrey, and Irina have learned that one is essentially alone. A shocked Olga hides behind a screen refusing to hear, while Irina, who just confessed her despair and disillusionment, meets Masha's confession with the silent response of tacit approval. Her long-suppressed confession spent, Masha vows "silence . . . silence . . ." (166–67).

But if the night of raging fire is nearly over, the torrent of confessions is not. Andrey, who clearly had had and wasted potential, promise, and purposefulness, breaks his self-imposed silence about his wanton gambling and its concomitant threat to his sisters, his abdication of responsibility as the head of the family, and his cuckoldry. Initially, Andrey employs language defensively, but then his linguistic control is broken disjunctively by pauses. The sisters, exhausted by the long evening of calamities and confessions, refuse to listen to him. Powerless to respond in anger or to offer compassion, the sisters convey by their silence their annoyance with, and censorious exclusion of, their brother. Indeed, Andrey admits more to himself than to them that in marrying Natasha he had thought they would be happy, and we recall Andrey's passionate confession of love to Natasha which concluded act 1 and stands in direct contrast with this broken, disjunctive speech. Gone is the promise of love, the joy of marriage, the longing for future. Andrey negates all the positive qualities of Natasha which he has previously enumerated, and the negations serve to establish an erasure of words in time, as he tries to erase their memory in his mind. Weeping, Andrey begs for the understanding and the forgiveness of his sisters, "Dear sisters, darling sisters, you must not believe what I say, you mustn't believe it . . . *(goes out)*." Because Chekhov has chosen a tumultuous night in which the family is thrown together in need and in trial to help themselves and others, their confessions, otherwise awkward and melodramatic, do not seem unnatural. However, repetitive confessions have a cumulative effect, so that the final prayer which Irina utters, "There's nothing in the world better than Moscow! Let us go, Olya! Let us go!" seems no more credible than Andrey's confession or Masha's assertion that she will maintain silence. Chekhov's characters can maintain neither silence nor speech; they inform by an integral interplay of both (168–69).

Act 3, characterized by its disorder, dispossessions, and dispersion, by its staccato confessions, its clanging fire bells and hysterical outbursts, by its claustrophobic entrapment in Olga's bedroom, is juxtaposed in Act 4 to the quiescent stillness of the autumnal garden, evoking an atmosphere of departure and death. Act 1, marked by the arrival of the soldiers, is complemented in act 4 by dispersion; the intricate paradigm of arrival/departure is reflected once again through echoing and choral speaking. Chekhov, a master of farewells, conveys unsuccessful attempts to communicate loss and forgetfulness and the sadness of departure by filtering the departure through several lenses. Just as in the conclusion of *Uncle Vanya* when Marya, Astrov, Vanya, Sonia, and Marina acknowledged the departure of Serebryakov and Yelena, similarly, Irina and Tchebutykin take note of the departure of Fedotik and Roddey. The mood is restive. Andrey quietly wheels the baby carriage while Irina confesses her uneasiness about Tusenbach to Tchebutykin. Moreover, Masha, anxious about the arrival and imminent departure of Vershinin, also seeks out the companionship of the old doctor. Whereas her baby sister, loquacious as always, chats with Tchebutykin about her anxiety, Masha, as in act 1, is taciturn, maintaining her withdrawal from conversation and obviously distracted by her thoughts. Sitting close to the doctor she hesitates and then decides against revealing her pain. Could words possibly define or delimit it? Instead of speaking of her agony, Masha changes the direction of her thoughts and asks the old doctor a question which has probably been in the recesses of her mind for years that is dredged to the surface by present events. "Did you love my mother?" she inquires. The response is immediate: "Very much." But to her next question: "And did she love you?" Tchebutykin's silent response communicates his unwillingness or inability to reveal that confidence. His refusal to give an immediate, affirmative reply suggests that the love was unrequited, but essentially Tchebutykin maintains the enigma by leaving the past love undefined. Trying to conceal her personal loss through language, Masha attempts to speak about Andrey, but her voice breaks off. She can neither be quiet nor concentrate on one subject. The wait is agonizing. Reiterating the motif of departure, Masha takes note of the birds escaping. Distraught about the duel, Masha links her personal loss to that of the Baron and by implication, although unstated, to her sister Irina, so happily expecting to depart tomorrow to marry Tusenbach and begin a new life. Characteristically, Tchebutykin responds, "It doesn't matter," but he pauses, as if to imply that Masha is not to believe him. Postponing his departure for the duel, Tchebutykin appears to contribute to the eventless atmosphere in act 4 which is building into an intolerably static and emotionally suffocating one.

After much intimation, Tusenbach arrives to speak to Irina, but they succeed in talking about nothing. His parting speech to her is poignant and emotional, broken by pauses in which he seeks to cover up the truth of the duel and reveal the truth of his love. On the subject of the duel he is silent; on the subject of her love for him she is silent. Both silences, however, stunningly underscore the lack of confirmation. Styan views the Baron's silence as a "gesture of helplessness," but I would add that his chosen silence is not one of dumb apathy.[38] It is a fertile silence of awareness and acceptance. Indeed, so sensitive and perceptive does Tusenbach appear that Irina wants to accompany him, but in alarm he goes off, only to turn around and call "Irina" for the last time. She asks, "What is it?" but, covering up the fact that he has no one thing to say, he asks, in a magnificent Chekhovian touch, to have coffee made for him. Irina's silent response to his request and departure is crucial; Chekhov's directions are explicit: "Irina stands lost in thought," then silently sits in a swing, presumably to await his return (177–79).

Time has been of constant concern throughout this play: the specific time for departures, the time of the duel, the undefined passing of time indicated by Olga's new position as head mistress, and Natasha's new offspring, Sophie. Set against the coming and going in the garden, Andrey, normally taciturn with the others, converses with Ferapont, who has in the last four years lost even more of his hearing faculties than was obvious in his last tête-à-tête with Andrey. The motifs of longing and escape, purpose and uselessness are reiterated, but Ferapont is unable to respond to Andrey. Finally the long-awaited Vershinin has arrived, but from the moment of his arrival we are made aware that time has been spent elsewhere. There are only a few brief moments for farewell. Using the stock phrase, "Forgive me if anything was amiss," Vershinin gives this commonplace a deeper resonance of implicit acknowledgment of self-deception by the pause which follows it.[39] Olga, despite her refusal to face the fact of her sister's love affair with Vershinin, is deeply saddened and speechless at his departure. We note in her silence the agony of separation that she feels personally and feels vicariously for Masha. Awkwardly waiting now for Masha's arrival from the recesses of the garden where she has been secluded anticipating her lover's arrival, Vershinin asks, "What am I to theorize about? . . . *(Laughs).*" Without his philosophy, Vershinin is lost; it is his defense against vulnerability, despair, and the creeping ravages of time. Continually consulting his watch, he is anxious about time passing: the time which seemed to drag so long in anticipation is now contracted, compressed, and fleeting in departure. Masha sobs violently and Vershinin's characteristic articulateness disintegrates into disjunctive phrases broken by silences: "I . . . must go . . . I am late. . . ." The wrenching of separation is conveyed by their emotional, primarily nonverbal responses (181–82).

Vershinin's departure dovetails with the arrival of Kuligin; obviously Masha's husband had discreetly waited for the departure of her lover. Intending to console her and claim her as his wife, Kuligin is nonetheless embarrassed by Masha's breakdown, which anticipates and foreshadows that of Irina. In the excitement of Vershinin's departure, Irina, awaiting the arrival of her lover, is forgotten by the others who try to calm the distracted Masha muttering disjointed words from the refrain which has haunted her for years. Fluctuating between hysteria and emotional control, Masha struggles to resume or restore her former life. Irina comes to console Masha and to silently share a farewell embrace; ironically, within moments it will fall to Masha, the more experienced in love and loss, to embrace and console her bereaved sister. Similarly, it falls to Tchebutykin, the doctor, oldest friend, and pseudo-father, to convey the truth of Tusenbach's death. Reiterating his characteristic "it doesn't matter," the exhausted Tchebutykin sings, "Tarara-boom-dee-ay," while the three sisters huddle together. Essentially separate individuals, their words and silences echo the different way in which each perceives loss in love and in life, as well as the devices, linguistic and other, by which they attempt to shield themselves from the agony of separation and the absurdity of existence.

Gone is the promise of vitality and love and contentment, gone the dream of Moscow, gone the possibility of escape. Characteristically, Chekhov neither defines nor delimits their words and their silences. Maintaining the ambivalence of mood by which he has realistically and emotionally shown the psychic lives of these characters, Chekhov underscores the contrast between the words of the three sisters and their stillness, their earnestness, with Tchebutykin's careless singing. Styan accurately suggests that "to define our final sensations by the final words of the three sisters, simply because they speak, is to treat fictions as truths, characters as mouthpieces, and to disregard the contribution of the whole series of impressions."[40]

Chekhov symphonically concludes his masterpiece of mutability and perpetuity by linguistically reinforcing flux and fixity. Olga bravely and confidently declares, "We shall know what we are living for, why we are suffering," but her pause more honestly conveys the prevailing doubt and hesitation. The fervently hopeful words of the three sisters, like their embrace, are undercut by the silent response of resignation, anticipated loneliness, and retreat into illusion. Indeed, once again escape into the future obliterates present pain. The conclusion of this static drama is only apparently quiescent, belying cyclical, psychological, and social flux. By the masterful use of the specific and obvious in concert with the imprecise and tacit we learn that Natasha and Protopopov are securely entrenched within the Prozorov home and the three sisters will disperse, just like the brigade which has so recently departed. Thus this drama of coming and going ends by reflecting on the transitory nature of beauty, of life, and of love, ending as it began, by reflecting on the quotidian and the enigmatic.

The concluding scene of *The Three Sisters* beautifully illustrates the typifying characteristics of Chekhov's mature drama: resonance of impression, synthesis of expression and suggestion, silence of the playwright. Focusing on the motifs of love, loneliness, and loss, all emotions essentially untranslatable, Chekhov delicately and implicitly conveys ontological solitude through suggestion and evocative pauses.

In dramatizing immediacy and unintelligibility through a language of silence, Chekhov has not only achieved verisimilitude in his own drama, but also prepared the way for subsequent linguistic innovation in modern theatre. Our attention first turns to the Theatre of Silence which emerged on the dramatic horizon after World War I, descendent of Maeterlinck and Chekhov and child of global hostility.

NOTES

1. Robert W. Corrigan, "The Plays of Chekhov," in *The Theatre in Search of a Fix* (New York: Dell, 1973), 131.

2. A. Skaftymov, "Principles of Structure in Chekhov's Plays," trans. George McCracken Young, in *Chekhov: A Collection of Critical Essays*, ed. Robert Louis Jackson, Twentieth Century Views (Englewood Cliffs, N.J.: Prentice-Hall, 1967), 69–87. This valuable essay poses and attempts to answer the question of unity of form and content in Chekhov's plays.

3. See Maurice Valency, *The Breaking String* (New York: Oxford University Press, 1966), for an excellent study of Chekhov's predecessors in the Russian theatre, influences on his oeuvre, the role of the short story, and his career as a playwright.

4. On the issue of Chekhov's social criticism, see Maxim Gorky, "Fragmentary Reminiscences," in *Anton Tchekhov: Literary and Theatrical Reminiscences*, trans. and ed. S. S. Koteliansky (1927; reprint, London: Benjamin Blom, 1965), 98–101. Gorky maintains that no one before Chekhov depicted bourgeois existence with such merciless truth. See also Robert Brustein, *The Theatre of Revolt: An Approach to Modern Drama* (Boston: Little, Brown, 1962), chap. 4, "Anton Chekhov," 135–79, for a discussion of Chekhov's rebellion against the quality of Russian life.

5. Quoted in David Magarshack, *Chekhov the Dramatist* (New York: Hill and Wang, 1960), 84.

6. John Lahr, "Pinter and Chekhov: The Bond of Naturalism," *Drama Review* 13, no. 2 (Winter 1968): 137–45; rpt. in *Pinter: A Collection of Critical Essays*, ed. Arthur Ganz, 60–71, Twentieth Century Views (Englewood Cliffs, N.J.: Prentice-Hall, 1968), hereafter cited as *PCCE*.

7. Brustein, *Theatre of Revolt*, 137.

8. Chekhov to Grigori Rossolimo, *The Selected Letters of Anton Chekhov*, ed. Lillian Hellman, trans. Sidonie Lederer (New York: Farrar, Straus, 1955), 252–53.

9. Bernard Beckerman, "Artifice of 'Reality' in Chekhov and Pinter," *Modern Drama* 21, no. 2 (June 1978): 153–61.

10. See Magarshack, *Chekhov the Dramatist*, for a distinction between plays of a "direct" and "indirect" action; see also Francis Fergusson, *The Idea of a Theatre* (Princeton, N.J.: Princeton University Press, 1949), 163–72, for a study of the scene as a dramatic form.

11. Regarding Maeterlinck's contribution to Chekhov's evocative, eventless drama, see Valency, *The Breaking String*; F. L. Lucas, *The Drama of Chekhov, Synge, Yeats and Pirandello* (London: Cassell, 1963).

12. Chekhov's muted images, gray landscape, tonal resonance, and the evocative mood of memory and melancholy are reminiscent of Verlaine's symbolist poetry.

13. See Brustein, *Theatre of Revolt*, for an interesting discussion of those forces of darkness (such as mediocrity, vulgarity, and illiteracy) which "intrude" into the Chekhovian world and displace accomplishment, humanity and education (148–50).

14. Beverly Kahn, *Chekhov: A Study of the Major Stories and Plays*, Major European Authors (Cambridge: Cambridge University Press, 1977), 312.

15. Corrigan, *Theatre in Search of a Fix*, 131–33.

16. Brustein, *Theatre of Revolt*, 153.

17. William Alexander Gerhardi, *Anton Chekov: A Critical Study*, rev. ed. (1923; reprint, London: MacDonald, 1974), 28.

18. Chekhov to Alexei Suvorin, *Selected Letters*, 189.

19. Beckerman, "Artifice of 'Reality,' " 155.

20. Brustein, *Theatre of Revolt*, 155.

21. Kahn, *Chekhov*, 10.

22. In a letter to Maxim Gorky, 3 January 1899, Chekhov defines grace: "when a person expends the least possible quantity of movement on a certain art" (*Selected Letters*, 239).

23. Corrigan, *Theatre in Search of a Fix*, 133.

24. Fergusson, *Idea of a Theatre*, 172–73.

25. For further consideration of the quantitative nature of the pause, see James Kolb, "Language, Sounds and Silence" (Ph.D. diss., New York University, 1974), especially chap. 2. Regarding the multivalent use of the unspoken in Chekhovian drama, consult Siegfried Melchinger, *Anton Chekhov*, trans. Edith Tarcov, World Dramatic Series (New York: Frederick Ungar, 1972). For perceptive commentary on the interplay of structure, setting, symbol, and language, see J. L. Styan, *Chekhov in Performance: A Commentary on the Major Plays* (Cambridge: Cambridge University Press, 1971).

26. Corrigan, *Theatre in Search of a Fix*, 133–34.

27. Chekhov to Suvorin, 1 April 1890 (*Selected Letters*, 98).

28. Chekhov to Gorky, 3 January 1899 (ibid., 230). Regarding Chekhov's insistence on laconism, see Ivan A. Bunin, "A. P. Tchekhov," in *Anton Tchekhov: Literary and Theatrical Reminiscences*, trans. and ed. S. S. Koteliansky, wherein the poet quotes Chekhov, "It is very difficult to describe the sea. Do you know the description a schoolboy gave in an exercise? 'The sea is vast.' Only that. Wonderful, I think" (87).

29. Chekhov to Suvorin, 1888 (quoted in Brustein, *Theatre of Revolt*, 147).

30. Melchinger, *Anton Chekhov*, 4.

31. Ronald Hingley, *Chekhov: A Biographical and Critical Study*, rev. ed. (1950, London: George Allen and Unwin, 1966), 49.

32. See Valency, *The Breaking String*, 32–47.

33. Vladimir Nemirovitch-Dantchenko, "Tchekhov and the Moscow Art Theatre," in *Anton Tchekhov: Literary and Theatrical Reminiscences*, trans. and ed. S. S. Koteliansky (1927; reprint, London: Benjamin Blom, 1965), 135–38.

34. Vladimir Nemirovitch-Dantchenko, *My Life in the Russian Theatre*, trans. John Cournos (Boston: Little, Brown, 1936), 162–63. See also Brustein, *Theatre of Revolt*, 154, for an interesting footnote in which the critic observes, "It is a pity that so many modern realists have followed Stanislavsky's approach to reality and not Chekhov's."

35. Regarding the brilliance of revelation by innuendo, see Styan, *Chekhov in Performance*, 182–83.

36. Ibid., 186.

37. See Kahn, *Chekhov*, 303–4, for an interesting discussion of the interrelationship of compressed space and the interminable night. See also Brustein, *Theatre of Revolt*, 158–59, for a discussion of this scene as a prelude to dispossession.

38. Styan, *Chekhov in Performance*, 214–15.

39. Ibid., 225.

40. Ibid., 236.

4

Bernard

Jean-Jacques Bernard, whose name is frequently linked to the post–World War I avant-garde *Théâtre du Silence*, is best known for his intimate dramas about subconscious desires in conflict with conscious life. In *The French Drama of the Unspoken* May Daniels observes that the expression *théâtre du silence*, as employed by critics in the 1920s, did not have the rigidity of a scientific term. Rather, it was used broadly to describe any intimate drama and was interchangeable with the term *théâtre intimiste*.[1] Bernard, who protested that "en réalité, il ne s'agit pas de silence et il n'y a aucune théorie," preferred the specificity of the explicit *théâtre de l'inexprimé*.[2] The unexpressed, including the eloquent use of silent response and bivalent, quotidian dialogue which implies more than it superficially communicates, informs both the medium and the meaning of Bernard's silent drama.

Crucial to Bernard's *théâtre de l'inexprimé* is the distinction between *silences* and *silence* which the dramatist emphasizes in his essay "De la valeur du silence dans les arts du spectacle." Whereas silences are the intervals between responses whose value is limited to exceptional cases, silence, according to this playwright, encompasses:

> tout ce que les personnages ne veulent ou ne peuvent dire, c'est toute la série des pensées ou des désirs qui échappent aux mots, qui ne peuvent s'échanger que par allusion indirecte, voire par le regard ou par l'attitude, c'est toute la gamme des sentiments inexprimés, inavoués ou inconscients.[3]

If men do not always express their most profound thoughts, argues Bernard, it is because they often camouflage them in shame and hypocrisy. Most often, however, men do not reveal their emotions "parce qu'il n'en ont pas conscience ou parce que ces sentiments arrivent à la conscience claire sous une forme tellement méconnaissable que les mobiles réels n'en sont plus perceptibles."[4] Essentially, silence as employed by Bernard is not an evocation of absence, but of presence. Unspoken and unspeakable, silent responses are conscious and unconscious, revelatory and communicative.

Bernard typically juxtaposes reticent and loquacious characters to underscore the conscious and unconscious suppression of information. The concealment is obvious on the part of characters like Martine in *Martine*, Marie-Louise in *L'Invitation au voyage*, and Francine in *Nationale 6*, who excuse their laconism on the basis of personality. Less conspicuous is the behavior of talkative characters like André in *Le Feu qui reprend mal*, Julien in *Martine*, and Olivier in *L'Invitation au voyage*, who similarly experience the inability or the reluctance to verbalize and define their disquieting emotions, but prefer the distorting disguise of speech to direct attention away from psychological truths.[5]

Bernard's experimentation with dramatic form, content, and linguistic methodology is a function of his intention to reveal the mystery of life and human personality. Characteristically, the dramatist exteriorizes the interior life of a character through evocative expression and implicit suggestion, rather than conventional, consequential dialogue. Maintaining that expressed emotions lose impact, Bernard elicits and intensifies ambiguity and mystery by the polarities of intellect and intuition, fixity and flux, illusion and reality, speech and silence.[6]

This playwright achieves a synthesis of phenomenal and psychological experience through a fusion of thought and technique. Therefore, we postpone examination of his idiosyncratic use of silence to consider the impact of Freudian psychology, Bergson's intuitive philosophy, and World War I on postwar literature in general and on his silent theatre in particular.

Prior to World War I, Paris was a city of major importance to the European theatre. Despite the innovations of Antoine and Lugné-Poë, however, French theatre was traditional in format and production, primarily comprised of well-made plays and boulevard comedies characterized by their explicitness, rhetorical eloquence, and literary appeal. Even if there had been no war, the revitalization of the French theatre was inevitable in light of scientific studies in the first decades of the twentieth century, primarily those of Freud and Bergson, which intensified rather than dissipated the mystery of existence.

But there was a war, with far-reaching and irrevocable effects on society and art. Global conflagration ruptured established spiritual order and directly provoked the birth of a new literary and ideological world that addresses the issues of relativity, instability, violence, and dehumanization. The lesson to be learned from the war, insists Benjamin Crémieux in *Inquiétude et reconstruction*, is that the individual's right to liberty did not exist any more, whereas the lesson to be learned from the postwar period is more radical: "rien ne dure et peut-être rien n'existe."[7] Essentially, the rejection of reality took two specific forms: refusal through negation (Dadaism) and refusal through evasion.

The immediate impact and the lingering effects of the war need not be sought in the number of plays in which it is the subject, but rather in the subject as structure in postwar drama. Reflecting a world of disquietude, disjunction, and distrust, postwar drama found its form in the coalescence of observation and introspection, memory and experience. Doubt, instability, and physical and emotional mutilation explain in good part the rejection of eloquent, definitive statement and societal concerns, along with the search for linguistic authenticity and emotional verisimilitude. The dramatist turned inward to the individual, the only reality which was immediately perceptible.

In the opinion of Crémieux, the central theme of postwar literature is the individual, not as object of exaltation, but as subject of examination. The artist concerned himself with defining the individual, isolating his implacable, irreversible qualities and illuminating the secret of his personality.[8] One understands, therefore, why the theories of Freud and Bergson, which had appeared prior to the war, were in the ascendant afterward.[9] Essentially emphasizing relativism applied to personality and chronicity, these theorists complemented the general attitude of distrust in reasoning man which the war intensified. Postwar drama, focusing its attention on the interior nature of man, minimized the role of the intellect and maximized that of the emotions. Freud's theories on the unconscious and its influence on the conscious, illuminating inner conflicts and repressions, had significant application in a drama typified by escape from reason and reality. Helmut Hatzfeld suggests, moreover, that as a result of the artistic discovery of the subconscious and the emphasis on introspection, entirely new love relationships, particularly abnormal and conjugal, were analyzed for the first time.[10] Bergson's philosophy of *durée* and intuitive knowledge informs the postwar reliance on intuition, fixity, and silence. In *Durée et simultanéité: A propos de la théorie d'Einstein*, Bergson argues that time which endures is not measurable, that *durée* is "une mémoire intérieure au changement lui-même, mémoire qui prolonge l'avant dans l'après et les empêche d'être de purs instantanés apparaissant et disparaissant dans un présent qui renaîtrait sans cesse."[11] The relationship between stasis and use of the unexpressed has been previously discussed. With *durée* the progression of phenomenal time, to which language is inextricably linked, ceases, with the result that sequential speech also ceases. Memory, which intrudes upon reality and continually disrupts the continuous flow of anthropocentric chronicity, imposes its own disjunctive order, or rather chaos, of mind and time. The playwright who seeks authentic dramatization of apparent, external fixity and actual, internal fluctuation from thought to thought and from past to present, must rely on silent response. Furthermore, Bergson's philosophy of immediate perception is similarly linked to the devaluation of speech and the revaluation of silence.

Freud, Bergson, and World War I clearly had considerable impact on the nature and thematic concerns of postwar theatre, but the revival of French theatre after the war took diverse forms. For the purposes of considering Bernard's *théâtre de l'inexprimé*, we must evaluate the impact of these formulative forces on his theatre. Essentially, the Freudian concept of the subconscious is implicit in Bernard's plays: although he did not rely on Freudian psychology to exteriorize the psyche, psychoanalysis, with its emphasis on inner conflicts and repressed emotions, presented him with a new and powerful dramatic technique. He was, to use Daniel's term, an "observant psychologist" who carefully chose types of characters who were a mystery to others and to themselves. His silent plays may be divided into two categories: plays which concern themselves with unexpressed emotions of which the character is aware, such as *Martine*, and plays which concern submerged, repressed emotions unrealized by the character, as in the case of *Le Printemps des autres*.[12] Similarly, we may isolate the influence of Bergson's philosophy on Bernard's apparently static structure which belies internal flux. Sylviane Bonnerot suggests in *Le Théâtre de 1920 à 1950* that "la volonté de supprimer les effets dramatiques de diluer l'action dans une durée" so that the silence and monotony filter hidden aspirations is principally related to the intimate drama of Vildrac and Bernard.[13] We observe, for example, that the memory of the American soldier and the memory of war continually invade and intrude upon the seeming serenity of André and Blanche in *Le Feu qui reprend mal*, much as the memory of Julien is disruptive in *Martine* and that of Robert is disquieting in *Nationale 6:* that Julien informs Martine that past experiences can be recaptured and relived at will recalls the Bergsonian concept of duration. Bernard's silent dramas, moreover, are characterized by their reliance on intuitive, rather than conceptual, knowledge. His characters both perceive without benefit of ratiocination and communicate without benefit of verbal denotation. Martine "knows" that Julien is infatuated with her, Olivier that Philippe is the source of his wife's disquietude; Francine that Robert will propose marriage.

In *Mon ami le théâtre* Bernard admits that the war was a turning point in his career, offering other subjects than those he had employed in prewar theatrical experiments. Philosophically the dramatist recalls, "il n'était plus question de jouer."[14] Daniels confirms that Bernard saw active service and that exposure to warfare deepened a sensibility already manifest in *L'Epicier*, three short sketches published prior to the dramatist's mobilization in 1914.[15] The effects of the war may be observed in Bernard's increased sensitivity to and awareness of suffering, waiting, real or imagined threats, the prolonged duration of separation, the ambivalence of reunion, loneliness, monotony, and disquietude. A troubled melancholy colors the unspoken silence of impasse, complicity, resignation, expectation, and confusion, indicating the unspeakable silence of the witness to atrocity. In *Les Enfants jouent, Le Feu qui reprend mal*, and *Martine* the thematic preoccupation with war is overt and explicit. Conflagration, with its attendant disruption and disquietude and its unspeakable silences, informs Bernard's postwar drama when emphasis is on the internal, implicit portrayal of unconfessed, repressed emotions. The themes of evasion and isolation, unrealized and unrealizable aspirations, and social and personal disunity find form in this drama through disjunctive speech and the unity of silence.

Essentially, World War I determined in great part not only the subject, but also the structure of Bernard's *théâtre de l'inexprimé*. In Bernard's intimate drama the most fascinating battles take place in the mind and in the home. The individual struggling with the disparate parts of himself conveys this psychological conflict implicitly to the other members of the household and to the audience through all that is not explicitly expressed. The disunity of conjugal relationships is reflected by passive interactional communication in which the combatants, armed with silence or with speech, both advance and withdraw. An interesting contrast may be drawn between Strindbergian brain battles, which rely on caustic, piercing dialogue, as in *The Father* and *Miss Julie,* and Bernard's silent battles.[16] But Bernard is concerned neither with a test of wills nor with a test of wits; his attention focuses on the no-man's land, interminable and illimitable, which separates a couple. In the presence of an undefined and undefinable enemy, the emotions unleashed dissipate, but not before they have wounded the serenity and security of the other person and left frustration in their wake.

In addition to other sources of inspiration, Bernard found both inspiration and example in Maeterlinck's silent drama. Like Daniels, Dorothy Knowles has emphasized the importance of Maeterlinck to the development of Bernard's dramatic methodology; and the playwright confirms his indebtedness in *Mon ami le théâtre.*[17] Specifically referring to Maeterlinck's bivalent dialogue, Bernard explains the dualism of his own dramatic expression: "Il y a sous le dialogue entendu comme un dialogue sous-jacent qu'il s'agit rendre sensible." Furthermore, the dramatist maintains that he has not discovered an original dramatic technique, but merely renewed, after Maeterlinck, a fundamental tenet of the theatre: "Dès que nous avons vraiment quelque chose à dire, nous sommes obligés de nous taire."[18] Bernard shares with Maeterlinck the belief that silence is the medium of direct communication and that fundamental truths are distorted by the spoken word.

We observe in Bernard's plays a focus on interior states of being, substitution of the effects of an event for the event itself, use of nuance and suggestion to evoke mood, use of symbols, particularly windows and shutters to elicit interior and exterior space and entrapment, and an apparently quiescent structure which belies cyclical and psychological fluctuation. Like his predecessor, Bernard situates his dramas in realistic settings in order to elicit the dramatic but subtle tension inherent in intimate relationships. He also draws heavily upon the fairy tale with its archetypal characters: delicate, vulnerable princesses, virile princes, fairy godmothers, wicked witches, and wise old men. In modern dress Martine, Marie-Louise, and Francine await the Prince Charming who will release them from their imprisonment in boredom; in *Le Feu qui reprend mal* and *L'Invitation au voyage* concerned fathers advocate moderation and dispense worldly counsel; in *Le Printemps des autres* the mother-figure, Clarisse, metamorphoses into a wicked witch, preventing the reconciliation of Gilberte and Maurice. Whereas Maeterlinck employs archetypes and the paradigm of innocence to convey mystical truth and the universality and continuum of human experience, Bernard employs archetypes and the paradigm of innocence to underscore evasion and idyllic escape from reality, the predominance of doubt and vulnerability, and the universality of psychological truths. Whereas Maeterlinck evokes an atmosphere of spiralling anxiety, Bernard elicits deepening frustration; whereas Maeterlinck employs enigmatic utterances and the silent responses of awe and communion to suggest the ambiguity and mystery of spiritual existence, Bernard employs disjunctive speech, the unexpressed, and the silent responses of confusion and impasse to underscore the ambivalence and mystery of psychological experience. Maeterlinck employs repetitions to weave a pattern of compulsiveness and to imply the stressful situation of growing fear; Bernard, on the other hand, employs repetitions to elicit an atmosphere of distraction and disunity, emphasizing the widening alienation between the speaker and another, between the speaker and his own thoughts.

We have seen that the central focus of Maeterlinck's static drama is the silent progression, intrusion, oppression, and finality of death. Like Maeterlinck, Bernard concentrates upon the approach, progression, oppression, and passage of the intruder, but his intruders, human and abstract, are disruptive rather than deadly. Bernard considers the multivalent concept of intrusion: What constitutes invasion of personal and psychic space? Do withdrawal and complicity aid and abet the invasion of privacy? When does a welcome visitor become a dreaded intruder? Characteristically, the playwright does not provide answers for the spectator, just as he does not provide his characters with precise information. Not unlike Maeterlinck's pilgrims, his characters are helpless, vulnerable victims to unknowable, uncontrollable intrusions, but significantly, in this post–World War I drama, the threat is from within as well as from without. In *Martine*, for example, Bernard weaves an intricate pattern of intrusions in each tableau: in the first tableau Alfred intrudes upon Martine and Julien, in the second Jeanne intrudes upon Martine and Julien. In tableau three Jeanne intrudes upon Martine and Alfred, and in the climactic fourth tableau Martine intrudes upon Jeanne and Julien. Finally, the play concludes in the fifth tableau with the agonizing intrusion of both Jeanne and Alfred on Martine and Julien. In *Le Feu qui reprend mal* and *L'Invitation au voyage* unseen intruders effect a devastating influence on the relationships under consideration. The effects of these multiple human and abstract intrusions are alternatingly immediate and long-lasting, perceptible and cumulatively effective, obvious and subtle, real and imagined. Typically in Bernard's silent theatre reality intrudes upon illusion, doubt upon truth, jealousy on love, and disquietude on security.

Besides Freud, Bergson, Maeterlinck, and World War I as influences on the formulation of Bernard's themes and techniques, we note striking areas of compatibility between Chekhovian drama and that of Jean-Jacques Bernard.[19] In *Mon ami le théâtre* Bernard confides that on the suggestion of his friend Cesare Lodovici he read Anton Chekhov and "nous avons subi tous deux l'influence de Tchekhov."[20] Bernard shares with Chekhov an emphasis on suggestion, concision, and resonance. Like the Russian playwright's, his theatre is distinguished by its "artifice of reality," to use Bernard Beckerman's term—the seemingly arbitrary landscapes, character details, and aimless dialogue. Bernard also subtly balances subjectivity and objectivity, interiority and exteriority, undefined, incompleted intimations and clearly delimited specificity of detail, psychological time and phenomenal chronicity to achieve emotional realism.

Bernard exploits the daily flow of the customary and habitual to dramatize continuity and perpetuity, employing intricate arrival/departure patterns, pertinent "acts of God," the season, and the date to illustrate fluid and fixed moments in time. In *Martine*, for example, nature figures importantly in his subtle portrait of life as it is, graphically revealing a pattern of cyclical deterioration. In the first act, for example, the burning hot July sun forces Julien and Martine to seek the protection of a large apple tree. In act 2 the harvest scene is suggested by Julien's recitation of Chénier's poetry and by the repeated symbol of the horn of plenty, but the resplendent tree is nearly barren in act 3. In act 4 we observe Christmas preparations and learn of Jeanne's pregnancy, whereas in act 5 Jeanne and Julien, returned to Grandchin to bury Mme. Mervan, speak about their baby, now old enough to smile, and congratulate Martine on her pregnancy.

In *L'Invitation au voyage*, on the other hand, Bernard conveys chronological progression through Marie-Louise's vacillating tastes in poetry, men, and music. In the first act, the protagonist enjoys Chénier's poetry, but in act 2 Baudelaire, Philippe's favorite, takes Chénier's place on the coffee table and in Marie-Louise's heart. At the conclusion of the drama, however, after the heroine has returned from her rendezvous with Philippe, she convinces Olivier that her romance with the latter is terminated by replacing Baudelaire in the bookshelf and playing the tune from Chopin which she had been playing at the beginning of the play. Despite the seemingly quiescent conclusion, Bernard's inconclusive resolution to this drama, and to his other silent plays, implies the tedious continuity and the ever-present need for evasive illusion. Loss displaces promise; weariness, vitality; waste, beauty; resignation, hope.

In his *théâtre de l'inexprimé*, Jean-Jacques Bernard is more concerned with the protraction of time than the progression in time. Sharing with Maeterlinck and Chekhov the theme of waiting, he places his characters in authentic situations in which the wait is inevitably prolonged and nearly unendurable. Waiting is invariably for loved ones, real or imagined, and whatever the specific duration of the wait, whether short or long, the ordeal appears interminable. In Chekhov's dramas, Irina begins to lose faith that she will go to Moscow, Treplev that he will ever see Nina again, Varya that Lopachin will propose marriage; in Bernard's plays Blanche waits for André, Jeanne for Julien, Marie-Louise for Philippe, Martine for Julien. The torment is not limited to delicate princesses, however: Alfred pines for Martine; Merin père anticipates the return of his son, Olivier impatiently expects the return of Marie-Louise.

Simultaneously with the alternatingly swift and slow temporal progression, Bernard exposes the fluctuating state of intimate relationships and the mutable condition within each character. Simplifying plot to focus upon a few characters, the dramatist achieves psychological verisimilitude by directing attention away from action to emotion, from process to motive. The simulation of aimless, fluid speech and thought, as in Chekhov's plays, appears to be an irrational and accidental arrangement of words, but what seems intermittently fixed and fluid is in fact achieved by intricate counterpointing of speech and silent response. Chekhov employs choral speaking, overstatement, understatement, and negation to cast doubt on what is said; Bernard characteristically relies upon the unexpressed to create and accentuate indistinctness and imprecision because his theatre is primarily the art of the unexpressed. It is, as he explains, "moins par les répliques mêmes que le choc de répliques que doivent se révéler les sentiments les plus profonds" (1:5).

Bernard, like Chekhov, focuses upon the universal, evanescent, insubstantial, ambivalent, and undefined emotions of love, loss, and loneliness. His silent drama elicits self-regarding, inwardly directed sentiments and the mystery of manipulative forces. In order to show life as it is, Bernard defines his characters by their solitude and their estrangement from life, rather than their involvement in it.[21] Efforts to break out of the imprisonment of isolation are foiled or gently mocked: confidants are mismatched; confessions have the special quality of alienating rather than uniting the characters. Le Feu qui reprend mal, L'Invitation au voyage, and Martine illustrate the paradigm of the jealous lover pushing his wife or sweetheart to confess infidelity. Similarly, in L'Invitation au voyage, Martine, and Le Printemps des autres Bernard employs female confidants who invariably intensify disquietude rather than dissipate it. The frequent repetitions of "dites-moi" and "tais-toi" underscore the dichotomy between those who press for clarification through verbal denotation and those who shun it. We observe that Martine and Marie-Louise do not verbalize their emotions, because they either cannot or do not want to define or delimit the elusive. Others, like Blanche and Clarisse, refuse denotation because they shrink from the unspeakable. Their silence emphasizes their repulsion at emotions which are alien to them and not socially acceptable. Typically, Bernard's characters deny the presence of a problem, preferring conscious and unconscious evasions which merely perpetuate the undefined malaise. In Le Feu qui reprend mal André avoids the fact that he has brought his war home with him; in L'Invitation au voyage Olivier avoids the fact that Marie-Louise's affection cannot be bought; in Martine Alfred avoids the fact that Martine loves another man; in Nationale 6 Michel avoids the fact that Francine's dream will never materialize. Bernard's theatre is one of exposure, not exposition. Relying upon a paradigm of deception and denial, the dramatist reveals the web of evasive deceptions which his characters weave for themselves. Isolated and lonely, they perpetuate the illusion of communication through speech and of unification through love. But this modern playwright dispels illusions and destroys deceptions, concluding his théâtre de l'inexprimé in the silence of the unexpressed and the unconfessed.

Crucial to understanding Bernard's use of the unspoken is the relationship between World War I, psychology, symbolist and naturalistic techniques, deceptive stasis, and cyclical flux to this dramatist's linguistic innovations. Fusing subject and structure, the characterizing elements of Bernard's methodology are these:

    1. indirect, disjunctive speech

2. quotidian dialogue implicitly conveying more than it explicitly communicates
3. repetition
4. negation
5. pauses
6. mute characters
7. silent scenes
8. silence as a metaphor for isolation
9. silence as a metaphor for invasion
10. silence of the playwright

Disjunctive speech, eliciting imperceptible fluctuation both within the mind of the speaker and between speakers, is well suited to the realistic dramatization of exterior and interior experience. By their halting or compulsive speech patterns, by their hesitation to find a word to express what they wish to communicate, or leave unspoken, Bernard's characters convey emotional stress, natural reticence, confusion in unfamiliar situations, and the desire to avoid communication. A few characteristic passages clearly focus what the dramatist has intentionally left indistinct and imprecise. In *Le Feu qui reprend mal* Blanche and André, reunited after four years, are both excited and relieved:

Blanche: Je ne peux croire que tu sois vraiment là . . . Que de fois j'ai rêvé de ce moment! Et il est arrivé. Est-ce vrai? Est-ce vrai?
André: Nous sortons du cauchemar. Ah! comme tu as dû souffrir!
Blanche: J'ai des milliers de choses à te dire . . .
André: Dis.
Blanche: Je . . . Des tas de choses . . . je . . . Je ne sais plus . . . Toi, dis-moi, c'est le plus pressé . . .
André: Pas aujourd'hui . . . C'est trop long. . . .

(1:31–32)

Obviously enthusiastic about the return of her husband, Blanche wants to unburden herself of the worry and loneliness she has borne in his absence but finds that words inhibit the flow of emotion. For Blanche feelings are more directly and authentically conveyed without defining them, whereas for André sentiments that he does not want to define, that he does not want to reveal to Blanche or to himself, are delayed for another, more convenient occasion.

Unlike the joyful hesitancy which informs this reunion, a conversation between Gilberte and Clarisse in *Le Printemps des autres* illustrates the disjunctive quality of emotional stress and the avoidance of communication. Juxtaposing two distinct personality types, Bernard implies the distance between two intimate speakers, between a thought and its verbalization, between illusion and reality. Clarisse's halting, measured response to her daughter's ebullient, disordered monologue reflects her efforts to contain her emotions and conceal her disappointment while maintaining the façade of interest. "Gilberte . . . Gilberte

. . . ," Clarisse murmurs in a strangled voice, "c'est vrai que tu es belle . . ."
(1:208). In light of Clarisse's suggestive conversation with Maurice, to which
we are privy, her evasiveness is not only authentic, but also predictable.

A similar avoidance of topic is painfully revealed in the following exchange
between Olivier and Marie-Louise in *L'Invitation au voyage*. Olivier, searching
for the words to define his feelings of disquietude, continually disrupts his own
speech and refines his thoughts as he jumps from one subject to another without
apparent logic or continuity:

> *Olivier:*   Voilà . . . combien de temps? . . . plus d'un an que j'ai cette
>   impression. On dirait que la vie t'a mûrie, ma chérie. C'est vrai,
>   la vie a mûri ma petite fille . . . Tu es grave, enfant, n'est-ce
>   pas? Et notre bonheur t'avait conservée enfant . . . Il n'y avait
>   que de l'insouciance dans ces bons yeux-là . . . Mais maintenant
>   . . . *(Il lui touche le front.)* qu'y a-t-il la derrière? Je sense des tas
>   de pensées . . . si profondes . . . si cachées . . .
> *Marie-Louise:* Mais non, Olivier, mais non . . . Pourquoi me dis-tu tout cela?
>   (1:302)

In refusing to deal with the issues that her husband has raised and tried to
clarify, in refusing to continue Olivier's line of questioning, Marie-Louise disassociates herself from the subject under consideration and effectively short-
circuits the lines of communication between them.

Whereas Maeterlinck employs superficial, colloquial dialogue whose simplicity conceals profundity, Bernard employs superficial, colloquial dialogue whose
simplicity conceals inhibitions and hidden motivations. Bivalent dialogue, peculiar to the *théâtre de l'inexprimé*, operates simultaneously on objective and subjective levels. A quotidian conversation between Julien and Martine, for example,
appears aimless and impersonal, but the sophisticated Julien consciously directs
the flow of conversation so that their explicit discussion of eggs and butter and
flowers and nature is implicitly sexual. Similarly, a casual tête-à-tête between
Clarisse and Maurice in *Le Printemps des autres* ostensibly concerns itself with
Maurice's horseback riding and flirtatious relationship with Mme. Desgrées.
The concerned mother-in-law adamantly warns her errant son-in-law, "Vous ne
savez pas quelles souffrances provoque un geste maladroit. Vous ne savez pas ce
qu'un regard de vous mal dirigé peut blesser un coeur qui vous aime" (1:236). It
is only at the conclusion of the play that Clarisse fully comprehends the implication of the words she has uttered to Maurice; indeed, it is she, not Maurice,
whose misdirected emotions break Gilberte's heart.

In *Nationale 6*, moreover, a casual conversation between Robert and Francine,
which apparently pertains to Robert's competence as a painter, Antoine's as a
writer, and Francine's as a model implies more than it superficially and
specifically states. In fact, so provocative and suggestive are Robert's implications of affection that Francine erroneously anticipates a proposal of marriage to
be forthcoming on the basis of these connotative allusions:

Robert:	. . . Parfois, c'est triste, le métier de peintre.
Francine:	Je ne peux pas le croire . . .
Robert:	Combien de fois a-t-on cette chance? Peindre la pureté, la candeur, l'ingénuité . . . Et avec le modèle vrai! Mais le plus souvent, le peintre qui prétend d'avoir réalisé cela, il est un peu de Marseille, te, il s'est vanté. Car il a fait comme tout le monde. Pour peindre la pureté, il a pris . . . Ah! quel mensonge, quel trompe-l'oeil! Quelle duperie! Et pourtant avec ça on fait des choses magnifiques: des madones avec des courtisanes, comme Raphaël, des jeunes filles au bain avec des . . . oui, enfin!
Francine:	Des quoi, monsieur Robert?
Robert:	Enfant chérie, naïve petite perle, vous êtes exquise . . .[22]

Robert later confides to his father that he was only teasing Francine, that he did not mean what he implied, but Francine, interpreting both his words and the emotions they conveyed, had assumed that Robert meant more than he explicitly stated.

The coalescence of disjunctive and bivalent dialogue constitutes an essential element of Bernard's linguistic methodology. Undefined thoughts and unconfessed sentiments evoke and intensify an atmosphere of apprehension and frustration. The unexpressed stimulates the imagination of the spectator to complete the idea or emotion suggested. But we have seen that the exchange of confidences in Bernard's theatre, while apparently aimless, casual, superficial, and realistically accurate, leaves more unstated than confessed. In *Martine*, for example, when Martine offhandedly asks Jeanne about Julien, Jeanne, always ready to converse about her favorite subject, does not suspect, or does not reveal if she does suspect, that Martine has more than a casual interest. Similarly, at the conclusion of *L'Invitation au voyage*, Marie-Louise and Olivier intentionally leave unspoken their most profound emotions, hers of disappointment, his of relief. When Marie-Louise states that Philippe is dead for her and for them and sits down to play her favorite Chopin tune, we intuit what Bernard has intentionally left imprecise and evocative.

The pause, static and nonprogressional, is a principal component of Bernard's technique to stall the progression of thought, action, and time. Cumulatively effective, hesitations reinforce the impression that more is left unstated than is verbally communicated. This dramatist's treatment of the unspoken includes the silence of impasse, anticipation, reflection, expectation, isolation, and complicity. Bernard typically employs reticent and slow-thinking characters whose hesitations are realistic to emphasize the different speeds at which people think, using the pause to allow for meditation on the spoken dialogue, to show psychological interaction, and to convey the nonverbal transference of an idea. In the poignant scene between Martine and Mme. Mervan, for example, the warm-hearted woman, in her role as Martine's fairy godmother, attempts to comfort the young girl and convince her to marry Alfred. Mme. Mervan's monologue is punctuated by pauses wherein she questions Martine and supplies her own

responses. Martine concludes, "Ça m'est égal. . . ." She offers no confirmation
of comprehension or agreement, but Mme. Mervan, with the spectator, intuitively perceives by Martine's hesitation, coupled with the lack of verbalized
objection, that she will accept Alfred's forthcoming proposal (1:165–66).

Often indicative of turning points in the psychological action, pauses are
frequently employed by Bernard in silent scenes. In the following excerpt from
the concluding scene of *Le Printemps des autres*, Clarisse is busily preparing for a
hasty departure for herself and Gilberte. When Maurice calls to inquire about
his estranged wife, Clarisse hesitates before responding and then reiterates two
times that she has not seen Gilberte, although her daughter is standing in the
room with her. Clarisse's fabrication elicits a heated and critical exchange between the two women:

> *Gilberte:* Tu ne veux donc pas mon bonheur?
> *Clarisse:* Je ne pense qu'à cela . . .
> *Gilberte* *(rageuse):* Ce n'est pas vrai. *(Clarisse la lâche, effrayée.)* Mais oui, pour-
> quoi as-tu répondu que je n'étais pas là? Et tout ce que tu m'as dit
> sur lui! Non, tu ne veux pas notre bonheur. Je connais bien tes
> sentiments maintenant . . .
>
> (1:258)

But Gilberte does not know her mother's deepest sentiments. In fact, when she
surmises that her mother hates Maurice but encounters her mother's adamant
denial, Gilberte is confused. "Alors? alors? alors? . . . ," she echoes, trying to
grasp the elusive explanation for her mother's unusual behavior. Bernard's stage
instructions call for the women to take stock of each other and to square off as if
they were enemies. And indeed, they are. Clarisse, who in the pause has
become increasingly more conscious of hitherto unconscious emotions, finds the
new information unspeakable. She begs Gilberte, who similarly recoils from the
unspeakable reality of an incestuous love, "Tais-toi . . . tais-toi . . . *(Brusque-
ment.)* Va-t'en . . ." (1:258). Significantly, after her moment of recognition,
Clarisse is mute for a long time, only slowly regaining her composure and her
ability to engage in conversation.

Though repetitions in this scene convey emotional disturbance, repetitions
are generally employed in Bernard's silent drama, as they are in Maeterlinck's
and Chekhov's, to reinforce the impression of fixity implied by pauses. A
speaker reiterates a word or expression in order to fix it in his mind and effectively block the free flow of other thoughts. In the concluding scene of *Martine*,
to cite an illustrative example, Martine continually repeats the word "La Tous-
saint" in order to fix in her memory the rendezvous with Julien. Unlike the
conclusion of *Uncle Vanya* when each character repeats the same expression and
thus reveals his particular, personal reaction to the departure of Yelena and
Serebryakov, Martine, alone, reveals by repetition of the expression the subtle,

psychological fluctuations within her mind as she anticipates loss, loneliness, and physical and emotional entrapment with Alfred. Repetitions are also indicative of compulsive behavior. In *L'Invitation au voyage* Marie-Louise's periodic mention of Buenos Aires, South America, and anything even remotely connected with Philippe is perceived by Olivier as a compulsive pattern indicating the cause of Marie-Louise's malaise. When Olivier confronts Marie-Louise, he is met with a wall of avoidance and resistance. Marie-Louise's repeated denials are of less importance than her need to convince Olivier and herself that her husband has inaccurately perceived her words; but we are convinced, with Olivier, that Marie-Louise protests too much.

Bernard characteristically employs repetitions to suggest a mood of distraction. In *L'Invitation au voyage*, for example, an exchange between Olivier and Gérard reveals the disquietude gripping the husband which he cannot, or will not, verbally define. Each time Olivier answers a question with a question or repeats an entire phrase, he convinces us of the psychic distance separating him from Gérard and from reality. Lost in his own thoughts and distracted by Marie-Louise's delayed return, he can neither concentrate on the questions put to him nor maintain even the semblance of colloquial conversation. Similarly, in *Nationale 6*, Michel's excited, disjunctive monologue, a flow of disconnected thoughts, is juxtaposed to Elisa's absentminded responses and distracted repetitions of "oui." While Michel verbalizes the happiness that both share because of Francine's anticipated engagement to Robert, Elisa conveys in her silences and reiterated affirmations the confirmation of all the dreams she has had for her daughter and herself. Not only do repetitions imply distraction, they also convey withdrawal and evasion. In *Martine*, for example, the young heroine pleads with Alfred to desist from his persistent declarations of love. Alfred insists that Martine consent to marriage and acknowledge the rightness of their relationship; in calling repeatedly for his silence, Martine attempts to block not only the verbal denotation of his affection but the emotion itself.

The themes of evasion, avoidance, withdrawal, and isolation are nonverbally expressed by the muteness of the characters in Bernard's theatre. Martine's silent response to the news of Jeanne's pregnancy is a classic example of linguistic paralysis. Shocked, caught in a web of emotion she does not understand, she can neither speak nor move. Her silent presence becomes untenable for Jeanne and Julien, who finally ask her directly to leave them alone. Similarly, Martine is struck dumb by Julien's confession of his affection for her at the conclusion of this drama. She appears placid, but within her mind one thought battles another: Julien's love for her; the impossibility of a life based on their affection; her entrapment in marriage with Alfred; her pregnancy; the finality of the sale of the Mervan estate. As tears well in her eyes, it is impossible for her to compete with her nonverbal thought processes to initiate and complete a sentence. But significantly, linguistic paralysis in Bernard's theatre also reflects withdrawal and willed rejection. Disoriented after Julien's departure and unable and unwilling to make a transition between profound thoughts and casual, realistic speech, Martine maintains her self-imposed silence to protect the privacy of these thoughts.

Unlike Maeterlinck, who achieves his most striking effects through the antithesis of speech and silence, and Chekhov, whose linguistic methodology synthesizes expression and suggestion, Bernard makes a distinctive contribution to silent theatre through the diminuation of dialogue which can culminate only in silent response.[23] By means of lucid, precise, resonant expression this dramatist conducts the situation and the emotion to the point at which the emotion speaks for itself.[24] Essentially, Bernard prepares the moment by increasing awareness of the presence of the unexpressed through disjunctive speech, pauses, and repetitions, while simultaneously decreasing verbal denotation. Silence thus conveyed is the sum of all that has been spoken and all that has been left unsaid. In these dramas of "poetic realism," to use Marcel Doisy's term, the deafening silence, drowning out superficial expressions, inundates a character with hidden, private impressions. The following excerpt from *Nationale 6* is drawn from what was to have been an engagement party. Antoine's disjunctive speech reveals the anguish and strain he endures by saying less than he feels. Carefully choosing the words of the announcement of his imminent departure, he speaks directly to Francine by addressing all gathered:

> Antoine (*péniblement*): En tous cas . . . en tout cas . . . je peux vous dire une
> chose . . . c'est que je garderai un . . . un bon . . . un excellent
> souvenir . . . de vous trois . . . oui, de vous trois, madame Elisa . . .
> et c'est avec regret . . . que . . . vraiment . . . oui, mais il faut que les
> meilleures choses aient une fin, voyez-vous . . . (*un silence.*)
>
> Michel (*angoissé*): Vous . . . vous ne pensez pas encore partir?
>
> Antoine: Si . . . il faut . . . je suis triste de vous le dire . . . demain . . .
> (*Nationale 6*, 105)

The playwright, aware that he has prepared a moment of speechless intensity, indicates in his stage instructions that all gathered should be absorbed in their soup, in their private thoughts, in their private agonies. The silence of this moment, like the silence of resignation which concludes *Martine*, the silence of impasse which concludes *Le Feu qui reprend mal*, and the silence of confusion and repulsion which concludes *Le Printemps des autres*, is inextricably linked to time. Because language occurs in time, the silent scenes which typify Bernard's drama focus on the fixity of *durée* and the flux of psychological time. An impression of continuity is nonverbally conveyed by the ticking of a clock at the conclusion of *Martine* and by the repetition of the Chopin tune at the end of *L'Invitation au voyage*, but these explicit examples of perpetuity implicitly convey the fluidity and constancy of psychological experience that is inaccurately translated through denotative expression.

The striking withdrawal of the playwright from silent scenes illuminates

Bernard's respect for restraint in art and the artist. The reticence of Bernard's characters mirrors his own. The dramatist admits in prefatory comments on *Martine*, quoted in D. A. Rhodes's *The Contemporary French Theatre*, that "J'étais seulement porté à chercher la vérité des coeurs, non dans les phrases bruyantes et les moyens artificiels, mais dans ces profondeurs de l'être que ne peuvent toujours se manifester par des mots."[25] For Bernard, the subject demands its own structure. The depths of being, which refuse delineation, delimitation, and definition may be indicated, in the opinion of this artist, by evocative, resonant, imprecise suggestion. Bernard passes judgment on neither the unspoken nor the unspeakable emotions which he elicits. Reflecting his limitation as a human being and as an artist, he underscores doubt and disquietude in his silent theatre by intentionally leaving more unexpressed than confessed. Authentic to the human psychological condition, Bernard, like Chekhov and Maeterlinck, refuses to limit his portrait by precision but characteristically leaves questions unanswered: What was the nature of André's imprisonment? Did Jeanne's husband know about her affair with Lubin? What happens between Marie-Louise and Philippe? Will Gilberte and Clarisse see one another again? By this technique the playwright intensifies the mystification and confusion of the audience. Artistic creation necessitates choice; Bernard shows that the multiplicity and mystery of phenomenal and psychic experience is conveyed through silent response.

Le Feu qui reprend mal, which premiered 9 June 1921 at the Théâtre Antoine, is the first of Bernard's postwar plays that fuses form and content. The themes of war, disjunction, conjugal interaction, evasion, and isolation as well as the paradigm of separation and reunion are communicated through indirect, bivalent dialogue, pauses, repetitions, denials, silent scenes, and Blanche's muteness about her infatuation with the American soldier. *Martine*, presented eleven months later, on 9 May 1922, by Les Compagnons de la Chimère, directed by Gaston Baty, similarly concerns itself with love, longing, and loss communicated through essentially nonverbal techniques.[26] In *Martine*, however, the dramatist sophisticates his presentation of the unexpressed. Subtle, nuanced, and resonant, *Martine*, generally considered Bernard's masterpiece and a classic of the *théâtre de l'inexprimé*, is a psychological portrait of a young country girl whose infatuation with Julien disrupts her tranquility and irrevocably alters her life. Characteristically reticent, Martine expresses neither her joy nor her sadness; but Bernard elicits the fluctuations of her heart and mind through what is said to her and how it affects her. Significantly, Martine's unsuccessful attempts to verbalize and impose linguistic order on her tumultuous emotions contribute to the authenticity and poignancy of this essentially static portrait.

It is *Martine* which we will subject to exegesis to illuminate Bernard's particular use of the unspoken as it evolves and develops within the text. In the drama comprised of five short tableaux, the unexpressed and silent scenes both characterize and inform the separate tableaux and link one to another. Thematic, bivalent duologues are connected through a series of recurring motifs, the constant presence of Martine, who is spoken about even when she is mute or absent, and disruptive intruders. In order to understand Bernard's distinctive use of silence, we need to establish the significance and fluctuating rhythm both within and between conversational units.

In the initial tableau, Martine, who has sought protection from the summer noonday heat, lies contentedly under an apple tree. The intense heat, silence, and physical stasis combine to evoke a sensation of fixity. After a few moments, however, Martine's curiosity is aroused by the approach of someone walking along the road, and she abruptly sits up to get a closer look. "Qui est-ce?" she murmurs to herself. Pausing to consider who it might be, she instinctively rearranges her rumpled dress and piles her beautiful hair in a more orderly fashion on her head. Within a few moments, when the blurry image is more clearly definable against the blinding glare of the sun, Martine is able to determine that it is a young man, but before she can decide who would be walking in this heat and why he looks familiar, Julien is standing above her. In the casual and credible verbal interaction which follows, Julien introduces himself and asks to share her shade. Their quotidian dialogue rapidly becomes seductive as Julien deftly directs the chain of thought from the beauty of the day to the beauty of Martine's name to the beauty of her hair. As the subject matter becomes more and more intimate, Martine and Julien leave unexpressed their growing physical attraction and excitement. Characteristically, Bernard prepares for a silent scene through disjunctive, connotative phrases and pauses in which a character hesitates to find an appropriate word to express his feelings or, more realistically, intentionally refrains from conceptualizing what is irrational. Therefore, when Julien suggests, "Nous nous sommes cachés, aussi, nous . . . sous le pommier . . . ," additional verbal communication is superfluous. Martine is so overwhelmed by their silent communication, however, that she attempts to short-circuit its flow through speech. Muttering repeatedly and disjointedly, "Vous ne voulez pas . . . vous ne voulez pas . . . ," Martine gains Julien's attention and calls him back to reality. "Quoi?" he responds, not understanding what she is asking or why. Tacitly, her inability to verbalize her thoughts completely and his to concentrate on her incompleted remarks evoke *l'état d'âme*, suggesting the separation between emotion and thought, thought and its verbalization, and fantasy and reality. More eloquent and revelatory is the couple's silence of affirmation and communion (1:97–103).

The heat of their passion, mirrored in the hot July sun, alchemically transforms the common, physical reality of the apple tree and two passing strangers into an extraordinary, golden kingdom in which the Prince Charming, Julien, needs only to let down Martine's golden hair to gain access to the fairy princess. In the absence of speech, chronological progression ceases; in the protection and protraction of *durée*, the two lovers need not explicitly express their physical and emotional pleasure or delineate their deep longing that the present moment be interminable. Julien, intoxicated and intoxicating, convinces "Fée" Martine that they must return to their altar of love. Solemnly and silently they consummate their love and consecrate their oath.

So intense is their emotion that Bernard introduces an intruder to shock the lovers back to reality, to break the dramatic tension, and to account realistically for the return to verbal communication. In a repetition of the motif of the unexpected arrival, the fixity of fantasy is displaced by the flux of reality. Alfred's intrusion disrupts the intimacy of the couple; and as they pause to don social masks to conceal their sexual excitement, the unstated presence of their disappointment is oppressive. Julien's chivalric protection of Martine is noteworthy: allowing her time to quiet the clamor in her mind and heart, he reinforces the image of the frail, dependent princess lovingly defended by her prince. In fact, he calmly reassures Martine, even if it is not true, "N'ayez pas peur . . . Il ne regarde pas de notre côté. Le soleil est trop aveuglant" (1:106).

Julien quickly and easily engages in conversation with Alfred. Implicitly, through their casual conversation, previously unexpressed and crucial pieces of information are revealed which color and irrevocably alter the progression of Martine and Julien's budding romance. Whereas Prince Charming had introduced himself to Martine as Julien, to Alfred he identifies himself as Mme. Mervan's grandson recently returned from the war. A stupefied Martine can only utter, "Vous êtes . . ."; then her words drift into silence as she fights against the completion of this horrible thought. Shocked into muteness, Martine steadily observes Julien, her thoughts spinning off in all directions: the intimacy they have just shared, the intimacy she shares with Mme. Mervan, the knowledge of his fiancée's imminent arrival, the ramifications of Alfred's intrusion, the difference in their social strata. Alfred's intrusion has embarrassed and upset Martine, and coupled with her physical and emotional excitement and her ambivalent feelings toward Julien, her withdrawal is authentic and credible.

But Alfred, obvious where Julien has been subtle, outspoken where Julien has been suggestive, abrasive where Julien has been gentle, leaves no doubt in Julien's mind about the intimacy which Martine and Alfred have shared. Alfred reveals what Martine's reticence and imprecision have consciously concealed; thus, when Alfred casually comments in parting that he will see Martine at home in the evening, a daily occurrence obviously taken for granted, he is genuinely shocked by her refusal. Pressed for an explanation, Martine responds, "Parce que non . . . ," leaving unstated the fact that Julien has displaced him in her heart (1:106–8).

With Alfred's departure, Martine and Julien are reunited, but their perfect union has been tainted by the intrusion of reality. Unexpressed passion, longing, and pleasure, which had informed their previous duologue, are supplanted by distress, disappointment, and disorientation. Obsessed with the arrival of Julien's fiancée, Martine becomes withdrawn and reticent. Julien protests that they were never formally engaged, but the pauses which disrupt his chain of thought are more eloquent and revelatory than his weak denials. Julien tries to draw Martine out of her protective shell by resuming a superficial exchange about Grandchin, and as before the dialogue operates simultaneously on objective and subjective levels. Distracted by the news of Jeanne's arrival, Julien concludes "Midi s'éloigne et le pommier nous est déjà moins nécessaire." Ironically, his words imply more than they explicitly express and more than he realizes. As Julien's voice drifts off in reverie, one may speculate that once out of the protection of the apple tree, the locus of their passion, these lovers will never return to the altar of their love nor recapture the special magic of the moment.

Whereas earlier in the day and in their brief relationship, Julien won easy access to Martine's charms, now he must play the wounded war hero to cajole a withdrawn Martine into walking arm in arm with him. Happily she takes his hand, but sensitive to his every word, she recoils abruptly when he identifies them as "deux amoureux." The tableau concludes on an uneasy silence when his question to her "qu'est-ce que vous avez?" goes unanswered (1:109–14).

The initial tableau has introduced important recurring paradigms: interiority and exteriority, arrival and departure, flux and fixity, tranquility and disquietude, vision and blindness, and the extraordinary and ordinary. The fluctuating rhythm of emotions and motifs, moreover, mirrors the ebb and flow between exterior stimulation and interior reaction, chronological temporality and psychological continuum. The unexpressed will take the form of bivalent dialogue, silent protagonist, silent scenes, and—peculiar to Bernard's theatre—the presence of the unexpressed.

Set within the interior of Mme. Mervan's comfortable country home, tableau 2 is linked with the previous tableau by Martine, the subject of an intimate tête-à-tête between grandmother and grandson. Indeed, Julien's preoccupation with Martine has prompted Mme. Mervan's interrogation, but we observe that in response to the old woman's specific questions Julien, alternatingly halting and hesitant, reveals more by what he does not say than by what he does. When Mme. Mervan presses him, "Que veux-tu d'elle?" insisting that he define his intentions toward Martine, Julien's response is evasive and imprecise: "Ah! grand'mère, le sais-je, ce que je veux? . . ." While admittedly skirting the issue, his response nonetheless evokes the river of disquietude which runs deep within this recently released soldier. Julien defends his ambivalence and indecision by the fact that he has analyzed neither his feelings nor his intentions. Whereas in tableau 1 Julien impetuously and readily gave himself up to an infatuation with Martine, it is increasingly clear that the infatuation is a defensive evasion directing his attention from ambivalences which disturb him: his joy at being alive, safe and free in France; his sense of contentment with Mme. Mervan related to his ecstasy with Martine; his reluctance to yield the flexibility of the present to the fixity of marriage and commitment; his desire for calm, bucolic experiences to quiet the clamor and still the bestiality of war.

Left alone, Julien's thoughts turn to Jeanne, but it is Martine who materializes outside his window. His speech falters, and he motions her inside. Interiority and exteriority inform their dialogue as the companions recall memories from their evenings together to be stored in a memory bank, available always for recall. The flow of conversation moves outward as Julien, overcome by the beauty of the field, calls Martine to the window to share his experience. Noting that she is visibly upset, he inquires, "Qu'est-ce que vous avez?" but Martine can only reply, "Je ne sais pas . . . je ne sais pas . . ." before she falls into his arms. The suddenness and openness of Martine's reaction surprise Julien, who pauses before pleading, "Dites-moi, Martine. . . ." Because he is concerned and confused, Julien's voice drifts off and Martine, who does not know how to verbalize her emotions, prefers to dismiss her anxiety with "Ce n'est rien." Julien will not accept in Martine the avoidance and imprecision he had previously shown in his conversation with his grandmother. Pressing Martine to define her feelings, Julien asks, "Que voulez-vous dire?" But even if Martine could have tried to speak, a bell in the garden warns the couple of the untimely arrival of Jeanne. Both are momentarily paralyzed by the intrusion, but Julien recovers quickly, and tidying the mask as he did in tableau 1, makes Jeanne welcome (1 : 121–25).

Making the swift transition from Martine to Jeanne, from new passion to old flame, from simplicity to sophistication, from innocence to experience, Julien offers his hand as a welcoming gesture. We note that Jeanne and Julien's animated conversation is in stark contrast to Martine's linguistic and physical paralysis. Apparently struck dumb by the physical reality of the fiancée, Martine is unable to speak and unable to move, although Mme. Mervan repeatedly calls her out of the room, for she, ironically, is the intruder imposing on the privacy of the others. When she finally departs, her presence is noted by Jeanne, who inquires, "C'est la bonne?" A troubled Julien hesitatingly responds, "Non, non . . . ," and pausing while he goes to close the door, Julien tries to think of a more acceptable response. Julien identifies Martine as "une petite voisine," which Jeanne wisely intuits as a synonym for flirt. Significantly, Martine remains the focus of conversation even when she is absent from the scene. Julien's initial displeasure at Jeanne's arrival begins to be displaced by pleasure; it becomes increasingly obvious to Julien, and to the spectator, that Julien has deceived Martine and himself about the nature of his relationship with Jeanne, just as Martine had misrepresented hers with Alfred.

In stark contrast with Julien's disjunctive exchange with Martine, Julien and Jeanne explicitly communicate their fears, anticipations, and future plans through denotative language. Their duologue builds to a silent moment; but juxtaposed to Martine's ignorance of Chénier's poetry, Jeanne completes the citation which Julien had left incomplete. Though neither Jeanne nor Julien explicitly states the joy of reunion, such a reunion has subtly and definitely been accomplished (1 : 127–31).

At the conclusion of this tableau, we observe the cumulative pattern of coming and going, interiority and exteriority, tranquility and disquietude, expectation and arrival, and illusion and reality which have been important in it. Julien's physical and emotional disquietude and restlessness, which introduced the tableau, are supplanted by a sense of tranquility. His uncertainty about what he wants is displaced by a greater understanding of the role that Jeanne has played, and will play, in his life. Similarly, although Jeanne had been expected, Julien had had ambivalent feelings of expectation; after her arrival he observes how quickly the waiting time dissipates after reunion.

The solitary presence of Martine under the apple tree, now bereft of its glorious foliage, links the next tableau to the preceding scene. Shut out of Julien's life, Martine has made the pilgrimage to the altar of their love without him, and although unstated the implication is that Martine regularly prays at this church. The summer day has been displaced by the fall, the heat of their passion by that of Jeanne and Julien. In the hiding place stripped bare of its beauty and purpose, a pitiful Martine waits for someone who will not keep his appointment.

His approach unheard and unexpected, Alfred silently intrudes upon Martine's privacy with his physical and linguistic presence. The motifs of interiority and exteriority, tranquility and disquietude, coming and going, education and intuition, magical and ordinary are again reiterated. Julien had been gentle, seductive, and special; Alfred is aggressive, explicit, and common. Her hand demanded in marriage, Martine refuses to commit herself to him, refuses to hear his declaration of love, refuses to recognize his presence by verbal affirmation. For her, the silence of exclusion is the only appropriate response to his sacrilegious words and condemnatory silence. Their discontinuous tête-à-tête moves toward a silent confrontation of mutual frustration. Indeed, the cumulative effectiveness of Martine's repeated pleas—"Tu vas te taire"—convince Alfred that she wants his silence more than she does his affection. In their passive interactional confrontation, it is obvious that her silence has proved the more provocative and powerful weapon (1:133–36).

The paradigm of the unexpected intruder which figured importantly in tableaux 1 and 2 by disrupting silent scenes and reorienting quotidian dialogue once again effectively links this tableau to the preceding one. Whereas Jeanne had disrupted Martine and Julien's intimate duologue in tableau 2 and her arrival had been met with annoyance, her unexpected arrival in this scene is welcomed by Martine as a relief from Alfred's boorish brutalization. Embarrassed, frustrated, disappointed, and dissatisfied, Alfred is relieved to be sent on an errand for Mlle. Jeanne.

Alone, the two women remain chatting under the apple tree, their union, or misalliance, ironically mocking Martine's tête-à-tête with Julien under the same tree. Their disjunctive speech is realistic and psychologically authentic, alternatingly seductive and destructive, light and lethal. Jeanne scores continually against her reticent, vulnerable opponent who is not even a combatant in sophisticated brain battles. Characteristically, a seemingly distracted but calculating Jeanne inquires, "Est-ce que je vous ai dit que plusieurs fois, dans ces dernières lettres, il m'avait chargée d'amitiés pour vous?" With a blank voice, revealing shock and excitement, Martine disjointedly replies, ". . . Non . . . Monsieur Julien vous a . . ." Unable to complete the thought, Martine's voice drifts off.

Having put the knife in, Jeanne turns it. "Oui," she adds, "pour vous et les autres . . ." (1:140).

How are we to understand the symbiotic relationship between the two women whose superficial, colloquial interaction barely conceals the emotional tension between two who love the same man? The playwright leaves undefined the reasons for and the consequences of their mutual need in order to more fully reveal the complexities and ambivalences of relationships. One may speculate that Jeanne, driven by jealousy of Martine's magical powers and beauty, has understood that Julien's attraction for the country girl was based on these characteristics. Martine, on the other hand, while deeply scarred by the casual chats, is nevertheless dependent on Jeanne's confidences so that the existence of her fantasy lover is continually verified. Indeed, Bernard presents a fascinating study of feminine psychology, not by psychoanalyzing the individuals, but rather by presenting the multiplicity of their verbal and nonverbal responses and showing the emotional effects they have.[27] However, when Jeanne suggests that Martine use her as a confidant to unburden the unhappiness which is obvious to Jeanne, their duologue rapidly becomes an awkward silence. Martine's sadness, unexpressed and eloquent, embarrasses them both, and they try to reorient the conversation to a lighter subject such as the season and the approaching night. Within moments, however, unconsciously or intentionally, Jeanne is once again talking about Julien. The two women, arms locked, return to Grandchin, an unlikely duet mocking by their chatter the silent communion and affection of Julien and Martine which concluded tableau 1.

Time, a constant concern in plays of waiting, figures importantly in tableau 4, linking it to the discussion of chronological and psychological time which concluded the previous scene. As Alfred and Mme. Mervan make secretive preparations for Christmas dinner and Jeanne waits anxiously for Julien's arrival, the repetitive pattern of Julien's departures and arrivals reinforces the undefined continuity of seasonal progression. Now his wife, and soon to be the mother of his child, Jeanne paces as Julien did at the beginning of tableau 2, the physical restlessness implying emotional activity. Martine, whose physical presence links all the tableaux, brings Mme. Mervan an egg and takes up the vigil with the anxious young bride. Darning socks together and chatting aimlessly, Jeanne once again preoccupies herself with Julien; their casual chat once again moves toward a dumb silence. To Jeanne's confession, "je suis à peu près sûre que je suis enceinte," Martine is mute. Ironically, Jeanne adds, "n'en parlez pas encore." Martine can speak neither about this nor about anything else. Nor can she move. Significantly, in the most striking silent scene in this play, Martine's muteness is counterpointed to Julien's arrival and the loquacious, loving exchange of the newlyweds. Obsessed with one thought, that Jeanne is carrying the child that might have been hers, Martine is riveted in place as well as time. When directly addressed by Julien, Martine attempts to respond verbally, but she only manages to depart silently. In light of Jeanne's announcement, Mme. Mervan, returned from a visit with Martine's mother, entreats the young country girl to marry Alfred. The fourth act concludes with Martine's unexpressed affirmation and her eloquent, silent resignation and disappointment.

The final tableau commences as the preceding ones have, by linking thematically, chronologically, and symbolically the unspoken and undefined which inform Bernard's plays. Mirroring the Chekhovian paradigm of arrival and departure, reunion and separation in realistically acceptable situations, Bernard juxtaposes Julien's joyful return from war and his reunion with his family to his disconsolate departure at the death of that family. Tableau 1, in an open, beautiful, and extraordinary setting suggestive of reunion, vitality and sensuality, is supplanted in tableau 5 by the coarse, confined interior setting of Alfred Murieux's home. Expository exchange between Alfred and Julien reveals the progression of time and the series of acts of God which inform their lives. Interestingly, just as Jeanne had directed all conversations to the subject of Julien, so with Alfred Julien focuses attention on Martine and her pregnancy. Without looking at Alfred Julien inquires, "Et Martine supporte bien cela? . . ." to which her husband quickly responds, "Oh! Martine est solide, vous savez." Julien knows nothing of the kind. For him Martine is a fragile fairy princess. He is struck dumb by the arrival of a serious, hard-working country wife whose magnificent golden tresses are pulled severely away from her face. Aware that he is being indiscreet, Julien presses Martine to verbally express what is apparent but undefined. "Est-ce que vous êtes heureuse? . . ." Julien demands, but he cannot decipher her nonverbal response. He reiterates, "Vous ne dites rien . . . Vous ne voulez pas répondre?" Finally, Martine says that she is happy; however, Julien, doubting the veracity of her words, insists, "Il faut me dire la vérité." What is the truth? Whose truth is the truth? Does Julien really want to hear the truth? Bernard's imprecision is intentional and evocative. Martine presses Julien to explain why he wants the truth, and, faced with the question, he realizes that he has no reply. The silence which surrounds and underscores his question "Pourquoi?" suggests the difficulty in understanding, denoting, and classifying complex motivations. Julien continues with his interrogation, however, zeroing in on a carefully guarded emotion and ultimately leading to an eloquent and agonizingly silent moment (1 : 170–75).

Urging Martine to reveal her remembrance of their July together and admitting, "je n'y penserai jamais sans émotion," he succeeds in disorienting both Martine and himself. Since Bernard does not attempt to define or delimit the motivations of his characters, one is left to ponder, as critics have, whether Julien acts from a chauvinistic need to satisfy his ego, a strain of cruelty, the trauma of Mme. Mervan's death and the sale of the estate, the shocking appearance of Martine, or a change in his relationship with Jeanne since the birth of their child. Or do all these factors contribute to and offer explanation for Julien's behavior? Bernard's reliance on the unexpressed and silent response emphasizes rather than clarifies the mysteries of the uncharted territory of the psyche. Overwhelmed by his own emotion and Martine's tears, Julien admits to himself as much as to her that he does not understand what has motivated him. Divided between thought and deed, reason and the irrational, human ignorance and vulnerability and knowledge, Julien admits that he is not in control of his life. Focusing upon that which cannot be intellectually and logically explained and stubbornly refuses to be defined and verified, Bernard illuminates the central problem for modern man.

Significantly, the silence of the unspeakable and unknowable is disrupted by Jeanne and Alfred, who intrude upon the intimate and terribly painful moment between Julien and Martine. While the playwright has stripped his characters of illusions, he has not stripped his audience of theirs. Free to wonder about and to evaluate the loss of Martine's special love, we observe Alfred and Martine alone again. It is not Julien's absence which concerns us so much as the presence he has forced Martine to revive in her heart. But Alfred, typically boorish, intrudes upon Martine's moment of privacy with a casual remark that the Mervan estate has been sold. Martine hears him but refuses to understand. "Vendue?" As in Chekhov's late plays, *The Three Sisters* and *The Cherry Orchard*, the family home and all that it implicitly conveys yield to change. Yet the overwhelming impression of the concluding scene of this silent drama is one of fixity. Alfred closes the shutters, the clock ticks, he and Martine are silent. Whereas in tableau 1 Martine was spread out contentedly under the protection of the apple tree, now she is literally and figuratively trapped in her life with Alfred. Bernard's stage instructions call for a concluding silent scene that like the others typifies his theatre; it is effective because he has prepared the moment. Although unexpressed, Martine's anguish is deafening: isolated in this place and alienated from this man, Martine can look only to reverie for evasion.

In *Le Printemps des autres*, *L'Invitation au voyage*, *L'Âme en peine*, and *Nationale 6* Bernard extends his experimentation with the unexpressed and refines the techniques he had employed in *Martine*. In the opinion of Daniels, he contributed to the development of drama of today through his rejection of rhetorical drama and his linguistic innovation; but she maintains that Bernard's "concentration on pure emotion at the expense of the intellectual and reflective element in man indicates impoverishment of the human material of drama and the consequent lack of vitality in his work."[28] Daniels also is sharply critical of Bernard's excessively emotional characters, who lack both serenity and the will to meet the demands of life.

Daniels fails to see that Bernard's innovation in the theatre is not limited to linguistic methodology. Rather, we must approach Bernard's use of the unspoken and the unspeakable as dramatic statement and structure. Bernard dramatizes impoverishment, impotence, and immobility. By his reliance on the unexpressed and on disjunctive dialogue broken by pauses, his disoriented, distressed characters simulate, rather than intellectually interpret, the agonies and attitudes of the postwar period. Disjunction, disquietude, and determinism are integral factors of his drama, not the consequence of his use of silent response. Indeed, Bernard's use of the unspoken and the unspeakable and his focus upon withdrawal, isolation, and alienation anticipate and lay the foundation for post–World War II silent drama.

Ironically, in 1941 Bernard's imaginative world metamorphosed into a substantive reality. Interned by the Nazis, Bernard experienced an intensification of the quotidian reality he dramatized: the agony of isolation, the ordeal of captivity, the need to escape into illusion. We must now turn our attention to the historical period directly preceding World War II to consider the mutilation of speech, the predominance of silent response, and the crucial influence of these factors on the theatre which emerged from and reflects upon Holocaust and global conflagration.

NOTES

1. See May Daniels, *The French Drama of the Unspoken*, Language and Literature, no. 3 (Edinburgh: Edinburgh University Press, 1953), 112–16, where she argues that postwar dramas were exhibiting restraint and the value of the pause, but that not all intimate dramas employed silent techniques to achieve their purpose. On the contrary, most dramas of *théâtre de l'inexprimé* were intimate. For a discussion of the theory of silence, see John Palmer, chap. 4, "M. Jean-Jacques Bernard and the Theory of Silence," in *Studies in Contemporary Theatre* (1927; reprint, Freeport, N.Y.: Books for Libraries Press, 1969), 94–111.

2. See Jean-Jacques Bernard, "Le Silence au théâtre," *Bulletin de la Chimère*, no. 5 (May 1922), for his definition of the *théâtre de l'inexprimé* and his objection to a school of silence (reprinted in Jean-Jacques Bernard, *Théâtre* ([Paris: Albin Michel, 1925], 1:5–6; references hereafter will be to this edition unless otherwise indicated).

3. Jean-Jacques Bernard, "De la valeur du silence dans les arts du spectacle" (originally a lecture given at the Théâtre Montparnasse, 22 November 1930, quoted in Daniels, *French Drama of the Unspoken*, 172).

4. Ibid.

5. We observe that Bernard is dramatizing two silences: when there is an absence of speech and when there is a torrent of speech. This technique will be employed by post–World War II playwrights.

6. This study will concern itself with Bernard's plays, written between 1922 and 1935, in which psychological realism is achieved through the unexpressed.

7. Benjamin Crémieux, *Inquiétude et reconstruction: Essai sur la littérature d'après-guerre*, Inventaires (Paris: R. A. Corrêa, 1931), 17–18, and "L'Esprit d'inquiétude," 53–142. Regarding the impact of the war on literature, see Marcel Doisy, *Le Théâtre français contemporain* (Brussels: Editions "La Boetie," 1947), for a discussion of the historical precedent for an abyss between art and thought after conflagration and the resulting innovation in drama.

8. Crémieux, *Inquiétude et reconstruction*, 229.

9. On the subject of the formative influence of Freud and Bergson on postwar drama, see Serge Radine, *Essais sur le théâtre, 1919–1939* (Geneva: Les Editions du Mont-Blanc, 1944); Daniels, *French Drama of the Unspoken*, 101–2.

10. Helmut Hatzfeld, *Trends and Styles in Twentieth Century French Literature*, rev. and enl. ed. (Washington, D.C.: Catholic University of America Press, 1966), 75.

11. Henri Bergson, *Durée et simultanéité: A propos de la théorie d'Einstein* (Paris: Librairie Félix Alcan, 1926), 55.

12. Daniels, *French Drama of the Unspoken*, 174, 182.

13. Sylviane Bonnerot, *Le Théâtre de 1920 à 1950*, Ensembles Littéraires (Paris: Masson, 1972), 10.

14. Jean-Jacques Bernard, *Mon ami le théâtre* (Paris: Editions Albin Michel, 1958), 161.

15. See Daniels, *French Drama of the Unspoken*, 172–210: "Jean-Jacques Bernard: 1," for a thorough study of Bernard's early work and his progressive sophistication and internalization.

16. In Strindberg's *The Stranger*, where silence is an asset, not a liability, his use of the unexpressed more closely parallels that of Bernard.

17. Regarding the influence of Maeterlinck, see Daniels, *French Drama of the Unspoken*; Dorothy Knowles, *French Drama of the Inter-War Years, 1918–1939* (New York: Barnes and Noble, 1968).

18. Bernard, *Mon ami le théâtre*, 47–48.

19. Regarding the comparison of these two dramatists see Benjamin Crémieux, "Cronique dramatique: conclusions provisoires," *Nouvelle revue française*, 1 October 1927; see also Daniels, who maintains that Bernard did not read Chekhov until after he had written his early silent dramas (*French Drama of the Unspoken*, 210).

20. Bernard, *Mon ami le théâtre*, 55. In this text Bernard also compliments Georges Pitoëff, who was the first among their avant-garde group "rendre sensible toute la vie quotidienne que recèlent les ouvrages de Tchekhov" (82).

21. See Robert Emmet Jones, *The Alienated Hero in Modern French Drama*, University of Georgia Monographs, no. 9 (Athens: University of Georgia Press, 1962), 4. Jones maintains that isolation is the most essential theme in modern drama and that the heroes and heroines of all the major playwrights of this period are subjected, by themselves or by society, to exile from the quotidian world.

22. Jean-Jacques Bernard, *Nationale 6*, ed. Alexander Y. Kroff and Karl G. Bottke (New York: Appleton-Century-Crofts, 1950), 63–64 (references hereafter will be to this edition).

23. Daniels, *French Drama of the Unspoken*, 9.

24. Palmer notes the striking difference between Bernard's art of the unexpressed and that which characterized French drama, primarily culmination in tirade, loquacious characters, and scenes that served to frame the recitation of text (*Studies in Contemporary Theatre*, 95–98).

25. Bernard, quoted in D. A. Rhodes, *The Contemporary French Theatre* (New York: Appleton-Century-Crofts, 1942), 247.

26. World War I inspired diversity not only in themes and techniques, but also in production. The postwar theatre is generally regarded as the generation of *animateurs:* Jacques Copeau, Gaston Baty, Charles Dullin, Louis Jouvet, and the Pitoëffs. Gaston Baty's philosophy of the fusion of the disparate arts, attitudes toward dialogue, and emphasis on a poetic atmosphere figure importantly in the mise-en-scène of the *théâtre de l'inexprimé*. Significantly, Baty's views reflect the impact of Freud and Bergson. With regard to dialogue, Baty maintained, "le domaine du mot est immense puisqu'il embrasse toute l'intelligence, tout ce que l'homme peut comprendre et formuler. Mais au delà, tout ce qui échappe à l'analyse est inexprimable par la parole." For a comprehensive study of Bernard's involvement in the avant-garde theatre group Les Compagnons de la Chimère, other members of this group, and Baty's impact on the *théâtre de l'inexprimé*, see Daniels, "The French Theatre after 1918," chap. 5 of *French Drama of the Unspoken* (100–120). See also Bernard, *Mon ami le théâtre*, wherein he praises Baty for his tenacious faith in his art and the harmony and lucidity of his productions (37–42; 70–72).

27. Regarding the relationship between Jeanne and Martine, see Edmond Sée, *Le Théâtre français contemporain*, 2d ed. (Paris: Librairie Armand Colin, 1933), 156–57.

28. Daniels, *French Drama of the Unspoken*, 232.

Interlude
Altered Perspective: World War II—Culmination of the Crisis of Language

We come *after*, and that is the nerve of our condition. After the unprecedented ruin of humane values and hopes by the political bestiality of our age. . . . What man has inflicted on man, in very recent time, has affected the writer's primary material—the sum and potential of human behavior—and it presses on the brain with a new darkness.[1]

In *Language and Silence: Essays on Language, Literature and the Inhuman* George Steiner argues that the crisis of language culminating in retreat from the word and the elevated status of silence may be directly attributed to the political bestiality of this century.[2] The doubt which succeeded World War I was soon compounded by the certainty that everything is possible. Language, the prime carrier of culture and civilization, was perverted to become the compliant collaborator in inhumanity and silent witness to atrocity. From the iron logic of the Final Solution, there is no escape by reason.

Under the Reich, language acquired new dimensions and horrifying definitions. Not only was the unspeakable uttered repeatedly, observes Steiner, but language was prostituted to record, index, catalogue, and chronicle bestiality: human experimentation and extermination. Language was further adulterated by falsification; the "big lie," "indirect propaganda," "whisper" campaigns, and psychological warfare reached their zenith (or nadir) under Hitler.[3]

Curiously and paradoxically, the response to Nazi aberration in speech and act was essentially one of silence. "The world is silent," begins one of the last messages received from the Warsaw ghetto. "The world *knows* (it is inconceivable that it should not) and stays silent. God's vicar in the Vatican is silent; there is silence in London and Washington; the American Jews are silent. The silence is astonishing and horrifying."[4] In his study of American apathy, *While Six Million Died*, Arthur D. Morse argues that the world *did* know, that British, American, and European newspapers protested Nazi inhumanity while the United States, in receipt of official and unofficial evidence and corroborating memoranda, chose silence. The issue, it appears, was not one of knowing, but rather one of believing. To believe reports of genocide was to yield in some measure to the monstrous German intent. The absence of verbal response, more particularly in the form of outrage, from the American government and the Church, the two most powerful agencies operative during World War II, implied indifference, complicity, moral bankruptcy, and tacit sanction of Nazi policies.[5]

Precisely because it is the signature of humanity that has been stretched to accommodate the inhuman, language, insists Steiner, has exhausted its resiliency and its potential for literature. Collaborators, words are also victims. Arthur Adamov lamented the fact that "Les mots, ces gardiens du sens, ne sont pas immortels, invulnerables. . . . Dans la nuit tout se confond, il n'y a plus de noms, plus de formes."[6] In the absence of forms, the lyre of a dismembered Orpheus, to use Ihab Hassan's image, has no strings.[7] Silence, pleads Steiner. No more literature in our time.

But a literature that adjusts to the perspective of abnormality and distortion offers an alternative to silence.[8] Inhumanity in World War II extended from the Holocaust to Hiroshima. The writer who attempts to say what cannot be said, to communicate what eludes language, to convey a unique experience in the history of mankind, suggests Elie Wiesel, finds that language is inadequate to the task.[9] For many writers after World War II, there were no more names, no more forms, but there was a compelling need to speak about the unspeakable.

The attention of this study now focuses on postwar dramatists who authentically and obliquely reveal personal and global fragmentation through an elliptical, hesitant, dissonant, and disruptive linguistic structure.[10] Counterpointing noneloquent speech with the silent response of expectation, helplessness, immobility, and menace, the dramatist responds to alienation and isolation, to vulnerability and mortality, to survival and complicity, to bestiality and culpability, to metaphysical absolute and the relativity of historical fact.

In "Autour de Samuel Beckett: Devanciers, épigones et hérétiques," Pierre Brunel maintains that "le théâtre d'aujourd'hui pourrait sembler prisonner de son temps, puisqu'il naît de la confrontation de son auteur avec le monde dans lequel il vit."[11] Both timely and timeless, this theatre dramatizes the supposition that "we exist in no intelligible relation to the past, and no predictable relation to the future."[12] Subjective measurement supplants chronological measurement. Past, present, and future coalesce into a *durée* of memory and fantasy. Time serves as entrapment, for it coagulates and binds.

Similarly bound and constricted is the language which characterizes this drama. The repression of speech and the increased use of silence as dramatic structure and statement is of major concern to this study of contemporary drama. We observe that the outrage which rejects human identity and Western civilization is neither articulate nor direct. In his analysis of the ironic mode, Frye casts light on the nature and efficacy of linguistic reticence. Irony is evasive, indirect, discontinuous statement, reliant for its impact on the juxtaposition of images in the absence of causal connection: it is the art of saying little and meaning much, saying one thing and meaning something different.[13]

Oblique speech, innuendo, the reduction of the number of words, the extensive use of negatives, the use of the mute and/or inarticulate, the multiplicity of silent responses—all suggest entrapment and reinforce an impression of disorientation. "Il ne s'agit pas de 'parler de,'" urges Brunel, "mais d'être l'expression de."[14] Through a discourse of fragments punctuated and framed by the unspoken and the unspeakable the theatre which emerges after World War II can both "speak" about inhumanity and atrocity and simultaneously be the expression of it, can both reflect the refusal to speak and the inability to speak. A language of silence composed of both the unsaid and the unsayable reveals man fragmented from himself and from his world.

It is in the "negative creativity" of Samuel Beckett's drama that we find the epitome of the art of strangulation and the model for postwar linguistic experimentation.

NOTES

1. George Steiner, *Language and Silence: Essays on Language, Literature and the Inhuman* (New York: Oxford University Press, 1976), 4.

2. For Steiner's forceful and powerful argument on the crucial relationship between political inhumanity and language, see "The Hollow Miracle," in *Language and Silence*, 95–109.

3. For a discussion of falsification, "paper bullets," and psychological warfare, see Edmond Taylor, *The Strategy of Terror*, rev. ed. (Boston: Houghton Mifflin, 1942); Jay W. Baird, *The Mythical World of Nazi Propaganda, 1939–1945* (Minneapolis: University of Minnesota Press, 1974), 1–40; S. I. Hayakawa, *Language in Action* (New York: Harcourt, Brace, 1939). Hayakawa maintains that the political use of "two-valued" orientation in which everything is accounted for (hate/love; good/evil; Aryan/non-Aryan) reached its fullest expression under Hitler.

4. Quoted in Steiner, *Language and Silence*, 160.

5. See Arthur D. Morse, *While Six Million Died: A Chronicle of American Apathy* (New York: Ace, 1967), for a convincing, well-documented case for American and church apathy and genocide by proxy. Morse believes that Hitler exploited U.S. inaction and silent response.

6. Arthur Adamov, quoted in Steiner, *Language and Silence*, 52.

7. Ihab Hassan, *The Dismemberment of Orpheus: Toward a Post-Modern Literature* (New York: Oxford University Press, 1971), considers the postmodern spirit and its genesis in terrorism.

8. See Ihab Hassan, *The Literature of Silence: Henry Miller and Samuel Beckett* (New York: Knopf, 1967).

9. Elie Wiesel, *One Generation After* (New York: Random House, 1965).

10. As was the cast in post–World War I France, the theatre in post–World War II France (as well as Britain, Germany, and the United States) experienced diverse experimental activity. In this regard, see Martin Esslin, *The Theatre of the Absurd*, rev. ed. (Garden City, N.Y.: Anchor-Doubleday, 1969); see also Ruby Cohn, *Currents in Contemporary Drama* (Bloomington: Indiana University Press, 1969).

11. Pierre Brunel, "Autour de Samuel Beckett: Devanciers, épigones et hérétiques," in *La Mort de Godot: Attente et évanescence au théâtre*, ed. Pierre Brunel, Situations, no. 23 (Paris: Lettres Modern Minard, 1970), 13 (hereafter cited as *La Mort de Godot*).

12. Frank Kermode, *The Sense of an Ending: Studies in the Theory of Fiction* (London: Oxford University Press, 1967), 102.

13. Northrop Frye, *Anatomy of Criticism: Four Essays* (Princeton, N.J.: Princeton University Press, 1957), 61.

14. Brunel, "Autour de Samuel Beckett," 16.

5
Beckett

The nature and function of language and silence in Samuel Beckett's plays are, more than any other factors, the clearly distinctive elements of his theatre. So innovative is Beckett's use of the unspoken and the unspeakable as dramatic structure and statement that analysis of his techniques is fundamental to our understanding of the unexpressed in post-World War II drama. *En attendant Godot*, *Fin de partie*, *Krapp's Last Tape*, *Happy Days*, and *Footfalls*, plays in which the dramatic tension derives from the interdependence of speech and silence, will be considered as illustrative of Beckettian form—the evocative and subtle interplay of constricted, bivalent expression and expansive, eloquent silences.

For Becket form and content are inextricably linked; "the one is a concretion of the other, the revelation of a world."[1] Essential to an understanding of the coalescence of speech and silence integral to Beckett's drama is the distinction between *silences* and *Silence*. *Silences* are the intervals between verbalized responses that indicate separation (and that steadily increase in the Beckett canon to overtake and nearly obliterate the spoken word). *Silence*, on the other hand, is the Void, the Nothing, the ultimate language of the self that is unattainable. It is in the silences that the presence of ephemeral Silence is evoked.

In *Textes pour rien* Beckett cautions, "Nommer, non, rien n'est nommable, dire, non rien n'est dicible."[2] Beckett's art rests on this negative definition of naming and speaking: the unknown is unknowable, unnameable, unspeakable. The mind's inability to comprehend the irrational combined with the finite word's inability to contain and express the infinite explain in great part the frustration of the compulsive Beckettian quester in search of self. The actual self remains isolated, alienated, and exiled from the essential self. The quest is impossible.

Like his characters, the artist in search of the unspeakable may become trapped in the labyrinth of words—his own and others. "Il faut dire des mots," explains the narrator of *L'Innommable*, "tant qu'il y en a, il faut les dire, jusqu'à ce qu'ils me trouvent, jusqu'à ce qu'ils me disent . . . ils m'ont peut-être porté jusqu'au seuil de mon histoire."[3] On the threshold, writer and characters continue to employ words while seeking Silence. "Ce n'est pas le vocabulaire qui manque à l'auteur pour exprimer l'inexprimable," observes Claude Mauriac in

L'Alittérature contemporaine, "mais plutôt le pouvoir d'enchaîner les mots selon l'absurdité du réel humain."[4] The author must struggle against the logic of speech in order to express what the words would seek to deny: the uncertain, the contradictory, the unthinkable. In Beckett's drama, where eloquence and logic are conspicuous by their absence, disjunction in language indicates disjunction from self, from the other, and from the unknown.

Speech, linked by syntactical and grammatical relationships, composes and segments time. It is sequential and takes time. Beckett maintains that "all that is realised in Time (all Time produce), whether in Art or Life, can only be possessed successively, by a series of partial annexations—and never integrally and at once."[5] Whereas awareness is instantaneous, and the "translation" of awareness into language takes time and is a linear extension in time, there exists a fundamental and irreconcilable conflict between absolute, instantaneous reality and verbalized reality.[6]

Words, like man, are prisoners of time. In order to break the bonds of time, in order to express the illogical and the infinite and simulate the instantaneous and the integral, Beckett has devised a language of cancellation. Frank Kermode maintains that Beckett's seemingly formless linguistic structure is in actuality a meticulous, multivalent reductive construction.[7] Through a shifting and slipping of tenses and the use of the infinitive—which defies tense as well as person—Beckett simulates the cancellation of time.[8] Both these techniques are employed at the beginning of *Fin de partie:*

> Clov   (*regarde fixe, voix blanche):* Fini, c'est fini, ça va finir, ça va peut-être finir. (*Un temps.*)
>
> . . . .
>
> Hamm: A—(*bâillements*)—à moi. (*Un temps.*) De jouer.
>
> (*Fin de partie,* 15–16)

Neither statement is trapped in time; rather, each is as valid today as it was yesterday and will be tomorrow. Beckett also cancels time through nonprogressional dialogue that calls attention to itself and to experience as nonprogressional.[9] Gogo's "Rien ne se passe, personne ne vient, personne ne s'en va" and Clov's "Toute la vie les mêmes questions, les mêmes réponses" illustrate this paradigm (*Godot,* 58; *Fin de partie,* 19).

Through echoing repetition in which the repeated word ceases to move through time, Beckett simulates the cancellation of psychological movement. Winnie's preoccupation with sounds reveals that she is trapped in the thought:

> Sometimes I hear sounds. (*Listening expression. Normal voice.*) But not often. (*Pause.*) They are a boon, sounds are a boon, they help me . . . through the day. (*Smile.*) The old style! (*Smile off.*) Yes, those are happy days, when there are sounds. (*Pause.*) When I hear sounds. (*Pause.*)[10]

A more exaggerated example of nonprogressional repetition may be found in Lucky's monologue:

Il est établi sans autre possibilité d'erreur que celle afférente aux calculs humains qu'à la suite des recherches inachevées inachevées de Testu et Conard il est établi tabli tabli ce qui suit qui suit qui suit.

(*Godot*, 59–60)

The repeated words would seem to indicate that Lucky, having lost the thread of his thought, is going back in time to recover it; the words are "cancelled" as they are repeated, while they simultaneously cancel the free flow of other thoughts.

Through qualifications, modifications, hesitations, and tentative retractions, Beckett simulates the obliteration of the thought as it is stated. As this exchange among Pozzo, Didi, and Gogo illustrates, Didi and Gogo qualify and refine their relationship with Godot and deny confusing Pozzo with him. Didi, moreover, verges on a denial of their wait:

Pozzo (*tranchant*): Qui est Godot?
Gogo: Godot?
Pozzo: Vous m'avez pris pour Godot.
Didi: Oh non, monsieur, pas un seul instant, monsieur.
Pozzo: Qui est-ce?
Didi: Eh bien, c'est un . . . c'est une connaissance.
Gogo: Mais non, voyons, on le connaît à peine.
Didi: Evidemment . . . on ne le connaît pas très bien . . . mais tout de même
 . . .
Gogo: Pour ma part je ne le reconnaîtrais même pas.
Pozzo: Vous m'avez pris pour lui.
Gogo: C'est-à-dire . . . l'obscurité . . . la fatigue . . . la faiblesse . . . l'attente
 . . . j'avoue . . . j'ai cru . . . un instant . . .
Didi: Ne l'écoutez pas, monsieur, ne l'écoutez pas!
Pozzo: L'attente? Vous l'attendiez donc?
Didi: C'est-à-dire . . .
Pozzo: Ici? Sur mes terres?
Didi: On ne pensait pas à mal.

(*Godot*, 30–31)

Through the delicate balance of speech and silences Beckett simulates the obliteration of the word as it is stated. As this rare "conversation" between Willie and Winnie reveals, the forward progression of language in time is canceled as the words seem to disappear into the void:

Winnie: . . . I beseech you, Willie, just yes or no, can you hear me, just yes or nothing.
 Pause.
Willie: Yes.
Winnie (*turning front, same voice*): And now?
Willie (*irritated*): Yes.
Winnie (*less loud*): And now?

Willie   (more irritated): Yes.
Winnie   (still less loud): And now? (A little louder.) And now?
Willie   (violently): Yes!

(Happy Days, 25–26)

Essentially, as these citations illustrate, Beckett employs words and silences to create the cumulative effect of cancellation.

Beckett's experimentation with dramatic form, content, speech, and silence is a function of his intention to grapple with the minotaur, Time, "the double-headed monster of damnation and salvation," in order to reveal the divided self and the suffering of being.[11] Beckettian drama is bound and constricted, stripped to the survival level of character, setting, action, and dialogue. Parallel-ing the use and simultaneous cancellation of words, he employs the structure of drama and then cancels it by ironic parody and artistic expression. "The theatre allows Beckett a double freedom," suggests Michael Robinson in The Long Sonata of the Dead, "the opportunity to explore the blank space between the words and the ability to provide visual evidence of the untrustworthiness of language."[12] A classic illustration of this is the resolution twice repeated in Godot, "Allons, y," and the playwright's instructions twice repeated, "Ils ne bougent pas" (Godot, 75, 134). Blank space functions as the background, the white canvas against which Beckett may project the words. Incorporated into his portrait of existence is the emptiness and evanescence of phenomenal and psychological experience.

Beckett's drama is characterized by a retreat from the word; physical, emo-tional, and linguistic entrapment; stasis as dramatic structure; evocation of evanescence; the motif of waiting; and the centrality of time.[13] These distinctive features suggest areas of compatibility with the other dramatists considered in this study of the unspoken in modern drama. Jacques Guicharnaud, referring specifically to Godot (but his comment is equally applicable to other early Beck-ett plays), notes that the absence of any intellectual debate—the constant state of tension and inaction—recalls symbolist drama.[14] We observe in Beckett's drama several typifying elements of symbolist drama, namely, the use of inti-mation and suggestion to evoke the psychic state, the use of symbols (particu-larly observation thresholds in Godot and windows in Fin de partie) to elicit interior and exterior space and entrapment, and the use of enigma and ambigu-ity (such as that which shrouds the identity of Godot and the appointment, the circumstances that prefigured "zero" conditions in Fin de partie, and the cause of the explosion of Winnie's parasol). The condition of waiting dramatized by Beckett in these early plays recalls the expectant mood that informs Maeter-linck's symbolist drama. Like Maeterlinckian pilgrims who wait for the Sister of Mercy in L'Intruse and the priest in Les Aveugles, Beckett's bums endure a prolonged and often painful wait. Winnie waits for bells to go to sleep, Hamm waits for painkiller, and Didi and Gogo wait for Godot.

Relevant to this comparative study of the unexpressed are the techniques employed by Maeterlinck and Beckett to simulate the condition of waiting and to elicit interior mood. Common to both dramatists is the use of confined settings to suggest psychic entrapment. The characters in *Les Aveugles* are trapped in the woods, just as Alladine and Palomides are literally locked in a crypt. Similarly, while not apparently entrapped, Didi and Gogo are meta-phorically tied to Godot. Clov and Hamm, on the other hand, are trapped within their room as Nagg and Nell are in their bins and Winnie is in her mound. More importantly, Beckett, like Maeterlinck, elicits psychological flux through the absence of action and the absence of speech. Silence contributes to the impression of fixity and suggests the fluidity of thought.

In Maeterlinck's drama enigmatic utterances, repetitions, unanswered ques-tions, and pauses intimate a mood of confusion and spiralling anxiety, as this citation from *Pelléas et Mélisande* reveals:

> *Mélisande:* Qu'y a-t-il, Yniold? Qu'y a-t-il? . . . pourquoi pleures-tu tout à
> coup?
> *Yniold*   *(sanglotant):* Parce que . . . Oh! oh! parce que . . .
> *Mélisande:* Pourquoi? . . . Pourquoi? dis-le moi . . .
> *Yniold:*   Petite-mère . . . petite-mère . . . vous allez partir . . .
>
> (2 : 58)

In Beckett's drama to wait is, as Martin Esslin suggests, "to experience the action of time."[15] The effect of this action, or more particularly inaction, is a deepening frustration and doubt, rather than escalating fear. Typically con-cerned with the nonappearance of Godot, this duologue in act 1 intimates frustration and uneasiness in repetitions and qualifications:

> *Gogo:* Il devrait être là.
> *Didi:* Il n'a pas dit ferme qu'il viendrait.
> *Gogo:* Et s'il ne vient pas?
> *Didi:* Nous reviendrons demain.
> *Gogo:* Et puis après-demain.
> *Didi:* Peut-être.
> *Gogo:* Et ainsi de suite.
> *Didi:* C'est-à-dire . . .
> *Gogo:* Jusqu'à ce qu'il vienne.
>
> (*Godot*, 17)

The nuanced repetitions of "vient" tacitly convey the frustration of repeatedly coming for an appointment that has yet to materialize. Didi's tentative retrac-tions, moreover, reveal the uncertainty that he and Gogo feel with respect to Godot's commitment to come. We also observe that the repetition of "et" rein-forces the impression of prolonged frustration. At the end of act 2 Didi and Gogo, exhausted by the wait, resolve to hang themselves tomorrow "à moins que Godot ne vienne" (*Godot*, 17, 133). The subtle modification from "jusqu'à"

to "à moins que" is startling. The cumulative effect of waiting and the movement toward despair is made evident obliquely by a shift in speakers. It is Didi,
long the one conscious of and insistent upon the wait, who now concedes "à
moins que."

The anxiety that Beckett's characters experience is the fear that language, like
the twilight of which Pozzo speaks, will become steadily paler and diminish
entirely before they run out of day. We exist, suggests Beckett, by virtue of our
ability to maintain the illusion of communication. Thus Beckett's characters use
words, magically as Didi notes, but the trick is increasingly more difficult to
perform. Monosyllabic words often serve to keep the linguistic ball rolling:
"oui," "non," "c'est vrai." In Beckett's drama stichomythic phrases, repetitions,
and pauses often serve to expose the anguish and effort of Beckett's characters to
sustain speech. Winnie's lament typically forestalls the intrusion of Silence and
lays bare her psychic state: "I can do no more. *(Pause.)* Say no more. *(Pause.)*
But I must say more. *(Pause.)* Problem here. *(Pause.)*" (*Happy Days*, 60).

Beckett parallels Maeterlinck in his use of disjunctive language to convey
rhythms of realistic speech patterns. But, essentially in Beckettian drama, fragmented speech in concert with silences exposes fundamental incompleteness
and disjunction both in the world and in the individual. As the jumbled fragments from *Krapp's Last Tape* illustrate, thoughts do not cohere:

> *(Gasping.)* Went to sleep and fell off the pew. *(Pause.)* Sometimes wondered in
> the night if a last effort mightn't—*(Pause.)* Ah finish your booze now and get
> to your bed. Go with this drivel in the morning. Or leave it at that. *(Pause.)*
> Leave it at that. *(Pause.)* Lie propped up in the dark—and wander. Be again in
> the dingle on a Christmas eve, gathering holly, the red-berried. *(Pause.)*[16]

Beckett employs stichomythic utterances not only to express anxiety and
incompleteness, but also to stalemate conversation. We note that this parting
exchange among Pozzo, Didi, and Gogo exemplifies Beckett's language of cancellation; the bums progress neither in space nor in time:

> *Gogo:*   Alors, adieu.
> *Pozzo:* Adieu.
> *Didi:*   Adieu.
> *Gogo:*   Adieu.
>   *Silence. Personne ne bouge.*
> *Didi:*   Adieu.
> *Pozzo:* Adieu.
> *Gogo:*   Adieu.
>   *Silence.*

(*Godot*, 65)

Despite their apparent differences, Chekhov and Beckett are masters of the
"artifice of reality." Whereas Chekhov impressionistically conveys a nuanced,

naturalistic portrait of reality, Beckett, on the other hand, portrays an "extended" reality, one that encompasses the seen and the unseen, the dream and the waking state, through simplification and magnification.[17] Both dramatists are distinctive in their use of a compressionistic style that distills the complexity of experience. We note that Beckett, like Chekhov, employs suggestion, concision, and resonance to evoke disappointment, disillusionment, and despair. Similarly, in Beckett's drama, as in Chekhov's, inertia devours energy, nostalgia concedes to melancholy, promise to loss, hope to resignation. Like Chekhovian doctors who bemoan their helplessness, resigned Beckettian bums concede, "rien à faire." Indeed, Beckett's studies of reductionism are more ruthless and devastating. Chekhov holds out the promise of future, albeit illusory, but in Beckettian drama, as Robbe-Grillet has observed, "ce peu qu'on nous avait donné au départ—et qui nous semblait être rien—se corrompt bientôt sous nos yeux, se degrade."[18]

Counterpointing alternatingly swift and slow temporal progression, Beckett, paralleling Chekhov, exploits the daily flow of the customary and the habitual to dramatize continuity and perpetuity, such as Winnie's attention to toiletries and Clov's sightings. Typically, Beckett employs paradigmatic and ritualized arrivals and departures to simulate fluid and fixed moments in time, even if they are diminished to Clov's "come and go" to the kitchen and Gogo's morning arrival from the ditch. Like their Russian counterparts, Beckett's characters are prisoners of time who speak incessantly about time. Pozzo has pressing appointments; Winnie does not want to "overdo the bag" for fear of having too much time before the bell for sleep. Suddenly, in a few years or in "one" day, time has slipped by unnoticed. With outrage and lamentation, or (in the case of Krapp) with ridicule, Beckett's characters, like Chekhov's, confront lost opportunities, tattered illusions and the passage of time. Hamm observes: "Nous perdons nos cheveux, nos dents! Notre fraîcheur! Nos idéaux!" (*Fin de partie*, 25).

Beckett's closest affinity to the Russian dramatist, however, is discernible in his subtle use of language. Paralleling Chekhov's simulation of aimless, fluid speech, Beckett relies upon understatement and overstatement to create the impression of ambiguity and indistinctness in speech and thought. Counterpointing, choral speaking, and negations serve both in Chekhovian and Beckettian drama to short-circuit communication or to cast doubt on what is being said. In act 1 of *The Three Sisters* the laughter of the men drown out Olga's fervent resolution to go to Moscow, just as in the concluding scene of act 4 Tchebutykin's characteristic "It doesn't matter" counterpoints the efforts of the three sisters to evade present loss by speaking about future promise. Similarly, in *Happy Days* Winnie provides her own counterpoint: "To sing too soon is fatal, I always find. (*Pause*). On the other hand it is possible to leave it too late" (*Happy Days*, 56). Contradictions, characteristic of Beckett's drama, may be viewed as a fusion of counterpointing and negation, as this concise and biting exchange between Nagg and Hamm reveals:

Hamm: Salopard! Pourquoi m'as-tu fait?
Nagg: Je ne pouvais pas savoir.
Hamm: Quoi? Qu'est-ce que tu ne pouvais pas savoir?
Nagg: Que ce serait toi. *(Un temps)*

(Fin de partie, 69)

Speech making, typical of Chekhovian characters (such as Vershinin's "future" speech, Trofimov's "All Russia is our garden," and Vanya's comparison between himself and Serebryakov), is transmuted in Beckettian drama. Pozzo, Hamm, Krapp, and Winnie, not to mention Lucky, all exceed at this "art" whose purpose is indeed diversionary. We observe that for Chekhov's characters the content of the speech is of primary importance. In *The Three Sisters,* for example, Masha is so impressed with Vershinin's ideas (the contrast to her husband Kuligin is striking) that she decides to stay to lunch. Similarly, in *The Cherry Orchard* we find Anna impressed by Trofimov. In Beckettian drama, on the other hand, the content serves the characters as a vehicle for their oration. Clov's parting speech is typical. Having been asked by Hamm for something from his heart, Clov engages in a long peroration on love, friendship, and suffering. Whether the subject is a beloved bookcase or the approach of twilight, orators crave approval. Whereas Pozzo demands "reviews," Winnie, although satisfied with the show of a finger, is aware that occasionally her performances reach great heights. And performance is exactly what Beckett's set pieces are. If Chekhov's characters spoke passionately, it was because it was a statement from their heart. This may still be the case for Beckett's characters, but self-conscious, they are as much concerned with the quality of the performance as the emotion that engenders it. Hamm, for example, is his most appreciative audience, continually calling attention to himself: "Joli ça." Essentially, in the Beckettian universe, characters perform for others and for themselves while waiting.

Defining his characters by their isolation and estrangement from life and from themselves, Beckett, like Chekhov, eschews confessions and confidences. We recall that in *The Three Sisters* Masha's efforts to confide her love for Vershinin and Andrey's to confess the life-lies on which he has been living, are both rejected by the weary sisters. Similarly, the conclusion of *Uncle Vanya* tacitly reveals Sonya's efforts to drown out Vanya's despair. Recalling the ontological loneliness of these characters, Gogo finds no consoling ear for his nightmares. "A qui veux-tu que je raconte mes cauchemars privés, sinon à toi?" he questions Didi. The rebuff is direct and inflexible: "Qu'ils restent privés" *(Godot,* 19). In *Fin de partie* Hamm blows his whistle to see if Clov is within listening range: "*(Il siffle. Un temps. Plus fort. Un temps.)* . . . Clov! *(Un temps long.)* Non? Bon" *(Fin de partie,* 111–12). Long pauses punctuate Hamm's monosyllabic speech. The unexpressed once again reinforces the impression that Beckett's characters are metaphorically, if not literally, isolated.

Symbolist, realistic, and surrealistic techniques; apparent stasis and cyclical flux; and a retreat from the word in response to the Holocaust and inhumanity—all figure importantly in Beckett's extensive use of the unspoken and the unspeakable. The elements of a language of silence employed by Beckett to dramatize discontinuity and disjunction are:

1. indirect, disjunctive speech
2. colloquial dialogue implicitly conveying more than it superficially and explicitly communicates
3. contrapuntal speech
4. unanswered questions
5. repetition and echoing
6. pauses
7. silences
8. mute characters
9. silence as a metaphor for isolation
10. silence as a metaphor for absence
11. silence of the playwright

Indirect, disjunctive speech that elicits imperceptible fluctuations both within the mind of the speaker and between speakers has been used variously by Maeterlinck, Chekhov, and Bernard to convey emotional stress, exhaustion, disorientation, and doubt. More than any other playwright who employs silence as structure and statement, Beckett exploits halting and groping speech patterns to reflect detachment both within the character and between characters. Disjunctive speech informs the stressful recitation of Hamm when he suspects that he is alone, or will be imminently, and similarly informs that of Winnie, who, troubled by the lack of denotative response from Willie, fears that she, too, is alone. Interrupted by unanswered questions, pauses, denials, and reversals, Willie's fragmented speech exposes an anxiety and isolation she would seek to deny:

> Words fail, there are times when even they fail. (*Turning a little towards* WILLIE.) Is that not so, Willie? (*Pause, turning a little further.*) Is that not so, Willie, that even words fail, at times? (*Pause. Back front.*) What is one to do then, until they come again?
>
> (*Happy Days*, 24)

For this dramatist, dialogue must authentically convey the confusion that he believes is intrinsic to what we term conversation. Confusion, claims Beckett, is not his own invention, but rather "all around us and our only chance now is to let it in."[19] What Beckettian dialogue lacks in continuity, it gains in authenticity. The following contrapuntal exchange among Pozzo, Didi, and Gogo from *Godot* illustrates what Beckett has intentionally left cryptic, chaotic, condensed, and confused. Gogo, disturbed because Lucky has not relieved himself of his burdens, repeatedly asks Pozzo, "Pourquoi ne dépose-t-il pas ses bagages?" Just as Pozzo is about to respond to the inquiry, now posed not only by Gogo but also by Didi, he is distracted by his preparations for the set piece on the twilight. Forgetting about the question, Pozzo is brought to attention by a duet of Didi's mime of a burdened carrier and Gogo's disjointed, inverted fragments:

> *(avec force.)*—Bagages! *(Il point son doigt vers Lucky.)* Pourquoi? Toujours tenir. *(Il fait celui ploie, en haletant.)* Jamais déposer. *(Il ouvre les mains, se redresse avec soulagement.)* Pourquoi?
>
> *(Godot*, 39–41)

Phrased in this manner, Pozzo promptly responds, "J'y suis. Il fallait me le dire plus tôt" (*Godot*, 41).

Bivalent dialogue, characteristic of silent theatre, operates simultaneously on objective and subjective levels, implying more than it superficially and specifically states. Much has been written about Beckett's use of simple colloquial language, seasoned with expletives and vulgarisms, whose appearance in *En attendant Godot* marks the debut of this language in hitherto eloquent French drama. Essentially, Beckett has fashioned a realistic medium of communication for his characters appropriate to their station in life and their elemental concerns. Characteristically, Beckett's characters make connotative observations that are undefined and unexplained. Winnie, for example, exclaims, "What a blessing nothing grows, imagine if all this stuff were to start growing. *(Pause.)* Imagine. *(Pause.)* Ah yes, great mercies" (*Happy Days*, 34). Similarly, we observe in this exchange between Clov and Hamm that more is implied than is explicitly stated:

> *Clov:*   Il y a tant de choses terribles.
> *Hamm:* Non non, il n'y en a plus tellement.
>
> *(Fin de partie*, 63)

The unexpressed stimulates the imagination of the spectator to complete the idea or emotion merely suggested.

In addition to unanswered questions, denials, and connotative, disjunctive expression, Beckettian drama is distinctive in its varied use of the technique of repetition. In Maeterlinck's symbolist drama, repetitions figured importantly and obviously to intensify mood and reinforce fixity. Chekhov, on the other hand, employed repetitions more subtly to elicit realistic speech patterns and perpetuate a condition. More recently, Bernard relied upon repetitions to suggest distracted and compulsive behavior. Beckett orchestrates all these variations. In his plays of "come and go," repeated motifs, phrases, and pauses that create and reinforce the impression of stasis are cumulatively effective.[20] We note that in Beckett's plays a character repeats a word or a phrase to fix it in his mind, to forestall the free flow of other thoughts (as previously discussed in relation to the language of cancellation), and to exploit to the fullest the only word he can think of at the moment. In *Godot*, for example, Didi's comment "Du calme" elicits Gogo's repetitive response: *"(avec volupté).—Calme . . . Calme . . . (Rêveusement).* Les Anglais disent câââm. Ce sont des gens câââms. *(Un temps.)" (Godot,* 20). Having exhausted the topic of "calme" Gogo must find new inspiration to stall the advancement of Silence.

In addition to the aforementioned uses of repetitions, this technique is employed by Beckett to simulate realistic speech patterns. The following conversation from *Fin de partie* is illustrative:

Hamm: Tes graines ont levé?
Clov: Non.
Hamm: Tu a gratté un peu voir si elles ont germé.
Clov: Elles n'ont pas germé.
Hamm: C'est peut-être encore trop tôt.
Clov: Si elles devaient germer elles auraient germé.

Annoyed by the persistence of Hamm's questioning and the seeds that have not sprouted, Clov concludes, "Elles ne germeront jamais" *(Fin de partie,* 27–28). Similarly, repetitions characterize Winnie's colloquial chatter. Limited in diversions and confined in space, Winnie must continually recirculate her few words to describe adequately the quotidian objects and concerns of her life.

To elicit and perpetuate mood, Beckett employs a broken-record technique, comparable to the echoing used by Chekhov at the conclusion of *Uncle Vanya, The Three Sisters,* and *The Cherry Orchard.* As previously noted, echoing subjects a thought or an emotion to multiple interpretation, similar to symphonic theme and variation. The resonant and evocative echoes may be the repetition of one character or several, individually or in concert, in sequence or interrupted by other statements. Essentially, each character is revealed by his idiosyncratic use and inflection of the phrase as the expression, subjected to mercurial interpretations, registers and reverberates throughout the play. The nuanced variations of "On attend Godot/C'est vrai"—which resonate throughout *En attendant Godot* and conclude acts 1 and 2—are an example of this paradigm. Spoken by both Didi and Gogo, the lines contribute to the evocation of mood and simultaneously assume a deeper resonance with each repetition.

The brief pause (three dots), the full pause, and silence may be considered the primary components of Beckett's linguistic construction. Static and nonprogressional, pauses and silences stall the progression of thought, action, and time. Performing structurally and linguistically, accumulated pauses and silences are responsible in great part for the oppressive sensation of entrapment and timelessness that pervades Beckett's world. Moreover, the repetitive use of gaps in the dialogue reinforces an impression of incompleteness, emptiness, and isolation and intimates that more is left unstated than is confessed. In another context, Beckett observed that there was no such thing as *"mere* relief." On the contrary, "relief has also to do work and reinforce that from which it relieves."[21]

In Beckettian drama pauses indicate a hesitation to find a word, to recover a lost thought, to quality or modify an expression and to allow time for response. We note that the multivalent function of the nonprogressional pause is evident in this passage from *Happy Days:*

> Do you think the earth has lost its atmosphere, Willie? *(Pause.)* Do you, Willie? *(Pause.)* You have no opinion? *(Pause.)* Well that is like you, you never had any opinion about anything. *(Pause.)* It's understandable. *(Pause.)* Most. *(Pause.)* The earthball. *(Pause.)* I sometimes wonder. *(Pause.)* Perhaps not quite all. *(Pause.)* There always remains something. *(Pause.)*
>
> (*Happy Days*, 51–52)

The profusion of pauses reveals that Willie does not respond, although Winnie has given him ample opportunity to do so. In the absence of Willie's denotative response, Winnie, hesitantly and haltingly, as the repetitions, negatives, and pauses indicate, maintains the momentum of speech. In *Footfalls* the time between responses is extended, intimating isolation and the strain of speakers to maintain even the illusion of communication:

> Pause.
>
> M: Mother. *(Pause. No louder.)* Mother.
>
> Pause.
>
> V: Yes, May.
> M: Were you asleep?
> V: Deep asleep. *(Pause.)* I heard you in my deep sleep. *(Pause.)* There is no sleep so deep I would not hear you there. *(Pause. M resumes pacing. Four lengths. After first length, synchronous with steps).* . . . .
> . . . . *seven eight nine wheel* . . . . . . *seven eight nine wheel.*
> *(Free.)* Will you not try to snatch a little sleep?
> M halts facing front at R. Pause.[22]

Long pauses and silences in Beckett's drama generally indicate a break in the dialogue of a longer duration than the pause and often underscore a culmination or a conclusion to a topic. In *Krapp's Last Tape*, for example, Krapp has been listening to a tape: "All that old misery. *(Pause).* Once wasn't enough for you. *(Pause.)* Lie down across her." The stage instructions call for a long pause during which Krapp wrenches the tape from the recorder, figuratively short-circuiting a continuation of topic (*Krapp's Last Tape*, 26–27). In addition, we note that Beckett employs silences to frame and accentuate words that are uttered between silences. In Pozzo's twilight speech, the orator builds to the climax of his speech and elicits attention through silences. His final comment, "C'est comme ça que se passe sur cette putain de terre," is preceded by silence and punctuated by a long silence (*Godot*, 51–52).

Silences, moreover, are employed by Beckett to indicate the increasing encroachment of Silence. In the lyrical passage from *Godot*, "Toutes les voix mortes," the stage instruction "Silence" recurs frequently, indicating that Didi and Gogo are losing their battle to drown out all the dead voices:

Didi: Ça fait comme un bruit de plumes.
Gogo: De feuilles.
Didi: De cendres.
Gogo: De feuilles.
   Long Silence.
Didi: Dis quelque chose!
Gogo: Je cherche.
   Long Silence.
Didi *(angoissé):*—Dis n'importe quoi!
Gogo: Qu'est-ce qu'on fait maintenant?
Didi: On attend Godot.
Gogo: C'est vrai.
   Silence.

                   (*Godot*, 88)

So desperate is Didi to maintain the flow of conversation that he reduces the demand "dis quelque chose" to "dis n'importe quoi!"

We note that Beckettian silences are operative not only throughout the plays, but they also figure importantly at the beginning and end of the plays to establish an impression of stasis. *Godot* begins and ends with a long pause; *Krapp's Last Tape* begins with elaborate nonverbal stage business and ends with the tape running on in silence; *Fin de partie* begins with nonverbal gestures and concludes on a frozen, silent tableau.

Like Maeterlinck, Chekhov, and Bernard, Beckett's treatment of silence extends to character as well as dialogue. Two characters in particular, Lucky in *En attendant Godot* and Willie in *Happy Days*, are "mute." Both speak sparingly (Lucky only once and Willie little and infrequently), and the fact that they speak is at least as important as what they say. For Didi, Gogo, and Pozzo, Lucky's recitation is anticipated as welcome diversion, although what he says is not well received. Similarly, for Winnie, the fact that Willie speaks at all constitutes a "happy day." Willie's occasional responses testify to his consciousness and assure Winnie that something of what is being said is being heard. We observe, moreover, that both these characters, who are obvious nonparticipants in the language game, are kept "alive" in the play by other characters referring to them or directly addressing them.

A master of concision, Beckett perceives of the artist's role as one of distillation, not amplification. "The time is not perhaps altogether too green," suggests the playwright, "for the vile suggestion that art has nothing to do with clarity, does not dabble in the clear and does not make clear."[23] Beckett asks rather than answers questions, alludes rather than definitively states. Through this technique Beckett mirrors the doubt and dread that grip his characters and intensifies the mystification and confusion of his audience. For Beckett, and for us, the search for certainty is impossible. The unstated remains unsayable.

Directed by Roger Blin, *En attendant Godot* received its first production in Paris on 3 January 1953 at the Théâtre de Babylone. In subjecting *Godot* to exegesis, I do not presume to clarify its essential and intended indistinctness, but rather to examine the varied use of the unspoken and the unspeakable. In the absence of the traditional theatrical trappings of sequential plot, conceptual dialogue, and physical action, thematic dialogue and silence have metamorphosed into structure and statement. Richard Schechner has observed that *Godot* is a "play of gaps and pauses." Closer examination will reveal the nature and function of these gaps and indicate that openness is not at the end, "but in many places throughout."[24]

In this two-act drama the bivalent duologues are thematically linked by symphonic motifs (one of the most telling is repetition itself), the unity of setting, the constant presence of Didi and Gogo, disruptive and diverting intrusions and the central symbol: Godot. Examination of the text will illustrate that the absent protagonist, Godot, makes his presence (or rather, absence) felt rather than known through tangible and intangible effects on Didi and Gogo; Godot's name, even an implicit suggestion associatively linked to his name (such as "on attend"), typically elicits verbal and/or physical paralysis. The fluctuating rhythm of Didi and Gogo's emotions and thoughts is evoked by the things that are said to them, by the effects these statements have on them, by the distinctive nature of their speech, and by what they say or choose to leave unspoken. We observe that Gogo's restlessness, anxiety, uncertainty, and despair are reflected in evasive naps and persistent questions that are often reiterated until Gogo provokes either a verbalized response or silent rejection. Didi, on the other hand, similarly plagued by boredom, fear, uneasiness, and uncertainty, reflects this linguistically through articulate statements qualified, modified, and interrupted by pauses and silences.

In order to understand the dynamics of Beckett's deceptively static dramatic and linguistic structure, we will need to establish the significance and fluctuating rhythm both within and between conversational units, the fluidity and continuity of which are directly attributable to the ability of the Beckett bums to keep the linguistic ball bouncing between them.[25] Although inextricably linked by recurring motifs, refrains, and phrases, for the purposes of this analysis the units will be considered separately within each act: Didi and Gogo alone; Didi, Gogo, Pozzo, and Lucky; Didi, Gogo, and Godot's messenger; and Didi and Gogo alone.

The initial conversational unit typifies the contrastive, associative, and nondirectional nature of Beckettian dialogue. Estragon, seated on the mound, repeatedly attempts to remove his boot. His panting, nonverbal, repetitive action and solitary presence evoke a sensation of exhaustion, frustration, and fixity. His first words, "Rien à faire" (soon to be a recurrent refrain), constitute a conclusive observation uttered to himself, but Vladimir, signaling his presence and his participation in the language game, responds to Gogo's words, "Je commence à le croire." Their reunion elicits the topic of their separation; the pressing issue is where Gogo spent the night and if he was beaten again. Meditating on Gogo's difficulties and his self-appointed role as Gogo's protector, Didi muses disjointedly, "Quand j'y pense . . . depuis le temps . . . je me demande . . . ce que tu serais devenue . . . sans moi. . . ." His voice drifts off, leaving unspoken what might have become, what is yet to become, of them both.

Through cooperative effort, Didi and Gogo manage to sustain a disjunctive conversation, finding inspiration in Gogo's boots and the Bible. Bored, Didi suggests, "Allons-nous-en." Didi's response, "On ne peut pas," encounters an incredulous and argumentative "Pourquoi?" Gogo has forgotten: "On attend Godot." Gogo's "C'est vrai" acknowledges and confirms the appointment. This first explicit mention of waiting directly conveys the expectant, anticipatory mood, unspoken and undefined, but nevertheless operative since the beginning of the play. The intimation "waiting for" informs us that a protagonist, absent for the moment, has yet to make a stage appearance (*Godot*, 9–16).

Exhausted by his questions about the appointment with Godot, such as "Tu es sûr que c'est ici?" and "Tu es sûr que c'était ce soir?" (Gogo typically presses for clarification while Didi typically retreats to indefiniteness), and the wait itself, Gogo short-circuits the conversation with a call for silence: "Taisons-nous un peu, tu veux." Gogo's escape in sleep is short-lived, however, because Didi, for whom isolation and silence are intolerable, awakens him to resume verbal interaction. Significantly, Didi refuses to submit to the intimacy of confession. Demanding that Gogo's dream/nightmare remain unspoken, Didi then repeats his demand, "Ne le raconte pas," because Gogo, distracted by his nightmare, had not heard Didi and has begun to speak. Rebuffed, Gogo coldly introduces the suggestion that they separate, and calm is once again displaced by animosity, eliciting figurative if not literal separation. Gogo haltingly makes physical and verbal advances to Didi but is repeatedly rebuffed by Didi's alienating silence of exclusion:

> *Gogo (Pas en avant):*—Tu es fâché? *(Silence. Pas en avant).* Pardon! *(Silence. Pas en avant. Il lui touche l'épaule.)* Voyons, Didi. *(Silence.)* Donne ta main! *(Vladimir se retourne.)* Embrasse-moi! *(Vladimir se raidit.)* Laisse-toi faire! *(Vladimir s'amollit. Ils s'embrassent.)*

Reunited, they once again reaffirm their commitment to waiting, but we note that there is no explicit mention of Godot's name. Between friends not everything must be stated; they are waiting for Godot (*Godot*, 16–21).

Didi and Gogo calmly divert themselves while waiting until the explicit mention of Godot and Gogo's characteristic questioning—at this moment directed toward clarification of their relationship to Godot—elicit the issue of entrapment. Gogo's repeated questions reveal his disquietude: "Et nous? . . . Je dis, Et nous? . . . Quel est notre rôle là-dedans?" Pressing the issue and revealing his entrapment in it, Gogo persists, "On n'a plus de droits?" Ignoring Didi's

laughter, Gogo presses for a resolution to the problem: "Nous les avons per-
dus?" he inquires. Vladimir corrects him: "Nous les avons bazardés." A muffled
silence of outrage severs the verbal ties that bind Didi and Gogo. The stage
instructions are explicit: both Didi and Gogo are physically and linguistically
paralyzed, sinking under the burden of what has previously remained unspoken.

Feebly Gogo breaks their silence and resumes their duologue, still gripped by
the thought of bondage. "On n'est pas liés?" asks Gogo, and a pause allows Didi
the opportunity to respond. But the silence of despair is quickly displaced by a
silent response to fear. Noises in the distance divert attention away from
thoughts of isolation and dependence to unite the two friends in mutual defense.
Intimated rather than stated, the two are apparently as committed to each
other's safety as they are to their wait. Frightened, Gogo begs Didi, "Allons-
nous-en," but the latter, rather than respond that they cannot because they are
waiting for Godot, employs a monosyllabic modification: "Où?" Neither Didi
nor Gogo has a response.

Despite the fact that the issue of entrapment has been displaced by a discussion of changed locales and the relative merits of carrots and turnips, it has
obviously been percolating in Gogo's mind. His mouth full of chewed carrot,
Gogo inquires and then asks again (because with his mouth full of carrot Didi
has not heard Gogo), "On n'est pas liés?"[26] Their exchange, punctuated by
questions and repetitions, reveals Gogo's entrapment in the thought and Didi's
evasion of the subject:

Gogo   (mâche, avale): Je demande si on est liés.
Didi: Liés?
Gogo: Li -és.
Didi: Comment, liés?
Gogo: Pied et poings.
Didi: Mais à qui? Par qui?
Gogo: A ton bonhomme.
Didi: A Godot? Liés à Godot? Quelle idée? Jamais de la vie! (Un temps.) Pas
        encore. (Il ne fait pas la liaison.)

Although Didi does not specifically admit doubt, his adamant denials punctuated by a pause cast doubt on his assertions, as does his qualified response
concerning Godot's name. "Rien à faire" concludes this pressing problem and
reveals an impasse in their conversation (Godot, 21–28).

This initial conversational unit has introduced several important motifs: com-
ing/going, interiority/exteriority, separation/reunion, security/danger, flux/
fixity, longing/disillusionment, and tranquility/anxiety. The fluctuating rhythm
of their psychic state, whether philosophical, argumentative, frustrated, or de-
spairing, is revealed in their disjunctive speech and their eloquent silences.

Shouts announce the arrival of intruders. Struck dumb with fear, Didi and
Gogo cringe together, their silence in striking counterpoint to the noise of

Pozzo's cries and cracking whip. Hesitant, Didi and Gogo are nevertheless relieved by the arrival of this man and his carrier whom they have indeed been expecting and with whom they have an appointment. Pozzo, repeating his name and allowing it to reverberate in the silence, receives no sign of recognition. The disjunctive, halting speech of the Beckettian bums reflects rather than directly defines their uneasiness about this intruder, on whose property it appears they are intruding. We note that as Didi and Gogo humble themselves before Pozzo, they leave unspoken their disappointment that Godot has failed to appear:

> Gogo   *(à Pozzo):* Vous n'êtes pas monsieur Godot, monsieur?
> Pozzo   *(d'une voix terrible):* Je suis Pozzo! *(Silence.)* Ce non ne vous dit rien?
>   *(Silence.)* Je vous demande si ce nom ne vous dit rien?
>   *Vladimir et Estragon s'interrogent du regard.*
> Gogo   *(faisant semblant de chercher):* Bozzo . . . Bozzo . . .
> Pozzo: Pppozzo!
> Gogo: Ah! Pozzo . . . voyons . . . Pozzo . . .
> Didi: C'est Pozzo ou Bozzo?

When Pozzo explicitly demands to know who Godot is, both Didi and Gogo are evasive. Their repetitions and denials punctuated by hesitations convince Pozzo that what he originally intuited, that the bums have confused him with Godot, is closer to the truth than what they disjunctively reveal:

> Gogo: Mais non, voyons, on le connaît à peine.
> Didi: Evidemment . . . on ne le connaît pas très bien . . . mais tout le
>   même . . .
> Gogo: Pour ma part je ne le reconnaîtrais même pas.

Pozzo's shouts for coat, whip, stool, and basket and Lucky's agitated "come and go" are contrasted with Didi and Gogo's silent observation. Whereas Gogo's disjointed, repetitive appeal for the bones—"Heu . . . vous ne mangez pas . . . heu . . . vous n'avez plus besoin . . . des os . . . monsieur?"—reveals his timidity and his tentativeness, Didi's momentary muteness, in one formerly loquacious, is similarly revelatory. After silently considering Lucky's inhuman treatment, Didi intrudes upon the conversation with outrage and anguish, the comments the product of his intense, silent meditation: "C'est une honte!" The speaker as well as his audience is silenced, awed by the audacity of the comment and struck dumb by the veracity of the message. Hesitation in Didi's voice, no longer reflective of timidity or humility, exposes his choking anguish and his difficulty in verbalizing the unspeakable suffering: "Traiter un homme *(geste vers Lucky)* de cette façon . . . je trouve ça . . . un être humain . . . non . . . c'est une honte!" Pozzo's response to the direct attack is understated and evasive: "Vous êtes sévères" *(Godot, 28–38).*

Pozzo, essentially ignoring what Didi said and Gogo echoed, diverts the conversation to a discussion of social amenities. In a notable reversal of roles the motif of departure is reiterated by Didi, who repeatedly beseeches Gogo, "Partons." However, when Gogo stalls for time, Didi announces, "*Je* m'en vais" (my emphasis). What remains unspoken is that Didi, more observant of, or more sensitive to, Lucky's suffering and Pozzo's shallowness, is willing to risk missing the appointment with Godot by leaving this place before nightfall.

Admitting, but not excusing, his inhumanity, Pozzo successfully entraps Didi into remaining by engrossing him in conversation about "Godet . . . Godot . . . Godin," the invisible thread that ties Didi and Gogo to this place and to each other.[27] The conversation, or rather the contrapuntal choral speaking that passes for conversation, concerns itself only momentarily with Godot. Rather, Gogo's repeated question, "Pourquoi ne dépose-t-il pas ses bagages?" and Didi's "Vous voulez-vous en débarrasser?" sustain interest in the silent carrier. Pozzo's abrupt mention of a schedule reminds us that Didi and Gogo, anxious and expectant, have made no explicit mention either of their appointment with Godot or their waiting for Godot. While Gogo characteristically distracts himself with his boots and Didi with his hat, Pozzo perorates on the twilight, his speech punctuated with dramatic pauses and hesitations to recover a lost train of thought, consider and praise his choice of words, elicit response, spray his throat, and jerk Lucky to attention. Having begun "Sauf le firmament," Pozzo is distracted by Didi, Gogo, and Lucky. "Qu'est-ce que je disais?" he asks himself and continues:

> Ah oui, la nuit. *(Lève la tête.)* Mais soyez donc un peu plus attentifs, sinons nous n'arriverons jamais à rien. *(Regarde le ciel.)* Regardez. *(Tous regardent le ciel, sauf Lucky qui s'est remis à somnoler. Pozzo, s'en apercevant, tire sur la corde.)* Veux-tu regarder le ciel, porc! *(Lucky renverse la tête.)* Bon, ça suffit. *(Ils baissent la tête.)* Qu'est-ce qu'il a de si extraordinaire? En tant que ciel? Il est pale et lumineux, comme n'importe quel ciel à cette heure de la journée. *(Un temps.)* Dans ces latitudes. *(Un temps.)* Quand il fait beau. *(Sa voix se fait chantante.)*
>
> (*Godot*, 38–53)

After Pozzo completes his set piece he invites reviews; subsequently, the conversation among Didi, Gogo, and Pozzo reaches an impasse. Gogo breaks the silence with an oblique reference to the wait for Godot: "En attendant, il ne se passe rien." The tedium of the wait and the minimal entertainment provided by Pozzo elicit the suggestion that Lucky, a nonparticipant in their verbal activity kept "alive" by occasional reference to his presence and pains, entertain all three with his dancing and thinking. Commanded to think, Lucky, obviously disoriented, begins to dance, and commanded once again, Lucky begins his recitation in midsentence: "D'autre part, pour ce qui est. . . ." Pozzo interrupts his speech and reiterates the activating command, "Pense." In contrast to Pozzo's set piece, Lucky's logorrhea, broken by his own interruption, "je reprends," has no punctuation, no pauses to qualify, gather thoughts, or dramatically empha-

size. Notably, repetitions (noted in the discussion of the cancellation of language) defy the logic, syntax, and progression in time integral to speech and
contribute to the impression that the torrential stream of words will not support
the burden of the thoughts.[28] Lucky's performance, unlike that of Pozzo, is
poorly received. The performer, instead of being praised, is silenced by the
removal of his thinking cap and physically trampled by Didi, Gogo, and Pozzo,
who have grown steadily more distressed in response to Lucky's oration.

After this disappointing diversion, Pozzo, Didi and Gogo resume their dialogue, and as before, Didi, distressed by Pozzo's inhumanity, suggests to Gogo,
"Allons." The motif of arrival/departure structures the conclusion of act 1 as it
has introduced it. Pozzo's verbalized intentions to depart are counterpointed by
the repetitions of "Adieu," which forestall departure and "oui, oui" and "non,
non," which reinforce stasis. A long, uneasy silence underscores Pozzo's successful departure and intimates that Didi and Gogo are once again left to their
own devices for diversion while waiting. Inspired by Pozzo's departure, Gogo
suggests that they also leave. The refrain, "On attend Godot," resounds, eliciting Gogo's "C'est vrai" punctuated by a pause (*Godot*, 53–66).

In the concluding moments of their wait for Godot on this day, Didi's observations about nonrecognition of the intruders, Pozzo and Lucky, signals the
arrival of another intruder: Godot's messenger. It appears, however, that he has
not just arrived, but rather has passed the time waiting for the departure of
Pozzo and his carrier. Why does Didi answer to the name "M. Albert"? Why
didn't Godot come? Is this the same messenger who, like them, does not remember from day to day, or is there another? There are no explanations.
Thwarted expectation accounts for Gogo's frustration and Didi's calm resignation. Through persistent questions Gogo reveals his previously unspoken and
undefined anguish and the disappointment he has tried to conceal and control.
Through verbal abuse directed against the boy, and through him indirectly to
his master, Gogo exposes an outrage that he has been kept waiting for so long
for no reason. Didi, on the other hand, displays a verbal control that belies the
mercurial flux of his emotions. Counterpointing one another, Didi and Gogo
alternately question and threaten the boy, whose disjunctive speech reveals the
depth of his fear and the limitations of his knowledge. His explanation, "C'est
monsieur Godot—," drifts off, the unfinished thought cryptically concluded by
Didi, "Evidemment." We intuit perfectly the telegraphic thought conveyed in
one word and followed by a pause that reveals the complexity and multiplicity
of silent reactions that Didi and Gogo leave undefined. Their despair is unnam-
able.

The boy has repeatedly been asked to approach and, encouraged by Gogo's
"Approche, on te dit," he does so fearfully. Disoriented by Gogo's question,
"Pourquoi tu viens si tard?" and Didi's "Tu as un message de monsieur Godot?"
the boy responds to the latter.[29] Typically, Gogo persists in his interrogation:

Gogo: Pourquoi tu veins si tard?

Le garçon les regarde l'un après l'autre, ne sachant à qui répondre.
Didi   *(à Estragon):* Laisse-le tranquille.
Gogo   *(à Vladimir):* Fous-moi la paix, toi. *(Avançant, au garçon.)* Tu sais
          l'heure qu'il est?
Garçon   *(reculant):* Ce n'est pas ma faute, monsieur.
Gogo: C'est la mienne peut-être?
Garçon: J'avais peur, monsieur.
Gogo: Peur de quoi? De nous? *(Un temps.)* Réponds!
Didi: Je vois ce que c'est, ce sont les autres qui lui ont fait peur.

Gogo's inability to quiet his emotions is indicated by his withdrawal from the
dialogue. Didi, however, persists, gaining the assurance that Godot will surely
come tomorrow. His disappointment and feeling of loss are expressed in the
understated "C'est tout?" The departure of the messenger leaves Didi and Gogo
alone, relieved of the burden of waiting but deprived of hope of Godot's arrival
on this day. Significantly, both Didi and Gogo leave unspoken their disappointment that Godot has not come, again (*Godot*, 68–72).

Although Didi claims to be encouraged by the boy's promise, the pause that
follows his recitation of the message to Gogo reveals his doubt. Didi and Gogo
evade the reality of their pointless wait by directing their attention to their
separation. Silence both precedes and punctuates "ce n'est plus la peine," leaving unspoken the comment that Didi made earlier in the day, "C'est trop pour
un seul homme." Having nothing more to say and no more reason to wait, Didi
and Gogo resolve to depart. Beckett's instructions are explicit: "Ils ne bougent
pas" (*Godot*, 73–75). Darkness finally descends and so does a paralyzed silence
that conveys the cumulative effect of the ordeal of waiting, casts doubt on the
trustworthiness of their words, and reminds us that the absent protagonist on
whom our attention has been fixed has not made an appearance.

The repetitive nature of this drama has occasioned general critical opinion
that acts 1 and 2 of *En attendant Godot* are, with few exceptions, parallel. Parallel, yes; identical, no. The parallels and the subtle differences in a play that is
scaled down to bare minimum cannot be ignored. We note that several important goals are accomplished by apparent binary duplication. Acts 1 and 2 serve
to reinforce one another, to restate and resound motifs and to indicate by the
coming of night, of Pozzo, of leaves, of messengers, and of attempts at recognition that time is passing.[30] Psychological fluidity is mirrored in the fluctuating
moods: expectant, optimistic, calm, anxious, and resigned. Pertinent to our
consideration of the unspoken in Beckett's drama is the observation that repeated actions, expressions, and emotions in act 2 assume the proportion of
ritual. Of even greater importance, however, is the fact that Beckett leaves a
great deal more unstated in act 2, obliquely communicating through an increased reliance on intimation. The most striking difference in act 2, and one
that realistically accounts for the increased number of pauses and silences, is
that the intrusions of Lucky, Pozzo, and Godot's messenger are of shorter
duration. Therefore, there is a greater need for Didi and Gogo to rely on their

own devices to maintain diversion while waiting. The strain of this effort, coupled with the strain of the wait, more obvious and wearing in their isolation, is intimated by the increased intrusion of Silence.

Act 2 commences with an inversion of the initial situation of act 1. Instead of Gogo there are his boots; instead of his oscillating efforts—stasis and silence—there is Didi's meditative, repetitive song and silent "va et vient." A barefoot Gogo returns, the reunion is once again consummated by embrace, and there ensues the now-familiar themes: the interdependence of Didi and Gogo, Didi's urinary problems, Gogo's beatings and pervasive uncertainty. Their reunion elicits the topic of contentedness, interesting because, while missing from the initial conversation of act 1, it was a theme developed in the concluding miniconversation with Godot's messenger:

Didi: Toi, aussi, tu dois être content, au fond, avoue-le.
Gogo: Content de quoi?
Didi: De m'avoir retrouvé.
Gogo: Tu crois?
Didi: Dis le, même si ce n'est pas vrai.
Gogo: Qu'est-ce que je dois dire?
Didi: Dis, Je suis content.
Gogo: Je suis content.
Didi: Moi aussi.
Gogo: Moi aussi.
Didi: Nous sommes contents.
Gogo: Nous sommes contents.

Echoing Didi's confirmation of contentedness, Gogo lapses into silence. What does one say after one has said "Nous sommes contents"? After consideration of this problem, Gogo typically poses another: "Qu'est-ce qu'on fait, maintenant qu'on est content?" The repetition of the word "content" and the need to echo one another's assertions, reveal that their mood is not one of contentedness. Leaving despair unexpressed and undefined, Didi and Gogo attempt to impose the illusion of contentedness through verbal expression, but speech neither actualizes nor concretizes ephemeral emotions. One waits for Godot; one is obviously not content (*Godot*, 77–84).

Increasingly, the silent commitment is to waiting and to passing the time while waiting. Incapable of separation, silence, and (by implication) salvation, Didi and Gogo converse calmly to drown out "toutes les voix mortes" that speak "toutes en même temps / Chacune à part soi." As previously noted, this passage is surrounded by silence and increasingly disrupted by silences; it is characterized by its reliance on repetition, echoing and the unspoken responses of communion, contemplation, and isolation. After a long silence that indicates Didi and Gogo's inability to maintain the flow of conversation, Didi expresses his anguish by a desperate call for help from Gogo: "Dis quelque chose!" Although Gogo's participation is minimal, the two together manage to escape

the grips of Silence and maintain a little duologue, only to find that they must
continue to find inspiration for another and another while waiting. Eager for
inspiration, Didi suggests picking up the dropped thread of a conversation left
incomplete earlier in the day, but Gogo finds that this time Didi has demanded
too much. Didi's solitary effort and agonizing search for lost ideas are recorded
by pauses and repetitions of "contents" and "attends":

> Attends . . . on s'est embrassés . . . on était contents . . . contents . . . qu'est-
> ce qu'on fait maintenant qu'on est contents . . . on attends . . . voyons . . . ça
> vient . . . on attends . . . maintenant qu'on est contents . . . on attends . . .
> voyons . . . ah! L'arbre!

The willow, which had figured importantly in their plans for suicide on the
night before, provides the stimulus for a new dialogue that momentarily preoccupies the bums. The few new leaves have convinced Didi and Gogo that they
have come to the wrong place, but they are hard pressed to remember yesterday. Didi attempts to refresh Gogo's memory and sustain their dialogue by
feeding him one image after another so that a picture of yesterday's events
eventually emerges. Although Gogo has obviously been barefoot since their
reunion, it is only at this moment, reminded of the wound that Lucky inflicted
on Gogo, that Didi directly comments about it. Associatively, the dialogue
moves from boots to the issue of departure, as the theme that initiated acts 1 and
2 is again reiterated. The ritualized exchange between Didi and Gogo reflects
nuanced variations, but typically neither explicitly reveals his disappointment
or deepening despair:

> *Gogo:* Je suis fatigué. *(Un temps.)* Allons-nous en.
> *Didi:* On ne peut pas.
> *Gogo:* Pourquoi?
> *Didi:* On attend Godot.
> *Gogo:* C'est vrai. *(Un temps.)* Alors comment faire?
> *Didi:* Il n'y a rien à faire.
>
> (Godot, 85–96)

The prolonged wait for Godot has had its effect on Gogo, who once again
seeks evasion in sleep. As Gogo sleeps we observe that Didi's reaction to separation and silence has markedly changed. Compensating for the lack of linguistic
diversion by active "va et vient," Didi, more accustomed to the silence and
obviously more tolerant of it, allows his friend to sleep. As before, Gogo bolts
awake from his nightmare, but whereas Didi is consoling, he adamantly refuses
to be Gogo's confidant. The nightmare must remain unconfessed. Sleep does
not provide Gogo with escape from reality, or to be more exact, the illusion that
he and Didi are waiting for Godot, "because it is," Rolf Breuer observes, "the
very waiting which creates the goal, for which the waiting then seems to be the
means."[31] Gogo, refusing to endure the agony of waiting, announces in nuanced

theme and variation his intention to depart: "Allons-nous-en"; "Je m'en vais"; "Adieu"; "Tu ne me verras plus"; "Je m'en vais." His repetitive comments, however, fall on deaf ears as Didi diverts himself with the discovery of Lucky's hat.

In the absence of Lucky's diversionary "thinking," Didi suggests that they employ his hat to provide them with diversion while waiting. When Gogo agrees to stay and play at "Lucky and Pozzo," his mention of departure is counterpointed and echoed by sounds of arrival; his wildly enthusiastic response to sounds of intruders reveals a deep well of doubt and fear that has given rise to this effusion: *"(triomphant).* C'est Godot! Enfin! *(Il embrasse Estragon avec effusion.)* Gogo! C'est Godot! Nous sommes sauvés!" Hysterical joy quickly metamorphoses into frozen, inarticulate terror. Didi and Gogo establish outposts as guards, long silences informing their anxious listening for the menace. As the ominous sounds dissipate, Didi and Gogo increasingly rely on such nonverbal activities as "doing the tree" and deep breathing, because as their increased silences reveal, it is steadily more difficult to find diversion while waiting. The question "Qu'est-ce qu'on fait maintenant?"—which has previously inspired the response "On attend Godot"—now elicits the reduced and echoed fragment, "En attendant." To Didi's delight the intruders Pozzo and Lucky arrive just as he and Gogo were running out of diversions before they were running out of day. Unexpressed, but intimated, is Didi and Gogo's disappointment that Godot has not come and their awareness that as the day progresses the likelihood of Godot's arrival fades with every moment (*Godot*, 96–108).

Resolved to heed Pozzo's cries for help, Didi and Gogo individually and in unison counter the cries with shouts of "Pozzo! Pozzo!" Their shouts receive a silent response of nonrecognition. When the bums finally succeed in extricating Pozzo from the muck, they resume that role as watchmen which they had held prior to Pozzo's less-than-impressive intrusion. Now blind, Pozzo presses Didi and Gogo for information about the location and the time of day, his insistent question "C'est le soir?" repeated until it elicits a response from Didi. In a reversal of the pattern of act 1, Didi perorates on "le soir," assuring Pozzo, "C'est le soir, monsieur, nous sommes arrivés au soir." Once Pozzo confirms that he is indeed Pozzo, and Lucky, his bearer, Didi, continually obsessed with diversion, requests a repeat performance, only to learn that Lucky, now literally mute, cannot sing, dance, or recite. Didi's question "Muet! Depuis quand?" evokes a harangue from Pozzo whose repetitive "un jour" obliterates the subject as it does time:

> Un jour, ça ne vous suffit pas, un jour pareil aux autres il est devenu muet, un jour je suis devenu aveugle, un jour nous deviendrons sourds, un jour nous sommes nés, un jour nous mourrons, le même jour, le même instant, ça ne suffit pas?

Pozzo's speech is met with a silent response of despair from Didi and a silence of evasion from Gogo, who has characteristically escaped into sleep. Without any verbalized expression of farewell, Pozzo departs (*Godot*, 108–28).

The noise of Lucky and Pozzo's departure is balanced by the silence of Didi and Gogo. Sobered by Pozzo's oration and its implications for their lives, Didi and Gogo display characteristic behavior. Gogo, exhausted by the tedium of waiting, escapes into sleep, while Didi, silent and agitated, resumes his "va et vient." But Didi soon awakens his friend, once more unable to bear the loneliness in silence he again feels so acutely. Instead of leaving the unspoken unexpressed, Didi asks questions that are by their nature unanswerable. In the questions, and by extension, the answers, what truth will there be? And whose truth? Yesterday's truth? Today's? Whereas the multiple series of questions simulate and underscore the personal and cosmic uncertainty, they also reveal that Didi shrinks less from the unspoken and the unspeakable than from words. "Je ne peux pas continue," mourns Didi, who after a contemplative pause does resume his inquiry. "Qu'est-ce que j'ai dit?" he demands. One recalls that words *said* at the beginning of the act, such as "content," convinced (to the extent that anything can be sure) Didi that saying something contributes to the illusion of its existence. Similarly, having said that he cannot continue, Didi is silent, considering the implications of his words. And, as before, his characteristic "va et vient" symbolically mirrors the mercurial fluctuations in his mind and his heart.

The intrusion of Godot's messenger distracts Didi from his self-analysis and crippling questions and reorients his attention to the fact that once again Godot has not kept his appointment. Although Didi never explicitly stated that he doubted Godot's late arrival when he informed Pozzo that it was already night, he must have intuited the nonarrival. Nevertheless, it remains for the messenger to confirm that Godot will not come today and to extend the bonds and the appointment to another day. As in act 1 the hesitancy of the boy's speech and his monosyllabic "oui" and "non" reveal his fear and limitation, but Didi's frustration and withdrawal into self are reflected by fewer and shorter questions. Allowing Gogo to sleep, Didi assumes both roles in the duologue with the messenger, pressing for information while venting his anger. Didi's distress and disappointment are most obvious in his disjunctive fragments broken by pauses to consider and reconsider the content of his message to Godot and to find the words to complete it. We observe that Beckett characteristically employs repetitions to reveal entrapment in a thought and to expose anxiety:

> Tu lui diras—*(il s'interrompt)*—tu lui diras que tu m'as vu et que—*(il réfléchit)*—que tu m'as vu. *(Un temps. Vladimir s'avance, le garçon recule, Vladimir s'arrête, le garçon s'arrête.)* Dis, tu es bien sûr de m'avoir vu, tu ne vas pas me dire demain que ne m'as jamais vu?

The boy, however, gives Didi neither verbal confirmation that he will deliver the message nor explicit indication that he has understood the message. When

Didi suddenly lunges at the silent messenger in a nonverbal expression of the futility of his words and of his wait, he frightens him away, losing even the empty assurances that yesterday's messenger had placated him with (*Godot*, 129–31).

Upon awakening Gogo is resolved to depart, and rather than encountering Didi's typical "On attend Godot," the latter echoes Gogo's "Moi je m'en vais" with "Moi aussi." The nearly imperceptible change in Didi, linked to the traumatic events of the evening and the cumulative effects of Godot's paradigmatic nonarrival, is obliquely conveyed by the fact that it falls to Gogo to initiate and maintain communication. Long silences punctuate their speech, reflecting their exhaustion and the tangible effects of Godot's absence. Moreover, we observe that Didi's responses are reduced to monosyllabic stichomythia:

> *Silence.*
> *Gogo:* Tu dis qu'il faut revenir demain?
> *Didi:* Oui.
> *Gogo:* Alors on apportera une bonne corde.
> *Didi:* C'est ça.
> *Silence.*
> *Gogo:* Didi.
> *Didi:* Oui.
> *Gogo:* Je ne peux plus continuer comme ça.
> *Didi:* On dit ça.

Echoing almost exactly the order of topics associatively discussed at the conclusion of act 1, act 2 concludes in silence. Instead of Gogo's "Allons-nous-en," it is Didi who suggests "Alors, on y va" and Gogo who responds "Allons-y." Beckett's instructions are explicit: "Ils ne bougent pas" (*Godot*, 131–34).

Samuel Beckett's *En attendant Godot* has irrevocably altered the nature of post–World War II drama.[32] In 1954 Eric Bentley observed that *En attendant Godot* is "not . . . a tombstone but a landmark."[33] It is indeed a landmark, marking the dramatic land staked out and cleared by Samuel Beckett and fixing the place, presence and potency of the unexpressed in contemporary drama. In *Godot*, as in other early plays, Beckett has employed a language of cancellation to evoke the impression of stasis and instantaneity and to elicit interior fluctuation. His exploitation of pauses and silences, which contribute to the sensation of fixity and which evoke evanescence and emptiness, may be considered his most notable contribution to the use of the unspoken as structure and statement. Linguistically structuring his dramas with repetition, nonprogressional pauses, unanswered questions, and silences, this playwright has authentically portrayed the confusion and uncertainty of experience while implying that less is more. Essentially, Beckett dramatizes the anguish of finite man at grips with the infinite, but the word, grasping at the unsayable, remains unsaid.

In *The Sense of an Ending* Frank Kermode has argued that "we are not connoisseurs of chaos, . . . we are surrounded by it and equipped for coexistence with it only by our fictive powers."[34] Beckett's fictive powers have given new life to twentieth-century drama; *Godot*'s children thrive.[35] We resume our examination of post–World War II drama of the unspoken and the unspeakable with a study of Harold Pinter, who has acknowledged the explicit and implicit influence of Beckett and of World War II on his drama.

NOTES

1. Samuel Beckett, *Proust* (New York: Grove Press, 1931), 67–68.

2. Samuel Beckett, *"Nouvelles" et "Textes pour rien"* (Paris: Editions de Minuit, 1954), 203–4.

3. Samuel Beckett, *L'Innommable* (Paris: Editions de Minuit, 1953), 261–62.

4. Claude Mauriac, *L'Alittérature contemporaine*, 2d ed. (Paris: Editions Albin Michel, 1969), 94–95.

5. Beckett, *Proust*, 7.

6. Richard Coe, *Samuel Beckett*, rev. ed. (New York: Grove Press, 1968), 17.

7. Frank Kermode, *The Sense of an Ending: Studies in the Theory of Fiction* (London: Oxford University Press, 1967), 115.

8. Susan D. Brienza presented an interesting paper on the slipping and shifting of tenses in Beckett's prose, an observation equally applicable to his drama ("Time in *How It Is:* 'Something Wrong There,'" paper presented at the convention of the Modern Language Association, New York, 28 December 1978).

9. Martin Esslin, *The Theatre of the Absurd*, rev. ed. (Garden City, N.Y.: Anchor-Doubleday, 1969), 63.

10. Samuel Beckett, *Happy Days* (New York: Grove Press, 1961), 53–54 (all references hereafter will be to this edition).

11. Beckett, *Proust*, 19.

12. Michael Robinson, *The Long Sonata of the Dead* (New York: Grove Press, 1969), 230.

13. Ludovic Janvier, *Pour Samuel Beckett*, Arguments, no. 27 (Paris: Editions de Minuit, 1966), argues that cycles of actions, gestures, words, characters, and days contribute to the sensation of stasis. It must be noted, however, that stasis is supported in Beckett by the unexpressed. In the absence of speech, and in Beckett, in the cancellation of speech, there is apparently no progression in time.

14. Jacques Guicharnaud with June Beckerman, *Modern French Drama from Giraudoux to Beckett* (New Haven, Conn.: Yale University Press, 1961), 194–96.

15. Esslin, *Theatre of the Absurd*, 31.

16. Samuel Beckett, *"Krapp's Last Tape" and Other Dramatic Pieces* (New York: Grove Press, 1960), 26 (references hereafter will be to this edition unless otherwise indicated).

17. Coe, *Samuel Beckett*, 2; Ihab Hassan suggests in *Literature of Silence: Henry Miller and Samuel Beckett* (New York: Knopf, 1967), 210–11, that the impact of surrealism on Beckett's work should not be overlooked.

18. Alain Robbe-Grillet, "Samuel Beckett ou la présence sur la scène," in his *Pour un nouveau roman* (Paris: Editions de Minuit, 1963), 99.

19. Beckett, quoted in Tom F. Driver, "Beckett by the Madeleine," *Columbia University Forum* 4 (Summer 1961): 21–25, reprinted in *Drama in the Modern World*, edited by Samuel A. Weiss, 455–56 (Lexington, Mass.: D. C. Heath, 1974).

20. Recurrence typifies Beckett's art whether in prose, play, or poetry. For an interesting study of repetition as linguistic/artistic structure, see Rosemary Pountney, "Samuel Beckett's Interest in Form: Structural Pattern in *Play*," *Modern Drama* 19, no. 3 (September 1976): 237–44. Pountney argues that Beckett initially creates a picture fragmentarily, then gradually reexposes fragments of it, forcing the audience continually to readjust.

21. Beckett to George Reavy, 13 November 1936, quoted in Deirdre Bair, *Samuel Beckett* (New York: Harcourt, Brace, 1978), 243.

22. Samuel Beckett, *Footfalls*, in *Ends and Odds* (New York: Grove Press, 1974), 42–43.

23. Samuel Beckett, quoted in John Fletcher, *Samuel Beckett's Art* (New York: Barnes and Noble, 1967), 17.

24. Richard Schechner, "There's Lots of Time in *Godot*," in *Casebook on "Waiting for Godot*," ed. Ruby Cohn, 179 (New York: Grove Press, 1967), hereafter cited as *CWFG*.

25. See Rolf Breuer, "The Solution as Problem: Beckett's *Waiting for Godot*," *Modern Drama* 19, no. 3 (September 1976): 225–36, for an incisive study of stasis as structure.

26. One is reminded of Charlotta in Chekhov's *Cherry Orchard* chewing on cucumbers while contemplating her uncertain parentage. This stage business serves both to underscore and to reduce the profundity of the words.

27. This phrase, broken by hesitations that realistically portray recollection, is reiterated several times in modified forms.

28. Lucky, whom Beckett so named because he was lucky to no longer have expectations (see Colin Duckworth, "The Making of *Godot*," in *CWFG*, 95), is rather like the prophetess Cassandra, chosen to be witness to suffering. He, like she, would prefer silence.

29. Duckworth, "The Making of *Godot*," 94, notes that in an early draft Beckett had included a note sent by Godot to Didi and Gogo to verify the appointment. While quieting their doubts, this symbol implied physical presence and severely limited the expansiveness of the abstract symbol, Godot, and was deleted.

30. Beckett was quoted in Bair, *Samuel Beckett*, 383, as saying that the leaves of act 2 of *Godot* are "only to record the passage of time."

31. Breuer, "The Solution as Problem," 230.

32. Ruby Cohn, *Back to Beckett* (Princeton, N.J.: Princeton University Press, 1973), 127. Cohn cites such specific areas of impact as mythic dimension, disjunctive speech, and confusion of chronology.

33. Eric Bentley, *The Life of the Drama* (New York: Atheneum, 1964), 100–101.

34. Kermode, *The Sense of an Ending*, 64.

35. Martin Esslin, "*Godot* and His Children: The Theatre of Samuel Beckett and Harold Pinter," *Experimental Drama* 14 (1965): 128–46; reprinted in *Modern British Dramatists: A Collection of Critical Essays*, ed. John Russell Brown, 58–70, Twentieth Century Views (Englewood Cliffs, N.J.: Prentice-Hall, 1968).

6
Pinter

Harold Pinter once said, "Life is much more mysterious than plays make it out to be. And it is this mystery which fascinates me."[1] Pinter's fascination with mystery informs in great part his idiosyncratic use of the unspoken and the unspeakable. The central focus of this examination of Pinter's plays will be the specific techniques he employs in order to explore and elicit the mystery and multiplicity of life and of human relationships. *The Room, The Birthday Party, The Dumb Waiter, The Caretaker, The Homecoming, Old Times, No Man's Land*, and *Landscape* will be considered to illustrate "what happens between the words, what happens when no words are spoken at all."[2]

Through the subtle, complex interplay of colloquial expression and evocative suggestion, Pinter achieves a coalescence of phenomenal and psychological experience. Crucial to an understanding of Pinter's art is the nature and function of speech and silence in his drama. In *The Pinter Problem*, Austin Quigley maintains that language, which is a pluralistic activity, assumes an "interrelational function" in Pinter's plays. In Quigley's view, the language of a Pinter play functions "primarily as a means of dictating and reinforcing relationships."[3] Silence, often the culmination of verbal interaction, is neither a failure of communication nor a failure of language.[4] On the contrary, argues Pinter, silence is communication; the unexpressed is an integral element of the linguistic function:

> We communicate only too well, in our silence, in what is unsaid, and . . . what takes place is continual evasion, desperate rear-guard attempts to keep ourselves to ourselves.[5]

In Pinter's plays silence may take two distinct forms that the playwright himself has identified:

> There are two silences. One is when no word is spoken. The other when perhaps a torrent of language is employed. This speech is speaking of a language locked beneath it. That is its continual reference. The speech we hear is an indication of that we don't hear. It is a necessary avoidance, a

violent, sly, anguished, or mocking smoke-screen which keeps the other in its place.[6]

Employed in this evasive manner, concludes Pinter, speech may be viewed as a "strategem to cover nakedness."

Martin Esslin has observed that Chekhov predates Pinter in the evasive use of language and the evocative use of silence.[7] Indeed, Chekhov is the playwright with whom Pinter is most often compared. We note that in addition to evasive expression, Pinter, like Chekhov, focuses attention on the unexpressed through an economy of expression. We recall Masha's understated response to Vershinin's florid "future speech": "I'll stay to lunch." In like manner, Firs's concluding remarks in *The Cherry Orchard*, "There's no strength in you, nothing left you—all gone," speaks volumes (*Chekhov*, 132–33, 117). Similarly, Aston's rebuff of Davies in *The Caretaker*, "I don't think we're hitting it off," and Ruth's to her departing husband in *The Homecoming*, "Don't become a stranger," imply more than they directly state.[8] Understatement, one of the most distinctive features of Pinter's language, and one that contributes to the impression of ambiguity and mystery, will be discussed more fully later in the chapter. I draw attention to compression of speech at this time because in Pinter's plays, as in Chekhov's, we are given less than we expect. More, much more, is left unstated, undefined and unexplained.

Like the Russian dramatist, Pinter employs seemingly realistic settings, aimless, colloquial dialogue, specific character details, and the daily flow of the customary and habitual to dramatize continuity and perpetuity. John Lahr suggests that Pinter shares with Chekhov an "uncompromising objective aesthetic" and a "bond of naturalism," or more particularly, a bond of Nature.[9] Nature figures importantly in Chekhovian drama, providing a background of associations with which we are familiar, and which graphically convey the cyclical and degenerative pattern of life. When Nature is invoked in Pinter's drama, however, it is as parody. In *The Caretaker*, for example, Aston's garden is glutted with inorganic, alien objects while his pond is empty of fish. In *The Homecoming* Ruth's description of America is as sterile and lifeless as the inhospitable Nature she portrays:

> *Pause.*
> It's all rock. And sand. It stretches . . . so far . . . everywhere you look. And there's lots of insects there.
> *Pause.*
> And there's lots of insects there.
> *Silence.*
>
> (*Homecoming*, 53)

While it may be argued that Pinter's portrait of Nature mirrors a changed consciousness in this century, it is important to determine how Pinter's realism (or "supra-realism," to use John Lahr's term) relates to his dramatic structure and statement. When asked to comment on the nature of his art, Pinter replied, "If you press me for a definition, I'd say that what goes on in my plays is realistic, but what I'm doing is not realism."[10] Pinter is no more a realist than was Chekhov, but he, like the Russian playwright, has designed an "artifice of reality." Whereas Chekhov "relies upon the interplay between a suggestive, half articulate figure and an explicit ground," argues Bernard Beckerman, Pinter "deliberately obscures or confuses the ground of action." Indeed, Pinter defamiliarizes the ground.[11] Hermetically sealed off from Nature (and from perceivable cyclical flow), Pinter's world expands to accommodate the ambiguous and the mysterious. Arthur Ganz believes that the feeling of dislocation that arises from the coalescence of reality and fantasy accounts for the sensation of menace that typifies Pinter's drama.[12] However, obvious in the early plays and steadily more subtle in the later ones, menace derives its effectiveness in great part from the unexpressed that is both unspoken and unspeakable. To define is to limit; to name, humanize. Thus, through innuendo, intimation and insinuation Pinter evokes the palpable presence of the ineffable in all its multiplicity and mystery.

The process of defamiliarization is promoted by the exaggeration of the familiar. John Russell Taylor suggests that meticulously rendered realistic settings, rituals, and speech patterns achieve a hallucinatory proportion when subjected to magnification.[13] By ironic inversion the real appears less real. The breakfast scene of *The Birthday Party* illustrates the distortion of the familiar.[14] Initially we accept as realistic the quotidian setting, Petey's reticence, and the banality of the conversation. However, when Stanley enters, his annoyance and agitation, scarcely concealed beneath the colloquial banter, seem strangely out of proportion to the events. We quickly learn that fried bread, cornflakes, and tea (as in other plays eggs, champagne, and cheese-rolls) are not merely foods to be consumed but foods to be contested. While the dialogue is explicit, the effect is vague and implicit. Is the milk sour or is it not? Is the house clean or is it a "pigsty"? Is Meg expecting visitors or is she not? "The desire for verification is understandable," concedes Pinter, "but cannot always be satisfied." Essentially he dramatizes a world in which there are neither "hard distinctions between what is real and what is unreal, nor between what is true and what is false."[15]

The sensation of defamiliarization is intensified by the most realistic of settings: the room. In rooms both cluttered and sparse (metaphoric of internalization of exterior reality), Pinter presents man at his most comfortable and most vulnerable. Pinter believes that given a man in a room, "he will sooner or later receive a visitor." This visitor, argues the playwright, will enter "with intent." Essentially, our attention focuses on the reaction to the intrusion, which may be "illumination or horror," and the reactions, if any, of the intruder, which may also be "illumination or horror."[16] The delicate balance between being safely at home and safely hidden is implicit in Pinter's dramatization of intrusion and fundamental vulnerability. Entrapping his characters in restricted surroundings, Pinter elicits the approach, progression, and oppression of intruders from without and from within. Intrusions, which are of three kinds—substantial (like Goldberg and McCann in *The Birthday Party*), insubstantial (like noises in *The Caretaker*), and ephemeral (like memory in *Old Times* and *No Man's Land*)— contribute to a sensation of disquietude. Essentially, Pinter expresses this un- easiness, which in *The Birthday Party*, *The Dumb Waiter*, and *The Caretaker* escalates to terror, through the unexpressed: fragmented speech, unanswered questions, and paralyzed silences. As this citation from *The Dumb Waiter* illus- trates, the cumulative effect of the repeated intrusion of the dumb waiter and the progressive intrusion of doubt are revealed in Gus's unanswered questions and a torrent of speech. Ben, who is also unnerved, expresses his anxiety, on the other hand, through a silence that counterpoints Gus's words:

Gus: What did he want us to light the kettle for?
Ben: For tea. He wanted a cup of tea.
Gus: *He* wanted a cup of tea! What about me? I've been wanting a cup of tea all night!
Ben *(despairingly):* What do we do now?
Gus: What are we supposed to drink?
  Ben sits on his bed, staring.
  What about us?
  Ben sits.
  I'm thirsty too. I'm starving. And he wants a cup of tea. That beats the band, that does.
  Ben lets his head sink on to his chest.
  I could do with a bit of sustenance myself. And what about you? You look as if you could do with something.
  Gus sits on the bed.
  We send him up all we've got and he's not satisfied. No, honest, it's enough to make the cat laugh. Why did you send him up all that stuff? *(Thoughtfully)* Why did I send it up?
  (*"Caretaker" and "Dumb Waiter,"* 113)

As Gus babbles for several more minutes, evading the uneasiness that grips him, his words intensify Ben's anguish that they are once again displeasing whoever it is who has been sending down requests in the dumb waiter. Ben had given his personal assurances: "Yes. Yes. Yes certainly. Certainly. Right away" (*"Caretaker" and "Dumb Waiter,"* 112). Any attempt to redeem themselves for stale Eccles cake, melted chocolate, sour milk, and moldy biscuits is lost. We observe that Ben leaves unexpressed his fear of consequences for their poor performance. Interrupting Gus to short-circuit his monologue, Ben mutters, "Time's getting on."

In these restricted rooms vulnerable to intrusions, instruments of chronolog- ical measurement from which one may assess the cyclical flow of time are notable by their absence. Pinter rejects both a definable past and a predictable future. In the suspension of specified chronological progression, Pinter achieves

the impression of fixity of stasis. The focus is deflected inward to capture the
fluctuating states of consciousness within each character. The impression of
disorientation precipitated by the absence of time is disjunctively articulated by
Davies in *The Caretaker* through repetitions and rhetorical questions:

> See, what I need is a clock! I need a clock to tell the time! How can I tell the
> time without a clock? I can't do it. I said to him, I said, look here, what about
> getting a clock, so's I can tell what time it is? I mean, if you can't tell what
> time you're at you don't know where you are, you understand my meaning?
> ("*Caretaker*" *and* "*Dumb Waiter*," 62)[17]

It is not only the absence of chronology but also the absence of speech that
intensifies the impression of stasis. Pinter, like other dramatists who have relied
heavily on the unspoken, simulates the impression of timelessness by employing
silence or disjunctive speech punctuated by pauses. Despite seemingly quiescent surfaces, the conclusion of each play confirms the swift passage of time. We
observe in Pinter's plays, as in Chekhov's, that concluding scenes may resemble
initial ones, and may linguistically echo them, but the effect of time's progression is subtly conveyed. In *Uncle Vanya*, for example, Astrov and Vanya exchange pleasantries both at the beginning of the play and at its conclusion, but
everything is different between these two men in their final conversation. Similarly, in *The Caretaker*, *The Birthday Party*, and *No Man's Land* we intuit differences. In Pinter's drama, however, where endings are typically left unresolved
and open-ended, we are in doubt as to the nature and degree of the change.

Pinter expands our awareness of mystery and increases the sensation of disorientation by sudden expansion of space and of arbitrary boundaries. Referring
specifically to *The Birthday Party*, John Lahr notes that when the set is thrown
into darkness "solidity evaporates" and "objects become spectres in the dark."[18]
This technique is similarly effective in *The Caretaker*. In Aston's darkened room
a dazed Davies shadowboxes with the humming sound and nozzle of the Elec-
trolux relentlessly pursuing him. His unanswered questions seem to be sucked
up into the void: "What's that? What? Who's that? What's that?" ("*Caretaker*"
and "*Dumb Waiter*," 44). Spacial fluidity is dramatically underscored by the
imposition of silence. In *No Man's Land* Pinter once again fuses spacial fluidity
with silence to intensify disorientation and elicit responses to menace and mystery.

Still another way in which Pinter defamiliarizes the familiar and contributes
to the sensation of ambiguity is through the confusion of names. We observe
that in Pinter's drama, where identity is inextricably linked to name, several
characters have assumed names. In *The Caretaker* Davies insists repeatedly, "the
name I call myself now, that's not my real name. My real name's not the one I'm
using, you see. It's different. You see, the name I go under now ain't my real
one. It's assumed" ("*Caretaker*" *and* "*Dumb Waiter*," 44). Davies is not the only
character lacking identity papers and hiding behind a pseudonym. Is Nat Gold-

berg's "real" name "Benny" or "Simey"? And why did Stanley Webber tell Goldberg that his name is "Joe Soap"? Will Ruth exchange her biblical name for the more elegant "Gillian" or the more exotic "Spanish Jacky"? Is Spooner a nickname or a surname, and is Spooner really Charles Wetherby? Pinter offers at least two alternatives for each name and leaves explanations for these deceptions unexpressed. Relying on multiplicity to create confusion, he intensifies ambiguity through intimation and insinuation.

Just as Pinter casts doubt on the trustworthiness of names, he similarly casts doubt on the meaning of words. We have observed that one of the ways that Beckett achieves a language of cancellation is by using words and then qualifying, modifying, and withdrawing them. Pinter's intent, however, is not to cancel the word, but rather to dislocate it from its familiar context in order to invoke uncertainty and mystery. By subjecting the word to parody and ironic inversion and by stripping it of specific referents, Pinter reduces speech to ambiguous fragments. The toasting of Stanley in *The Birthday Party* illustrates this paradigm. Goldberg employs a series of toasts more appropriate to religious occasions than secular ones. "Stanley," says Goldberg, "I wish you, on behalf of us all, a happy birthday. I'm sure you've never been a prouder man than you are today. Mazoltov!" The toast, more appropriate to the bar mitzvah, the thirteenth-birthday celebration of a Jewish boy, is immediately followed by "and may we only meet at Simchahs!"—a phrase generally reserved for funerals. After everyone has wished Stanley a happy birthday, Goldberg concludes the toast, "And well over the fast," apparently employing a toast that follows the fast of the Day of Atonement.[19] Goldberg has an appreciative, if uncomprehending, audience; Lulu and Meg applaud. Stanley, however, responds to the unexplained, undefined, and unconnected fragments with physical and linguistic rigidity (*"Birthday Party" and "The Room,"* 56–57).

Pinter employs several techniques to defamiliarize the familiar in order to elicit the presence of the unknown in the quotidian. The universal emotion, love (or more particularly, friendship), which defies the limitations of social stratification, time, and verbal expression, is particularly well suited to Pinter's dramatization of the ambivalent and the evanescent. Pinter's treatment of friendship encompasses a broad range of relationships (from acquaintance to guest to confidant) to reveal unexpressed tensions and reactions in both formal and intimate exchanges. Primarily, Pinter evokes the mercurial range of responses that friendship, or the lack of it, engenders. As this initial conversation between Ruth and Lenny in *The Homecoming* indicates, characters negotiate relationships by what they say or choose to leave unspoken. We observe that Ruth's reticence counterpoints with Lenny's loquacity and that direct questions receive monosyllabic responses:

Lenny: My name's Lenny. What's yours?
Ruth: Ruth.
   She sits, puts her coat collar around her.

Lenny: Cold?
Ruth: No.
Lenny: It's been a wonderful summer, hasn't it? Remarkable.
         Pause.
         Would you like something? Refreshment of some kind? An aperitif,
         anything like that?
Ruth: No, thanks.

(*Homecoming*, 28)

Despite the lateness of the hour and his state of undress (Lenny is in pajamas whereas the stranger in his livingroom is fully dressed), Lenny adopts the role and social responsibilities of the host—to maintain conversation with a guest, even if she is uninvited; to offer refreshment, even if there is none. As this citation indicates, Pinter, like Chekhov, draws his content from life as it is. Exaggerating and subjecting the familiar to ironic inversion, Pinter, through indirection, focuses attention on the insider and the outsider, on the overt and tacit interactional function of speech and silence.

The multivalent responses of friendship and emnity, and the fluctuating states between them, recall the drama of Samuel Beckett. Many fine studies have been devoted to the examination of parallels and differences between these playwrights. "If Pinter has been named Beckett's heir on the English stage," suggests Ruby Cohn, "it is because the characters of both lead lives of complex and unquiet desperation."[20] We observe that in the plays of both, doubt, static structure, and literal or figurative entrapment coexist to simulate and reinforce that desperation. However, the differing nature of that desperation informs in great part the content and function of their language. Beckett's characters are desperate to fill time while waiting for Godot, painkiller, the end of suffering. Literally and linguistically stripped bare of social context, Beckett's characters engage in a continual, indeed desperate, effort to maintain the flow of conversation. Moreover, Beckett's characters are desperate for confirmation that they exist, as Didi's insistent questioning of Godot's messenger, Hamm's requests for approval of speeches and stories, and Winnie's efforts to elicit response from Willie attest. Speech making, therefore, is a defense against the boredom and tedium of waiting, a defense against the void they feel within themselves and in their lives.

In Pinter's drama, however, characters, in social settings and situations, are desperate for connection rather than compliments. Thus we observe that Pinter's characters employ florid language to ingratiate themselves or drown out their own fears. In this set piece addressed to the voice upstairs controlling the dumb waiter, Ben reveals by his torrent of speech the effort to make an impression while not exposing weakness:

(*Speaking with great deference.*) Good evening. I'm sorry to—bother you, but we thought we'd better let you know that we haven't got anything left. We sent up all we had. There's no more food down here.

("*Caretaker*" and "*Dumb Waiter*," 111)

Ben's subtle shift from "I" to "we" obliquely conveys his insecurity; he cannot rely on himself to convince. We note, however, that in Pinter's drama what is a "rear-guard defense" for the victim becomes an instrument of aggression in the mouth of the victimizer. Mick, Briggs, and Foster all exceed in this art, which is intended not to encourage praise, but enforce an impression of power. Mick's violent "out-flooding of business jargon," notes Ganz, has an aggressive intention and a devastating effect on Davies, to whom it is addressed.[21] Significantly, these set pieces in Pinter's drama elicit silent responses. Speeches made by victims elicit the silence of rejection; speeches made by victimizers evoke the silence of bafflement and awe.

Symbols are crucial nonverbal elements employed extensively and precisely by Beckett and Pinter. Both playwrights draw their symbols from life; they are operative on realistic and symbolic levels. Carrots, turnips, bananas, and biscuits in Beckett's universe are displaced in Pinter's world by nationalistic delicacies of fried bread, roll-mops, Smith's crisps, and Cadbury's fruit-and-nut bars. Citing the examples of boots and shoes in *En attendant Godot* and *The Caretaker*, Ruby Cohn argues that symbols are instantaneously effective in Beckett's drama, but cumulatively effective in Pinter's.[22] We can examine Cohn's incisive observation by still another illustration of symbols that are organic, thematic, realistic, and common to both: optical equipment. Early in *Fin de partie* Clov establishes the telescope as a metaphysical symbol:

> *Hamm:* Quel temps fait-il?
> *Clov:* Le même que d'habitude.
> *Hamm:* Regarde la terre.
> *Clov:* Je l'ai regardée.
> *Hamm:* A la lunette?
> *Clov:* Pas de besoin de lunette.
> *Hamm:* Regarde-là à la lunette.
> *Clov:* Je vais chercher la lunette.
>   *Il sort.*
> *Hamm:* Pas besoin de lunette!
>
>   (*Fin de partie*, 43–44)

After turning his telescope on the audience and on Hamm, Clov fixes on the outside world. The impact of the first sighting is instantaneous: "Zéro." He reinforces this impression through repetition until Hamm presses him to define all that he sees in one word. Clov complies: "Mortibus." The blind Hamm continues to encourage Clov to report on the horizon, the waves, the sun. Later in the drama, having repeatedly dropped the telescope, Clov climbs the ladder warning, "Je vais regarder cette dégoûtation puisque tu l'ordonnes." His reports underscore his first sighting: "Rien . . . rien . . . rien . . . très bien . . . rien . . ." (*Fin de partie*, 102). Suddenly noticing life, he descends from the ladder and throws the telescope. In Pinter's *Birthday Party*, on the other hand, Stanley's glasses increasingly *become* symbolic, rather than immediately are so. In the breakfast scene, Stanley is seen reading the paper and "rubbing his eyes under his glasses." Later in the drama Stanley is threatened by Goldberg and McCann with a needle in his eye. At Stanley's party, the room darkened for a toast, a bright light is directed at Stanley's face, temporarily blinding him, and this is followed by the breaking of his glasses. Efforts to restore the frames are useless; they lack the lenses. Rendered essentially blind, Stanley can see nothing, or as Clov would say, "zéro." Through the use of nondiscursive symbolism, Beckett conveys more by saying less, whereas Pinter once again confuses us by a familiar object expanded before our eyes to symbolic proportion.

Crucial to Pinter's use of the unspoken is the relationship of symbolist and naturalistic—supranaturalistic—techniques, deceptive stasis and cyclical flux, and the quotidian to this dramatist's linguistic innovations. The characterizing elements of Pinter's methodology are:

1. indirect, disjunctive speech
2. colloquial dialogue implicitly conveying more than it superficially and explicitly communicates
3. unanswered questions
4. repetitions and echoing
5. pauses
6. silences
7. counterpointing through overstatement and understatement
8. mute characters
9. silence as a metaphor for isolation
10. silence as a metaphor for absence
11. silence of the playwright

Used variously by other playwrights of silent theatre, disjunctive speech assumes a special significance in Pinter's drama. Regardless of their social strata and the content of their speech, Pinter's characters reveal themselves by their rhythm, syntax, and choice of words. Disjunctive speech authentically simulates psychological and empirical experience by eliciting imperceptible fluctuations both within the mind of the speaker and between speakers. Halting and compulsive speech patterns and hesitations to find a word or evade direct communication are more obvious in Pinter's less articulate characters, but generally characteristic of all characters. A few citations from the plays exemplify discontinuity in conversation arising out of physical or emotional stress, unfamiliarity, natural reticence, uncertainty, and reversal or correction of a thought. We observe in *The Caretaker* that Aston's direct questions elicit evasive responses and what the playwright terms "rear-guard defense":

Aston: Where were you born?
Davies (darkly): What do you mean?
Aston: Where were you born?
Davies: I was . . . uh . . . oh, it's a bit hard, like to set your mind back . . . see

> what I mean . . . going back . . . a good way . . . lose a bit of track,
> like . . . you know. . . .
>
> *("Caretaker" and "Dumb Waiter,"* 25)

Later in the same play, Aston and Davies, now roommates, discuss the issue of caretaking responsibilities. By juxtaposing Aston's reticence with Davies's hesitancy and distrust, Pinter exposes the distance between two speakers and between a thought and its verbalization. As the following illustrative exchange indicates, no thought is completed as the tramp tries to negotiate his role, his responsibilities, and his continued presence in this room without revealing his insufficiencies and fears. Admitting that he has no experience as a caretaker, Davies attempts to respond to Aston's question, "How do you feel about being one?":

Davies: Well, I reckon . . . Well, I'd have to know . . . you know. . . .
Aston: What sort of. . . .
Davies: Yes, what sort of . . . you know . . .
    Pause.
Aston: Well, I mean. . . .
Davies: I mean, I'd have to . . . I'd have to . . .
Aston: Well, I could tell you. . . .
Davies: That's . . . that's it . . . you see . . . you get my meaning?
           ("Caretaker" and "Dumb Waiter," 42–43)

The coalescence of disjunctive and bivalent dialogue constitutes an important element of Pinter's linguistic structure. In these dramas of the unexpressed and unconfessed, the colloquial dialogue, while superficially accurate and appropriate to the social position of the character, the environment he finds himself in, and the social occasion, simultaneously leaves more unstated than is explicitly expressed. In *The Room*, for example, Rose chatters aimlessly about breakfast, the weather, and the people in the basement. Her casual manner conceals the intensity of her feelings about the cold and the basement, while her repetitive references to external cold and internal warmth insinuate more than is explained. In the absence of Bert's comments, the spectator must try to complete the thoughts that Rose has merely begun and make connections between ideas that she leaves disjointed. Similarly, in the concluding scene of *The Homecoming*, which directly follows the family's implicit proposal for Ruth's prostitution, the farewell comments intimate more than is stated:

Teddy: Good-bye, Lenny.
    They shake hands.
Lenny: Ta-ta, Ted. Good to see you. Have a good trip.
Teddy: Bye-bye, Joey.
    Joey does not move.
Joey: Ta-ta.
    Teddy goes to the front door.

Ruth: Eddie.
            Teddy turns.
            Don't become a stranger.
            Teddy goes, shuts the front door.

                                                                    (*Homecoming*, 80)

Unanswered questions, used by Maeterlinck to reveal growing anxiety, by Bernard to indicate evasion and distraction, and by Beckett to underscore fundamental uncertainty, are integral to Pinter's linguistic methodology. Employing a range of casual inquiries, unnerving interrogations, and terrifying inquisitions, this playwright creates ambiguity and disorientation and evokes the silent responses of baffled confusion and paralyzed terror. Seemingly casual and civil exchanges between strangers—or are they old friends?—at the beginning of *No Man's Land* and between partners of greater and lesser experience as in *The Dumb Waiter* are authentic and credible. Cumulatively effective, insidious, and probing questions expose spiralling agitation and/or hostility. In *The Birthday Party*, for example, Meg's casual comment that she is expecting other guests disturbs Stanley. He presses for additional information: "Who are they?" When she fails to satisfy his curiosity, he persists, "But who are they?" his agitated pacing mirroring his emotional fluctuation. Meg neither assuages Stanley's uneasiness nor offers comfort. Like a frightened child, Stanley punishes Meg by inflicting on her the terror that consumes him. "They're looking for someone," taunts Stanley. Reacting to Meg's growing hysteria, Stanley continues,"Shall I tell you who they're looking for?" Ignoring Meg's protestations, Stanley is unrelenting, "You don't want me to tell you?" Avoiding the question and its implications, a disquieted Meg counters and attempts to dissuade Stanley from further inquisition by name-calling: "You're a liar!" (*Birthday Party*, 24). Stanley's victimization of Meg anticipates his own. In a classic example of Pinteresque "torture by tirade," Stanley is reduced to nonverbal gurgles by the persistent and disorienting interrogation of Goldberg and McCann. Similarly, in a figurative boxing match between two unequal opponents (an image Pinter specifically delineates in *The Homecoming*), Mick's interrogation of the intruder, Davies, confuses the tramp, undermines his position in the room, and reduces him to silence.

Counterpointing through understatement and overstatement, employed by other playwrights to undermine what has been said, to authenticate realistic conversations, and to reinforce stasis by nonprogressional speech, is employed by Pinter to reveal the unspoken and to cast doubt on the trustworthiness of the speakers. Pinter's extensive and idiosyncratic use of this technique may be considered his distinctive contribution to silent theatre. We observe in *The Homecoming* what Bert O. States has termed "satirical formalism of expression," out of proportion to the context and inappropriate to the situation.[23] Through understatement and exaggerated overstatement Teddy and Lenny negotiate their relationship. We recall that when Lenny "takes" Ruth, dances with her and kisses her, Teddy's response is one of silence, a silence of complicity, surprise, and/or resignation. When Teddy takes Lenny's cheese-roll, however, his action occasions a long harangue from his brother. Angrily Lenny remarks, "Barefaced audacity," and pausing to consider his brother's seemingly un-motivated action, Lenny pursues the issue further. "What led you to be so . . . vindictive against your brother?" he demands. Directly counterpointing Ted-dy's taciturnity with his own linguistic range, Lenny lectures his brother, the professor, on the meaning of family, the importance of standards of behavior, and the value of respect and brotherly love:

> I'd have thought you'd have grown more forthcoming, not less. Because I want you to know that you set a standard for us, Teddy. Your family looks up to you, boy, and you know what it does? It does its best to follow the example you set. Because you're a great source of pride to us. That's why we were so glad to see you come back, to welcome you back to your birthplace. That's why.

In his summation, Lenny wonders if Teddy has paid sufficient homage to his family with "a bit of grace, a bit of je ne sais quoi, a bit of generosity of mind, a bit of liberality of spirit." Teddy quiets him with one word: "Yes" (*Homecoming*, 64–65).

Paralleling a technique employed extensively by Maeterlinck and Beckett, Pinter employs repetitions to intensify mood, primarily that of spiralling anx-iety, to reveal compulsive behavior, to reinforce the impression of fixity, to effectively block the free flow of other thoughts, and to convey a struggle to find a word and the fascination with it once found.[24] The following duologue from *The Caretaker* exposes a conflict between Aston and Davies for control and position in Aston's room. The repetition of "I" and "you" signifying their separateness obliquely conveys the steadily increasing psychic distance and hostility between them:

> *Aston:* I . . . I think it's about time you found somewhere else. I don't think we're hitting it off.
> *Davies:* Find somewhere else?
> *Aston:* Yes.
> *Davies:* Me? You talking to me? Not me, man! You!
> *Aston:* What?
> *Davies:* You! You better find somewhere else!
> *Aston:* I live here. You don't.
> *Davies:* Don't I? Well, I live here. I been offered a job here.

Aston considers bribing Davies, but the tramp exceeds his limits when he refers to Aston's shed as "stinking." Picking up and repeating this phrase, used earlier by Mick to describe Davies, Aston strikes back at Davies with "You stink." And, as a matter of fact, adds Aston, "You've been stinking the place out."

Concluding his comments, Aston once again reiterates his sentence of exile, "You better go" (*"Caretaker" and "Dumb Waiter,"* 68–69). Similarly, we note that the repetition of "friend" in *No Man's Land* reinforces motifs, underscores the impression of fixity, and reduces Spooner to silence.

In Pinter's plays, as in Chekhov's, echoing, nuanced repetitions reveal a disparity between the first expression and those that follow it, allowing the playwright to imply rather than explicitly state altered perspectives. Whereas in Chekhovian drama a phrase repeated by several characters conveyed different interpretations, the psychological state of the speakers, and typically appeared at the conclusion of the drama, in Pinter's drama, reiterated statements underscore reinforcement or indicate a reversal of the original meaning and echo throughout the play. In the initial scene of *The Homecoming* Teddy affectionately refers to his father as an old man and suddenly appears to be aware of his advancing age. Joey, trying to mitigate the coldness and lack of hospitality of the old man, dismisses Max, "You're an old man." For his frankness, Joey receives a crushing blow to the stomach from the "old man." In stark contrast, "old" acquires a different resonance at the conclusion of the play when employed by the old man:

> *Max:* I'm too old, I suppose. She thinks I'm an an old man.
> *Pause.*
> I'm not such an old man. *(To Ruth)* you think I'm too old for you?
> *Pause.*

Whimpering, moaning, and sobbing, the old man, more senile than sexual, crawls over to Ruth's chair begging, "I'm not an old man" (*Homecoming*, 22, 42, 81–82). Max's repetitive denials reverberate in the silence. And in the absence of any comment from Ruth, Joey, or Lenny, the playwright insinuates, rather than directly states, as Teddy originally observed, that Max is indeed an old man.

The brief pause (three dots), the full pause, and silence, suggests John Lahr, are the rhythms with which Pinter scores his plays.[25] Pauses are a principal component in Pinter's linguistic construction. According to the playwright, the pause is an inevitable aspect of communication: "The pause is a pause because of what has just happened in the mind and guts of the characters."[26] Static and nonprogressional, pauses are used variously to allow for meditation on the spoken dialogue, to convey continuing thought processes, to contribute to the developing tension and to forestall saying something. In the pauses the characters hide, judge, redefine, rearm or hesitate momentarily to receive needed confirmation. In the concluding scene of *The Birthday Party* we note that Petey's pauses reveal his attempt to hide, or postpone admitting, Stanley's absence:

> *Meg:* Where's Stan?
> *Pause.*
> Is Stan down yet, Petey?

Petey: No . . . he's . . .
Meg: Is he still in bed?
Petey: Yes, he's . . . still asleep.
Meg: Still? He'll be late for his breakfast.
Petey: Let him . . . sleep.

(*Birthday Party*, 86–87)

In addition to the aforementioned uses of the pause, we observe the effectiveness with which Pinter employs the pause to freeze the moment, thereby focusing attention on the mercurial range of words and their ability to reveal and conceal. In *The Homecoming*, for example, Ruth intentionally disrupts the flow of her speech with pauses to allow time for her words to reverberate in the silence and to allow time for her audience to comprehend what she merely implies:

Look at me. I . . . move my leg. That's all it is. But I wear . . . underwear . . . which moves with me . . . it captures your attention. Perhaps you misinterpret. The action is simple. It's a leg . . . moving. My lips move. Why don't you restrict . . . your observation to that?

(*Homecoming*, 52–53)

While the audience may restrict its observation to the movement of her legs and her lips, it does not fail to intuit, and correctly interpret, both her sexual connotations and her availability. Similarly, pauses effectively freeze the moment and focus attention on a leaking roof in *The Caretaker:*

  Pause.
Mick: You'll be tarring over the cracks on the roof.
Aston: Yes.
  Pause.
Mick: Think that'll do it?
Aston: It'll do it, for the time being.
Mick: Uh.
  Pause.
Davies (abruptly): What do you do—?
  They both look at him.
  What do you do . . . when the bucket's full?
  Pause.
Aston: Empty it.
  Pause.

(*"Caretaker" and "Dumb Waiter,"* 37)

Whereas pauses indicate hesitations in the linguistic action, silences, suggests the playwright, signal a clear-cut break. Like pauses, silences are inevitable, nonverbal communication occasioned by the linguistic action with the essential difference that silences indicate "something has happened to create the impossibility of anyone speaking for a certain amount of time—until they recover from whatever has happened before the silence."[27] As this instruction for silence indicates, a break in the conversation between Hirst and Spooner in *No Man's Land*, precipitated by the cumulative effect of Spooner's remarks, allows Hirst the opportunity to regain his composure:

> *Spooner:* Good lord, good lord, do I detect a touch of the maudlin?
> *Pause.*
> Hazel shit. I ask myself: Have I ever seen hazel shit? Or hazel eyes for that matter?
> *Hirst throws his glass at him, ineffectually. It bounces on the carpet.*
> Do I detect a touch of the hostile? Do I detect—with respect—a touch of too many glasses of ale followed by the great malt which wounds? Which wounds?
> *Silence.*
> *Hirst:* Tonight . . . my friend . . . you find me in the last lap of a race . . . I had long forgotten to run.
> *Pause.*[28]

Pinter employs silences, moreover, to connote isolation and separateness. We have seen in the aforementioned citation, and in a previously discussed duologue between Aston and Davies, that silences intimate withdrawal and exclusion. But as Max Wysick suggests, rightly, pauses and silences in Pinter's plays are largely "a function of character relationships—or of nonrelationships." Characters are not merely isolated, argues Wysick; they are "isolated *from* one another."[29] Separation is a kind of interaction. In *Landscape* Pinter relies extensively on this function of silence. We observe that Beth and Duff are essentially committed to individual worlds. This is not a new use of silence for Pinter, but rather an exaggeration of a technique employed in familiar, colloquial settings in *The Room*, *The Birthday Party*, and *No Man's Land*, for example. Indeed, it is a technique reminiscent of Chekhov and Beckett. Confidences are not exchanged; separation is not bridged by speech. In *Landscape* Beth and Duff never speak to one another. Their confidences, their confessions are stripped bare of even the illusion of communication. Although neither character hears the other, the audience is privy to their separate revelations. What is implicitly conveyed in the monologues that function as dialogue and the silences that reinforce the sensation of isolation is a basic irreconcilability between Beth and Duff, a fundamental experience of exclusion. Relying on suggestive words projected against a seemingly infinite landscape of silence, the playwright employs concomitantly the two kinds of silence he has previously delineated: a torrent of speech used to conceal uncertainty and a silence that brings us closer to nakedness.

Silences are also employed in Pinter's drama to end plays while maintaining the impression of incompleteness and irresolution. Comparable to a technique employed by Bernard, Pinter builds to silent, concluding scenes by a diminuation of speech and the cumulative effect of all that has been said and left unsaid. In *"The Dumb Waiter:* Undermining the Tacit Dimension," Quigley suggests that the long silent stares that open, punctuate, and terminate this play contribute to the impression of uncertainty.[30] Likewise, we observe that silent scenes subtly inform the concluding moments of *The Caretaker, The Homecoming, No Man's Land,* and *Old Times.*

One of the most important applications of silence in Pinter's theatre is the laconism of the characters. Naturally reticent, or assuming a passive interrelational role to assure the privacy of their thoughts and to escape the judgment of others, Bert, Petey, Kate, Sam, Teddy, and Aston are essentially uncommunicative and enigmatic. Their isolation is self-willed and often accompanied by a physical rigidity. When these taciturn characters do speak, however, their involvement in the speech process is at least as important as what they have to say. Thus when Sam confides to Teddy that he was the favorite of his mother, the information has the special impact of words never spoken before. Similarly, when Sam utters the unspeakable, the secret of an incestuous affair between Jessie and MacGregor, his remarks are met with a silent response and he himself collapses under the impact of the verbalized expression.

In Pinter's world, muteness is not only self-imposed, it is socially imposed. The imposition of silence in the early plays is typically bestial and brutal, as exemplified by Aston's shock therapy and Stanley's "torture by tirade." The dehumanizing process, however, need not be overt. In the later plays, subtle, tacit rejection is equally effective. In *Old Times,* for example, Kate simply says to Anna, "I remember you dead."[31] Anna is not heard from again. Similarly, Hirst's rejection of Spooner in *No Man's Land* sentences the latter to a silence from which there is no reprieve.

Still another application of silence in Pinter's drama mirrors a technique employed by both Maeterlinck and Beckett—that of focusing attention on an absent character. In *The Homecoming* continual references to dead Jessie keep her "alive" in the play and allow for subtle comparison between the former mistress of the house and the future mistress. The presence of the mysterious force operating the dumb waiter and requesting "Macaroni Pastitsio," among other things, is also elicited by Gus's persistent questions about it. Although Ben does communicate with the voice, the conversation is unheard by both Gus and the audience. Thus, the words of the absent being are indirectly conveyed through Ben and implied by his one-sided conversations. These absent characters, however, are not the only ones cloaked in mystery. How much are we to believe about any of Pinter's characters? How much is defensive fabrication?

Unlike some of his loquacious characters, Pinter maintains his silence. Sharing with many contemporary artists a nonanthropocentric vision of the world and of the artist's role, Pinter rejects the position of the omniscient author. This dramatist believes his characters are in search of an author to give them voice; his job is "not to impose on them, not to subject them to a false articulation."[32] Striving for authenticity in a world lacking the possibility of verification and clear distinction between what is real and unreal, false and true, Pinter offers an incomplete, unfinished portrait of reality.

No Man's Land, first directed by Peter Hall and presented by the National Theatre on 23 April 1975, concerns itself with many of the themes that Pinter has treated in earlier dramas: victim/victimizer, indifference/friendship, time/timelessness, fixity/fluidity, and madness/sanity. Through the increased use of memory and the sophistication of the unspoken and the unspeakable, Pinter has softened the portrait and sharpened our vision. It is this drama that we will subject to exegesis in order to illuminate Pinter's distinctive use of the unexpressed as it develops within the text. Thematic, bivalent duologues are connected through a series of motifs, the constant presence of Spooner, the unity of setting, the disruptive intrusions and the central symbol: the liquor cabinet. In order to understand Pinter's complex and multivalent use of silence, we need to establish the significance and fluctuating rhythm both within and between conversational units.

The initial duologue in *No Man's Land* is characteristically repetitive, contrastive, and associational. In a large, well-decorated but sparsely furnished room, Hirst, a cordial but reticent host, is pouring a drink for himself and for his guest, Spooner. While Hirst repeatedly refills and empties his glass, Spooner repeatedly thanks him for his kindness: "Thank you. How very kind of you. How very kind. . . . Terribly kind."[33] Continuing a conversation begun earlier in the evening, Spooner becomes increasingly more loquacious, but his repetitive, disjunctive speech, broken by pauses, exposes his uneasiness in the room. Spooner's efforts to expand the conversation and to extend his stay in the room are deflected by Hirst's clipped, monosyllabic responses, mildly threatening "You mean?" and silences:

> *Spooner:* I speak to you with this startling candor because you are clearly a reticent man, which appeals, and because you are a stranger to me, and because you are clearly kindness itself.
> *Pause.*
> Do you often hang about Hampstead Heath?
> *Hirst:* No.
> *Spooner:* But on your excursions . . . however rare . . . on your rare excursions . . . you hardly expect to run into the likes of me? I take it?
> *Hirst:* Hardly.
> *Spooner:* I often hang about Hampstead Heath myself, expecting nothing. I'm too old for any kind of expectation. Don't you agree?
> *Hirst:* Yes.

Establishing a measure of security, Hirst announces that he is a poet, but the absence of verbal response to his statements threatens Spooner's continued presence in the room. Pursuing clarification of his position Spooner inquires, "I have gone too far, you think?" Relieved to learn that Hirst has expectations for their continued verbal interaction, but somewhat disconcerted by the implications of Hirst's reply, Spooner again requests an explicit clarification. "That doesn't mean I interest you, I hope," inquires Spooner. The host, maintaining an emotional and psychic distance between himself and his guest, responds, "Not in the least," assuring Spooner that he is not in any danger of "positive liking." "Thank goodness for that," replies the guest, confusing us with his relief at rejection (*No Man's Land*, 15–20).

Essentially through counterpointing a loquacious character and a taciturn one, through overstatement, understatement, repetition, and disjunctive speech, Pinter implicitly conveys the uneasiness of both guest and host. This initial dialogue has introduced several important motifs: interiority/exteriority, verification/ambivalence, arrival/departure, and speech/silence. We note that Spooner's efforts to clarify meaning mirror those of Hirst and that this echoing pattern, characteristic of the play, will reverberate throughout.

Hirst's precise phrases counterpoint Spooner's redundancy and his continued efforts to make himself understood. The point Spooner is tediously trying to make through nuanced repetitions is missed by a distracted Hirst, but picking up the last word, "free," Hirst maintains the flow of conversation. "It's a long time since we had a free man in this house," observes Hirst, and the innuendo is not lost on Spooner. All he can manage is a choked "We?" Quickly Hirst covers with a hasty "I," but aware that he has revealed more than he intended, the host tries to divert Spooner from further inquiry by extending his hospitality. The intrusion of the unexplained and apparently inexplicable in this seemingly realistic setting is the first of many intrusions, both abstract and concrete, which typify the play. Why are there two mugs on the shelf? Why is having a hot beverage dangerous? More is left unstated and undefined than is explicitly expressed.

The inversion of their roles and the return to subjects discussed earlier are tacitly underscored by Spooner, who has now assumed bartending responsibilities. "You'll take it as it is, as it comes?" he inquires. With the mention of Jack-Straw's Castle, the past intrudes upon the present moment. Spooner pauses to savor the memory, and then recalling that he met Hirst at the same tavern, pauses again to consider his impressions of his host. Spooner verbalizes the uncertainty one most often leaves unspoken, his repetition of "wonder" freezing the linguistic action in doubt: "And I wonder at you, now, as once I wondered at him. But will I wonder at you tomorrow, I wonder, as I still wonder at him, today?" Hirst can neither answer Spooner's inquiry nor ease his mind. Whereas Hirst employs the first person active voice, "I cannot say," Spooner echoes with the passive, "It cannot be said," assuring us that the unknowable is also the unsayable. They have reached an impasse (*No Man's Land*, 21–26).

As the hour grows later and the alcoholic haze deepens, Hirst and Spooner exchange intimacies, the most private of which is identity.[34] Introducing himself, Spooner announces, "My name is Spooner," but Hirst's understated "Ah" neither confirms nor denies welcome, neither confirms nor denies recognition.

Continuing with his introductory remarks, Spooner notes, "I'm a staunch friend of the arts," and with a slipping of tenses we are in a long-lost pastoral world that Spooner has suddenly recalled. Although Hirst and Spooner do not appear to share common experiences in their present lives, it appears that they have shared past experiences. It is important to note that this shared past is not confirmed at this point of the drama or at a later point in the action. Ambiguity concerning their relationship to their past and to each other is crucial. Spooner's repetitive questions reveal his compulsiveness and his entrapment in reverie; they also imply that no answers are forthcoming from Hirst. Spooner encourages Hirst to commit himself, fearful that as before (on the issue of mugs), Hirst would expose a part of his private life and retrace and obliterate linguistically any revelation.

Obliquely responding to Spooner's insistent inquiry, "What happened to our cottages?" Hirst relates a perverse story. The host does not succeed this time, however, in maintaining an objective, linguistic, and psychic distance between himself and Spooner. Rather than being put off by Hirst's recitation, Spooner is seduced. "Tell me more," he begs. "Tell me more about the quaint little perversions of your life and times. Tell me more . . . Tell me more." A pause of anticipation follows Spooner's repeated requests for expansion of the information, but Hirst's denial, "There is no more," is calculated to short-circuit this line of communication. Simultaneously, the negation assures Spooner, and us, that more is left unspoken than is revealed.

Once again Spooner initiates a new turn in the dialogue, and as before, he finds inspiration in what has already been spoken about. Garlanded maidens in Hirst's story bring to Spooner's mind his wife on the lawn, and striking a delicate balance between past memory and present moment, Spooner asks Hirst about his wife. "What wife?" Hirst evasively responds. The unspoken assumes a palpable presence and pervades the room as a silence of contempt and alienation descends between them. In the silent moment, Spooner gathers his reserves and resumes his needling: "Her eyes, I take it, were hazel?" Hirst retorts with uncharacteristic obscenity: "Hazel shit," eliciting an overstated harangue from Spooner and a silence from Hirst.

We observe that as Spooner becomes increasingly more comfortable in Hirst's home, his speech becomes more and more aggressive, whereas that of Hirst, as evidenced by disjunctive phrases and silences, more and more defensive. Spooner's admonition to Hirst—"Heed me. I am a relevant witness. And could be a friend"—encounters Hirst's silent response coupled with a physical rigidity. Hirst barely manages a "No," but is this a denial of Hirst's wife's abandonment? A negation of Spooner's offer of assistance? An oblique rejection of Spooner? A tentative beginning to his last fragmented statement before collapsing? In an alcoholic stupor, Hirst disjointedly stumbles over his words: "No man's land . . . does not move . . . or change . . . or grow old . . . remains . . . forever . . . icy . . . silent." Hirst's silent exit is counterpointed by Spooner's ambiguous observation, "I have known this before. The exit through the door, by way of the belly and floor" (*No Man's Land*, 26–35).

Left momentarily alone in the room, Spooner investigates in serenity, but his mood is quickly disrupted by the sound of a door closing, concomitant with the threatening intimations of intrusion. Spooner's slow, methodical movement toward connection with Hirst and his tacit victimization of him, as evidenced by Hirst's physical and linguistic paralysis, are counterpointed by the physical and linguistic paralysis that grips Spooner as a result of the sudden intrusion of Foster. Like the host who welcomed Spooner into his home, Foster initiates the verbal interaction with a seemingly cordial, and realistically credible, question: "What are you drinking?" In a speech significant for the questions it asks rather than the information it conveys, Foster recalls a garrulous Spooner who formerly babbled nervously without waiting for a response:

> What are you drinking? It's bloody late. I'm worn to a frazzle. This is what I want. (*He drinks.*) Taxi? No chance. Taxi drivers are against me. Something about me. Some unknown factor. My gait, perhaps. Or perhaps because I travel incognito. Oh, that's better. Works wonders. How are you? What are you drinking? Who are you? I thought I'd never make it.

Whereas Spooner's repetitions conveyed uneasiness and a tentative attempt to negotiate a position, Foster's, on the other hand, are indicative of surprise and discomfort. He has come home "bloody late" to find a stranger in *his* living room. Repetitions of "How are you? What are you drinking?"—social amenities—alternate with the question of Spooner's identity that obsesses Foster, "Who are you?" Significantly, Foster's rapid-fire delivery allows Spooner no opportunity to respond; his silence is externally imposed. Foster's speech, implicitly underscoring the motif of interiority (insider) and exteriority (alien), reveals the fluctuations of Foster's mind. Vacillating between "I" and "you" (we recall the effectiveness of this technique in *The Caretaker*), Foster obliquely suggests by one word only—"our"—that there is yet another who Spooner may anticipate intruding into the room. In stark contrast to his loquacity earlier in the evening, Spooner manages only one response. Claiming to be a friend of the host, Spooner hopes that this statement will verify his right to be in the room. Silent in the presence of Briggs, who has just entered, and Foster, who talks at him rather than engage him in conversation, Spooner is reduced to an inactive participant in the interrelational language game: he is a relevant witness (*No Man's Land*, 36–42).

Hirst reappears, and his intrusion initiates a new conversational unit. Having awakened from a dream, Hirst is disoriented. "What day is it? What's the time? Is it still night?" he inquires. This first explicit mention of time draws attention to the fact that, supported by repetitions and nonprogressional pauses and silences, Pinter has fashioned a seemingly static universe, devoid of chronological progression. To the question "Is it still night?" Briggs contributes the explicit but imprecise "Yes." The impression of psychological fluidity, on the other hand, is mirrored in the profusion and fluidity of water imagery: waterfall, lake, water, drowning. The context, content, and characters of Hirst's dream remain undefined and unconfessed. Similarly unconfessed is any prior knowledge of Spooner. The absence of Hirst's verbal confirmation of their relationship, although not explicitly expressed, has the indirect effect of undermining the trustworthiness of Spooner's statement that he was a friend of the host.

Having guzzled several drinks, Hirst is disoriented not only by the nightmare, but also by his excessive consumption of alcohol. Past merges with present, nightmare with reality, death with life. The effect of the nightmare coupled with that of the liquor is revealed in Hirst's disjointed fragments:

> How kind of you. I wish you'd tell me what the weather is like. I wish you'd damnwell tell me what night it is, this night or the next or the other one, the night before last. Be frank. Is it the night before last?

> Help yourselves. I hate drinking alone. There's too much solitary shittery.

> What was it? Shadows. Brightness, through leaves. Gambolling. In the bushes. Young lovers. A fall of water. It was my dream. The lake. Who was drowning in my dream?

Spooner tries to reassure Hirst, but Hirst collapses under the combined weight of ephemeral memories, the reality of death and dying, and too much liquor. Spooner's efforts to help Hirst, however, elicit animosity from Briggs and Foster, who are threatened by the role Spooner has been steadily assuming. In subtle language (reminiscent of Lenny in *The Homecoming* and Mick in *The Caretaker*) Foster insists that Spooner has no knowledge of the world of "organisation." Reiterating "It's a world," Foster links together the many disparate characterizing elements of the world:

> This is another class. It's another realm of operation. It's a world of silk. It's a world of organdie. It's a world of flower arrangements. It's a world of eighteenth century cookery books. It's nothing to do with toffeeapples and a packet of crisps. It's milk in the bath. It's the cloth bell. It's organisation.

What Foster leaves unspoken, however, is that it is also a world of violence. Claiming that Spooner is a threat to Hirst's life, as he is to their security, the two sophisticated henchmen harass Spooner with invective, but their indirect comments are even more effective. Addressing his remarks to Briggs in Spooner's presence, Foster inquires, "Why don't I kick his head off and have done with it?" Confidently and malevolently, Briggs adds, "If you can't, I can," insinuating that if Foster's words fail to convince Spooner, his fists will not. Act

1 concludes in silence, as Briggs escorts the drunken Hirst out of the room and Foster entraps the alien in silence and darkness (*No Man's Land*, 42–50).

The initial conversational unit of act 2 is linked to the one that concludes act 1 and may be counterpointed, as well, to the one that begins act 1. The impression of stasis is subtly conveyed through shafts of light shining in the room, the door that is firmly locked, and the isolating silence. Spooner's allusive reflection, "I have known this before. Morning. A locked door. A house of silence and strangers," anticipates the intrusion of Briggs bringing an offer of light, sustenance, and companionship. Left alone again while Briggs goes to retrieve breakfast, Spooner reiterates the unexplained refrain, "I have known this before. The door unlocked. The entrance of a stranger. The offer of alms. The shark in the harbor." Each echoing repetition intimates that Spooner knows more about this house of silence and strangers than he specifically delineates, while Briggs's continual movement in and out of the room and his offer and withdrawal of friendship recall the motifs of interiority/exteriority, flux/fixity, and friendship/indifference. Characteristically taking advantage of Spooner's full mouth, his imposed silence, as it were, Briggs gives his captive audience an account of his friendship with Foster, concluding their tête-à-tête with a command to finish the bottle of champagne: "Doctor's orders." No explanation is requested and none received. Then, summoned by a command from an upper floor, Briggs departs. In the silent, solitary moment before Hirst reappears, Spooner reiterates the statement, "I have known this before," incorporating the latest data into the echoing refrain (*No Man's Land*, 59–68).

With the intrusion of Hirst, a new conversational unit is initiated. Immediately apparent is Hirst's openness, lucidity, and garrulity, which sharply contrast with his earlier manner. Spooner, on the other hand, formerly open and loquacious, has grown steadily more withdrawn and taciturn, mirroring the accumulated effect of implied rejection, verbal abuse, and unexplained detention. Informally addressing Spooner as Charles, as if he were an intimate, Hirst animatedly chatters about Oxford, mutual acquaintances, and Charles's well-being. Counterpointed with Foster's caustic comments, Hirst's cordial, salutory remarks punctuated by apparently cursory questions, are not intended to elicit information. Rather, the rapid-fire unbroken speech, typical of Pinter's victimizers, exposing psychological movement from subject to subject, leaves Spooner no opportunity to respond to untruths or to reject superficial observations. Essentially Spooner has no opportunity to reject the identity that has been foisted upon him. We are suddenly aware that we do not know if *Spooner* is a surname, a nickname, or an assumed name, or if in fact Hirst knows him. Confirming their friendship with specific details, Hirst places their last meeting in 1939, "the war looming." Casually Hirst inquires, "Did you have a good war?" but in allowing Spooner no opportunity to respond, the latter is reduced to silence. Pausing to gather the threads of memory, Hirst begins, in the guise of cordiality and camaraderie, a devastating attack on Spooner, all the more

chilling because of the icy civility with which the cold facts of seduction are laid
bare:

> She loved the cottage. She loved the flowers. As did I. Narcissi, crocus, dog's
> tooth violets, fuchsia, jonquils, pinks, verbena.
>
> *Pause.*
>
> Her delicate hands.
>
> *Pause.*
>
> I'll never forget her way with jonquils.
>
> *Pause.*

Spooner's silence reveals his imprisonment in a paralyzing rage and his unwillingness to affirm or deny the validity of Hirst's comments. Hirst returns to a
thread dropped earlier—the war—but this avenue of communication, as does
another on literary careers, leads to a dead end. In the final round of their
lingustic confrontation, Spooner's growing strength is revealed in the increasing
length of his speeches and his direct criticism of Hirst's "unnatural" and "scan-
dalous" behavior. The host, astounded by the outspoken behavior of the guest,
the direct, rather than circuitous speech, echoes the question previously asked
by Foster, "Who are you?" and the question not verbalized by Foster but
implicit in his inquiry of Spooner, "What are you doing in my house?" In an
exaggerated overstatement counterpointed by Spooner's silence of exclusion
and alienation, Hirst babbles as he continues to drink himself into a stupor. The
unexpressed, such as who is Spooner and what is he doing in Hirst's house,
remains undefined and unexplained (*No Man's Land*, 68–80).

Foster's intrusion into the room and conversation and his announcement that
it is time for Hirst's morning walk, remind us of the fluidity of chronological
progression. Although Spooner had told Briggs that he had an appointment to
keep, he now offers his services to Hirst as a secretary. In a contrapuntal
conversation the isolated thoughts of Hirst, Briggs, Foster, and Spooner cut
across and intersect one another. All are essentially isolated. As Spooner attempts to effect a more permanent connection with Hirst, Briggs and Foster
simultaneously employ obscenity to denigrate Spooner and drive a wedge between him and Hirst. In a long monologue in which Spooner pledges companionship, culture, compassion, and commitment, the guest concludes by saying,
"I'm yours to command." His remarks elicit the silent response of exclusion
from Hirst and a silence of resentment from Foster and Briggs, all complicitous
in their silence to alienate the intruder. Spooner makes one last plea, this time
appealing to Hirst's ego, but this long, overstated monologue is similarly countered by a stoic silence. Bernard Beckerman has observed that Spooner's remarks become more and more hollow, more and more pathetic when
counterpointed to Hirst's absolute and continued silence.[35] Although unspoken,
there is no doubt about the finality of Hirst's rejection (*No Man's Land*, 81–91).

The final conversational unit of *No Man's Land*, initiated by Hirst's terse suggestion, "Let us change the subject," is designed to short-circuit any further appeals from Spooner. The motifs employed linguistically and structurally reverberate, freezing us in the present moment while simultaneously recalling by nuanced repetitions the initial scene of the play. The most obvious motif is that of flux/fixity concomitant with interiority/exteriority. Whereas in the opening scene Spooner, now silent, raised the question of the salvation of language, Hirst concerned himself with the meaning of words. Similarly, Hirst, with the "aid" of Foster, struggles to understand the meaning of fixity:

Foster: You said you were changing the subject for the last time.
Hirst: But what does that mean?
Foster: It means you'll never change the subject again.
Hirst: Never?
Foster: Never.
Hirst: Never?
Foster: You said for the last time.
Hirst: But what does that mean? What does it mean?
Foster: It means forever. It means that the subject is changed once and for all and for the last time forever. If the subject is winter, for instance, it'll be winter forever.

We note in the above citation that Foster, as in his duologue with Spooner, employs words repetitively to reinforce the point he is making. Hirst, on the other hand, reveals his unease through persistent questions and obsessive repetition of "mean." Foster, with the assistance of Briggs, convinces Hirst that not only is the subject changed, it is also closed. The impression of stasis, crucial in this scene and operative throughout the drama, is once again created and underscored by references to fixed time, such as "forever" and "never," and by pauses. After a long silent moment in which the direction of the subject is changed, Hirst observes that he hears the sounds of birds. Although it is left unspoken, it is implicit in Hirst's observation that if he hears birds, then it is not winter. After a hesitation to gather his thoughts, Hirst recounts a dream, but unlike the one that awakened him last night, in this dream no one is drowning. Indeed, concludes Hirst, "There is nothing there." Spooner breaks his silence to point out to Hirst what Foster left unspoken in his clarification of "forever" and "never." Sentencing Hirst to a remote, frigid exclusion, Spooner observes, "*You* are in no man's land. Which never moves, which never changes, which never grows older, but which remains forever, icy and silent." Both preceded and punctuated by silences that frame the words and focus attention on them, and coupled with the impact of Spooner's solitary statement in the conversation, this explanation of no man's land elicits silence from all gathered.[36] Hirst's final toast, "I'll drink to that," confirms that he is once again lost in an alcoholic haze, out of touch with the meaning of Spooner's words and their implication. The play concludes in a frozen tableau leaving unresolved the nature and the future of these relationships (*No Man's Land*, 91–95).

Pinter's most recent work reveals a growing interest in memory and illustrates a more subtle portrait of the fragmented world. Even more than in the early plays words assume a chameleonlike quality and a multiplicity of connotation, while silence, expansive and mysterious, functions as a link between empirical and psychological worlds of experience. Pinter's intention may be summed up in an aesthetic theory expressed by Spooner: "What is obligatory to keep in your vision is space." Through his reliance on the unexpressed and the unspeakable, Pinter's defensive and disoriented characters experience rather than intellectually interpret the emptiness and the inexplicable in their lives.

We turn our attention now to the theatre of Edward Albee, whose use of silence reflects a transformation of Beckettian and Pinteresque techniques of the unexpressed.

NOTES

1. Harold Pinter, in an interview with John Russell Taylor, "Accident," *Sight and Sound* 35 (1964): 184.
2. Ibid.
3. Austin Quigley, *The Pinter Problem* (Princeton, N.J.: Princeton University Press, 1975), 54.
4. Ibid., 166.
5. Harold Pinter, "Between the Lines," Speech to the Seventh National Student Drama Festival in Bristol, *Sunday Times* (London), 4 March 1962, 25.
6. Ibid.
7. Martin Esslin, *The Peopled Wound: The Work of Harold Pinter* (Garden City, N.Y.: Anchor-Doubleday, 1970), 41.
8. Harold Pinter, *"The Caretaker" and "The Dumb Waiter"* (New York: Grove Press, 1961), 68; idem, *The Homecoming* (New York: Grove Press, 1965), 80 (references hereafter will be to these editions unless otherwise indicated).
9. John Lahr, "Pinter and Chekhov: The Bond of Naturalism," *Drama Review* 13, no. 2 (Winter 1968): 137–45, reprinted in *Pinter: A Collection of Critical Essays*, ed. Arthur Ganz, Twentieth Century Views (Englewood Cliffs, N.J.: Prentice-Hall, 1972), 60–71 (hereafter cited as *PCCE*).
10. Harold Pinter, "Writing for Myself," *Twentieth Century* 168 (February 1961): 174.
11. Bernard Beckerman, "Artifice of 'Reality' in Chekhov and Pinter," *Modern Drama* 21, no. 2 (June 1978): 157–58.
12. On this point, see Arthur Ganz, Introduction, in *PCCE*, 7–8.
13. John Russell Taylor, "A Room and Some Views: Harold Pinter," in *PCCE*, 112–13.
14. Harold Pinter, *"The Birthday Party" and "The Room"* (New York: Grove Press, 1961), 9–21 (references hereafter will be to this edition).
15. Harold Pinter, program of the Royal Court Theatre production of *The Room* and *The Dumb Waiter*, 8 March 1960, quoted in Esslin, *The Peopled Wound*, 33–34.
16. Ibid., 34.
17. Ruby Cohn, "The World of Harold Pinter," *Tulane Drama Review* 6, no. 3 (March 1962): 55–68; reprinted in *PCCE*, 80, notes that Pinter's victimizers tend to exhibit more brute power in their speech. We also observe that victimizers (Lenny, Ben, and Foster) possess chronological awareness, whereas victims (Davies, Gus, and Spooner) do not.
18. Lahr, "Pinter and Chekhov," 67.
19. Linked to the "fast," to the Day of Atonement, is the sacrifice of Isaac. Katherine H. Burkman, *The Dramatic World of Harold Pinter: Its Basis in Ritual* (Columbus: Ohio State University Press, 1971), 22–23, identifying the ritualistic core of Pinter's work, has suggested that this scene prefigures the sacrifice of the *pharmakos*, Stanley. Through Goldberg's "meaningless" phrases, Pinter may be obliquely conveying thematic concerns.
20. Cohn, "World of Harold Pinter," 78.

21. Ganz, Introduction, in *PCCE*, 10.

22. Cohn, "World of Harold Pinter," 80.

23. Bert O. States, "Pinter's *Homecoming:* The Shock of Nonrecognition," *Hudson Review* 21, no. 3 (August 1968), reprinted in *PCCE*, 153–54.

24. Esslin, in *The Peopled Wound*, offers a trenchant study of repetition in Pinter's drama (see chap. 4, "Language and Silence," 207–42).

25. See John Lahr, "Pinter's Language," in *A Casebook on Harold Pinter's "The Homecoming,"* ed. John Lahr, 123–36 (New York: Grove Press, 1971), for a concise study of pauses and silences (hereafter cited as *CHPH*).

26. Mel Gussow, "A Conversation (Pause) with Harold Pinter," *New York Times Magazine,* 5 December 1971, 132.

27. Gussow, "A Conversation," 132.

28. Harold Pinter, *No Man's Land* (New York: Grove Press, 1975), p. 32 (references hereafter will be to this edition unless otherwise indicated).

29. Max M. Wysick, "Language and Silence in the Stage Plays of Samuel Beckett and Harold Pinter," (Ph.D. diss., University of Colorado 1972), 130–32.

30. Austin Quigley, "*The Dumb Waiter:* Undermining the Tacit Dimension," *Modern Drama* 21, no. 1 (March 1978): 1–11.

31. Harold Pinter, *Old Times* (New York: Grove Press, 1971), 71 (references hereafter will be to this edition unless otherwise indicated).

32. Pinter, "Between the Lines," 25.

33. It has been suggested that literary allusions to Beckett, T. S. Eliot, and Tennessee Williams echo throughout *No Man's Land* (see Irving Wardle, "In a Land of Dreams and Actuality," review of *No Man's Land*, by Harold Pinter, *Times* [London], 24 April 1975, 10–11). Wardle maintains that the literary presence of Beckett, particularly *Endgame*, has never been more prevalent in Pinter's work. Steven H. Gale, *Butter's Going Up* (Durham, N.C.: Duke University Press, 1977), stresses the importance of Eliot and Williams (we cannot miss allusion to the kindness of strangers and Stella Winstanley). Most pertinent to our study is the disjunction between self and society that typifies the drama of these authors.

34. We might recall that the night of the fire in *The Three Sisters* encouraged the exchange of intimacies and precipitated attempts at confession.

35. Beckerman, "Artifice of 'Reality,'" 159. Beckerman notes that the effort of "voluble desperation striking against absolute and indifference" engenders the feeling that the life is draining out of the speaker.

36. Emphasis added. Beckerman, "Artifice of 'Reality,'" 159, believes that Pinter meant the inclusive pronoun "we." The dramatist's careful use of "I" and "you" in *The Caretaker* and earlier in this drama support my view, however.

The drama of Edward Albee, characterized by its explicit, direct, and caustic dialogue, would seem to be ill suited to a study of the unspoken and the unspeakable in contemporary drama. Close examination of the plays exposes a disparity between what is stated—often overstated—and what is left undefined and unexplained. *The Zoo Story, Who's Afraid of Virginia Woolf?, A Delicate Balance, All Over,* and *Listening* have been selected to illustrate the specific techniques that Albee employs to undermine denotative speech, to create confusion, and to evoke mystery.

Fusing form with content, Albee synthesizes phenomenal and psychological experience. Therefore, consideration of his use of the quotidian, realistic, and symbolistic techniques and the apparently static structure will anticipate and lay the foundation for our estimation of his characteristic use of the unspoken.

Like Chekhov, and more recently Harold Pinter, Albee creates a convincing "artifice of reality" by presenting familiar settings and situations, be they an impromptu visit of friends in *A Delicate Balance*, a chance encounter in *The Zoo Story*, or a death vigil in *All Over*. The daily flow of the customary and the habitual, such as Peter's visits to the park, underscores continuity, whereas ceremonial and social occasions, like Teddy's death, underscore fixed moments in time. Realistic character details are supported by seemingly aimless speech, authentic in vocabulary, syntax, and rhythm. Appropriate to the situation, realistic speech in Albee's drama functions in familiar, recognizable ways. In *The Zoo Story*, for instance, Jerry initiates a conversation and negotiates a relationship with a stranger through colloquial expression and common references. Their efforts to "place" the zoo recall those of Vershinin, Olga, Irina, and Masha in Chekhov's *The Three Sisters* to place the location in Moscow of their previous encounter. Equally recognizable is a mother-daughter quarrel in *A Delicate Balance*. Agnes's disjunctive speech exposes her efforts to impose control over her defiant daughter, a chaotic situation, and her own emotions. Referring to Julia's broken marriage, Agnes cautions, "You needn't make a circus of it," but Julia persists. Agnes's attempt to short-circuit conversation by another interruption is similarly ineffective:

Agnes: You're tired; we'll talk about it after . . .

Julia   *(Sick disgust):* I've talked about it!
Agnes   *(Quiet boring in):* I'm sure there's more.
Julia: There is no more.
Agnes   *(Clenched teeth):* There is a great deal more, and I'll hear it from you later when we're alone. You have not come to us in your fourth debacle . . .[1]

Her voice drifts off, leaving incomplete a sentence she will conclude in private. Pausing to consider a new strategy to effect control, Agnes softens her tone and obliquely suggests, "Perhaps after dinner."

In Albee's plays, as in Beckett's, language functions as a means of diversion while waiting. Like Beckett's characters who wait for Godot, for painkiller, for release from waiting, Albee's characters situated in realistic settings wait for uninvited guests to depart in *A Delicate Balance*, wait for invited guests to depart in *Who's Afraid of Virginia Woolf?* or wait for death in *All Over*. The motif of waiting is specifically delineated by Claire in *A Delicate Balance* and George in *Virginia Woolf*, but whether it is explicit or implicit, Albee's characters pass the time while waiting by exchanging reminiscences and confidences. Paralleling a technique employed by Chekhov, Albee situates his characters in confined settings where the stressful and exhausting circumstances are conducive to confession. Crucial to Albee's drama, as it is in Chekhov's, is the solitude of the character and his estrangement from, rather than involvement in, life. Efforts to break out of the imprisonment of isolation are foiled. Confessions, as the Mistress learns in *All Over*, have the ironic effect of alienating rather than uniting characters. Indeed, confessions are generally met with resistance, as is the case in *The Zoo Story*, or, as noted in the aforementioned citation from *A Delicate Balance*, disrupted by diversionary tactics. George's attempts to quiet Martha in *Virginia Woolf* are illustrative of this paradigm. George's "Martha . . . I warn you, Martha" escalates to "STOP IT, MARTHA!" (*Virginia Woolf*, 133–34). Martha's recitation is finally broken off when George lunges for her neck.

Albee, suggests Ruby Cohn, is "misinterpreted as a realist."[2] Providing a specific ground of association based on realistic setting, speech, and situation, he draws us into a suprarealistic world. Disoriented in this world, we are, as Anne Paolucci observes, "like Alice in a world of wonders."[3] We see familiar things exaggerated and minimized, confused and distorted. Closely paralleling Pinter, Albee establishes the presence of mysterious forces and elusive emotions through defamiliarization of the familiar and ironic inversion. Disjunctive and nonverbal responses reflect rather than explicitly define reactions to disorienting and fearful experience.

One of the ways in which Albee dislocates the familiar and contributes to the sensation of disquietude is through intimation and incomplete information. *A Delicate Balance* exemplifies an apparently realistic situation shrouded in mystery. The interior mood is one of confusion and spiralling terror. Uninvited, Edna and Harry drop in for a visit with their friends Agnes and Tobias. So close is their relationship that Edna, not Agnes's sister Claire, is Julia's godmother. In light of the nature and forty-year duration of their friendship, such a

social call would seem to be a usual occurrence, yet their less-than-cordial
reception is not explained. Similarly unexplained and undefined is the terror
that grips Edna and Harry and that has driven them to seek refuge with friends.
Claire compounds the mystery when she elliptically notes, "I was wondering
when it would begin . . . when it would start." A disoriented Tobias questions,
"Start? *(Louder)* START? *(Pause)* WHAT?" At the conclusion of this drama the
unidentified terror remains undefined (*Delicate Balance*, 58).

Employing a technique characteristic of Pinter's drama, and one that is responsible in great part for the defamiliarization of the familiar, Albee entraps his
characters in restricted surroundings. With the exception of Peter, figuratively
tied to his bench in the park, characters in the Albee plays under discussion are
confined to that most familiar of settings: the room. Intrusions into these rooms,
of an abstract and concrete nature, contribute to the impression of disorientation. Indeed, as Foster Hirsch maintains in *Who's Afraid of Edward Albee?* "once
characters open the door of their usually snug, enclosed living rooms to visitors
from the outside world, the delicate balance of their lives is threatened."[4] Focusing attention upon these invasions of personal and psychic space, Albee reveals
the oppression of these intrusions from within and without by the disjunctive
and silent reactions to them. In *The Zoo Story*, for example, Peter's solitude and
serenity are disrupted by the intrusion of Jerry. His distracted greeting,
"Hm? . . . What . . . I'm sorry, were you talking to me?" tacitly conveys his
displeasure (*Zoo Story*, 12).

In restricted rooms the impression of mystery and ambiguity is encouraged
by supplanting the recognizable order of chronological progression with the
chaos of psychological fluidity. Through the apparent cessation of chronological
progression underscored by the motif of waiting, Albee creates and reinforces
the sensation of captivity and stasis. Characters occasionally refer to the time
(Julia receiving the information, "nearly ten," and George noting the progression from two o'clock to two-thirty), but distracted, they seem unaware of its
progression. If clocks and watches are present, they are rarely consulted. Even
when Peter consults his watch in *The Zoo Story* his vague response, "I must be
getting home soon," contributes to the impression of indefiniteness, rather than
clarifying it. Similarly, in *All Over* questions concerning the time do not refer to
specific chronological time, but to the imminence of the man's death: "Will he
die soon?"[5] But when is soon, and what time is it now? Whether the wait is short
or long, whether defined or implicit, the effects and strains of intrusions and
waiting are evoked in Albee's plays through reliance on the unspoken.

Situations in Albee's plays that are apparently static are *only* seemingly so.
We observe that in each of these plays the initial situation, one of relative
inertia, builds inexorably into a frightening confrontation with the intruder and
with the self, and the concluding scene is characterized by a literal or
metaphoric death. In *The Zoo Story*, Jerry dies; in *Who's Afraid of Virginia Woolf?*
the imaginary sonny-Jim dies; in *All Over*, the dying man dies; in *Listening*, the
girl dies; and in *A Delicate Balance*, the friendship of forty years dies. The

playwright is concerned with private, daily, unexpressed deaths—betrayals and loss—and the verbal and nonverbal responses that they engender. Simultaneous with the swift and slow temporal progression and literal deaths, Albee exposes the fluctuating state of intimate relationships and the mutable condition within each character. By simplifying plot, focusing on a few characters and employing allusive references, the dramatist achieves psychological verisimilitude by directing attention away from the literal to the metaphoric and cosmic, from action to emotion. In the concluding moments of *Virginia Woolf*, for instance, Albee implicitly conveys the depth of loss that Martha experiences but leaves unspoken and undefined. Her disjunctive, monosyllabic responses, in stark contrast to her former coarseness and garrulity, reveal her altered psychic state and her difficulty in maintaining even the illusion of communication:

> *Martha:* It was . . . ? You had to?
> *George* *(Pause):* Yes.
> *Martha:* I don't know.
> *George:* It was . . . time.
> *Martha:* Was it?
> *George:* Yes.
> *Martha* *(Pause):* I'm cold.
> *George:* It's late.
> *Martha:* Yes.
> *George* *(Long silence):* It will be better.
> *Martha* *(Long silence):* I don't . . . know.
> *George:* It will be . . . maybe.
> *Martha:* I'm . . . not . . . sure.
> *George:* No.
>
> (*Virginia Woolf*, 240–41)

Albee further defamiliarizes the familiar through what Northrup Frye terms "demonic modulation," the deliberate reversal of moral associations of archetypes.[6] This playwright employs symbols extensively in his drama to communicate obliquely what he has intentionally left undefined, to reinforce motifs, and to maintain the universality of experience. In an interview with Michael Rutenberg, Albee argued that:

> People will read signposts into anything because they seem unwilling to suffer the experience on its own terms and let the unconscious come into full play. . . . This pigeon-holing and symbol hunting is merely an attempt not to suffer the experience the playwright wants the audience to suffer.[7]

In order to encourage the play of the unconscious, to forestall the displacement of the experience, and to inhibit the signification attached to known symbols, Albee counterpoints familiar apocalyptic symbolism with demonic symbolism. Moreover, by employing sacred symbolism in secular settings he achieves ambiguity and the impact of irony without direct statement.[8] In the concluding scene of *Who's Afraid of Virginia Woolf?* the dramatist offers no explanation for George's incantation of death rites in Latin as Martha recites the story of "Bringing Up Baby." The death that is implied and the emptiness that is evoked would seem to be the direct and intended result of Albee's defamiliarization of the familiar.

Inverted expectation is still another way in which Albee confuses the realistic ground of association and imbues his plays with an atmosphere of mystery and disquietude. An invitation for a nightcap after a party may be familiar, but the linguistic party game of "Get the Guests" that they play at George and Martha's is threateningly unfamiliar. A family gathered for a death vigil may be customary, but a wife of fifty years and a mistress of twenty arguing over whether to bury or burn their husband/lover is not. Similarly, a cry for Daddy's help would be appropriate and expected from a young child, but from thirty-six-year-old Julia, veteran of four marriages, it is not. In each of these circumstances the playwright confounds expectation in order to expose latent unexpressed tensions in a situation as well as to trace escalating responses to disorienting and fearful experience. The strain of waiting for death in *All Over*, for example, is mirrored in the daughter's disjunctive expressions and hesitation to avoid delineating her contempt and distress: "Stop it; stop it; stop it; you bitches, you filthy . . . you filth who allow it . . . you . . . you . . ." Her voice breaks off in frustration and exhaustion. Her mother, on the other hand, breaks the flow of her speech to look for the right word to express a sense of loss and disgust that extends beyond her immediate, impending loss: "Why don't you go home to your *own* filth? You . . . you . . . issue!" (*All Over*, 63).

Fusing the unusual with the familiar, realistic techniques with symbolic techniques, deceptive stasis and cyclical flux, Albee establishes and emphasizes the presence of the mysterious and unexpressed in the quotidian. The typifying elements of his linguistic structure are:

1. disjunctive speech
2. colloquial dialogue stripped of euphemism
3. counterpointing through understatement and overstatement
4. repetition and echoing
5. pauses
6. unanswered questions
7. mute characters
8. silence as a metaphor for isolation
9. silence as a metaphor for evasion
10. silence of the playwright

Disjunctive speech, which dramatizes imperceptible flux within the mind of the speaker and between speakers, is well suited to the portrayal of interior and exterior reality. Not unlike Chekhov and Pinter, Albee achieves authentic, realistic dialogue through an apparently irrational, subconscious choice and arrangement of words and hesitant, compulsive speech patterns that expose the efforts of the characters to express what they wish to express or wish to leave unspoken. The following citations from the plays illustrate discontinuity in a conversation or speech in situations of emotional stress, exhaustion, natural or defensive reticence, or avoidance of communication. In *A Delicate Balance* Tobias meets the challenge of Harry's probing question, "You . . . you don't *want* us, do you Toby?" Toby's repetitive speech, punctuated by questions, exclamations, hysterical laughter, and silences, exposes the flow of emotion he can neither contain nor comprehend:

(Softly, and as if the word were unfamiliar)

Want?

(Same)

What? Do I what?

(Abrupt laugh; joyous)

Do I WANT?

(More laughter; also a sob)

Do I WANT YOU HERE!

(Hardly able to speak from the laughter)

You come in here, you come in here with your . . . wife, and with your . . . terror! And you ask me if I want you here!

(Great breathing sounds)

YES! OF COURSE! I WANT YOU HERE! I HAVE BUILT THIS HOUSE! I WANT YOU IN IT! I WANT YOUR PLAGUE! YOU'VE GOT SOME TERROR WITH YOU? BRING IT IN!

After ranting for several minutes, Toby is exhausted and overcome with grief and pain. His speech drifts off into a plea: "Stay? Please? Stay? *(Pause)* Stay? Please? Stay?" (*Delicate Balance*, 164–67).

In *All Over*, on the other hand, the stress of waiting stimulates the Best Friend to recount previous and personal loss. Hesitation to find the right word, to emphasize others and ultimately avoid expressing what is too painful for him to admit characterizes his speech:

Each thing, each . . . incident—uprooting all the roses, her hands so torn, so . . . killing the doves and finches . . . setting fire to her hair . . . all . . . all those

times, those things I knew were pathetic and not wanton, I watched myself
withdraw, step back and close down some portion of . . .

(*All Over*, 28)

Similar to Jerry's dog story in *The Zoo Story* and Toby's cat story in *A Delicate
Balance*, Martha's "Bringing Up Baby" in *Virginia Woolf* illustrates still another
way in which Albee employs disjunctive speech authentically to reveal correc-
tions, reversals, repetitions, syntactical inversions, and interruptions typical of
storytelling:

> . . . and how he broke his arm . . . how funny it was . . . oh, no, it hurt him!
> . . . but, oh, it was funny . . . in a field, his very first cow, the first he'd seen
> . . . and he went into the field, to the cow, where the cow was grazing, head
> down, busy . . . and he moo'd at it! *(Laughs [to herself])* He'd moo'd at it . . .
> and the beast, oh, surprised, swung its head up and moo'd at him, all three
> years of him, and he ran startled, and he stumbled . . . fell . . . and broke his
> poor arm. *(Laughs, ibid.)* Poor lamb.
>
> (*Virginia Woolf*, 221)

Disjunctive, colloquial speech patterns in realistic social settings indicate
disjunction between participants in a conversation and within the thought of the
speaker. Implying that man employs language as a separating screen between
himself and reality (like the one that literally isolates the dying man from he
family in *All Over*), Albee makes a distinctive contribution to the drama of the
unexpressed by stripping speech of euphemistic expression. The "unspeakable," as it is employed by Albee, may be defined as expression generally
thought to be ill-suited to social conversation. This speech typically elicits
evasive responses and silences of embarrassment and rejection. In *The Zoo Story*
Peter does not respond directly to Jerry's observation that he will get cancer of
the mouth from smoking a pipe. Preferring to evade Jerry's comment and its
implications, Peter concerns himself with the medical terminology "prosthesis."
The Wife in *All Over*, reflecting the strain she is under by her choice of words,
announces that she will awaken her comatose husband in order to determine the
appropriate death rites:

> My darling, we merely want to know! Is it flame or worm? Your mistress tells
> me you prefer flame, while I, your merely wife of fifty years, the mother of
> your doubted children—true, oh, true, my darling—wants you to the
> worms.
>
> (*All Over*, 36)

Whereas her performance earns her measured applause from the Mistress, the
unspeakable recitation is as shocking to the Wife as it is to the others gathered.
She withdraws into a long, silent contemplation.

Counterpointing through overstatement and understatement has been employed by other playwrights, particularly Chekhov and Pinter, to undermine what has been said, to simulate realistic conversations that cut across one another, and to reinforce stasis by nonprogressional speech. Albee typically counterpoints a loquacious character with a taciturn one to indicate the conscious suppression of information or evasion of speech. The initial situation of *The Zoo Story* is characteristic. Jerry's enthusiastic overstatement is undermined by Peter's nonresponsive, monosyllabic understatement:

> Jerry   *(After a pause):* Boy, I'm glad that's Fifth Avenue there.
> Peter   *(Vaguely):* Yes.
> Jerry: I don't like the west side of the park much.
> Peter: Oh? *(Then slightly wary, but interested)* Why?
> Jerry   *(Offhand):* I don't know.
> Peter: Oh. *(He returns to his book)*
> Jerry   *(He stands for a few seconds, looking at Peter, who finally looks up again puzzled):* Do you mind if we talk?
> Peter   *(Obviously minding):* Why . . . no, no.
>
> *(Zoo Story*, 14)

Of even greater interest is this playwright's modification of the technique of counterpointing by which he juxtaposes two different statements in sequential order or separated by a time span. The time span allows the listener the opportunity to evaluate what he has heard, time to forget what he has heard, and a second opportunity to hear a conflicting version. Comparable to Pinter's use of counterpointing to cast doubt on the truthfulness of the narrator, Albee employs counterpointing to increase our awareness that less is confessed directly than is implied. In *Virginia Woolf*, for example, Nick hears two different versions of the boy who drank "bergin"; however, it is only after Nick has heard Martha's version that he intuits how much George left unexpressed.

Repetition is an essential element of Albee's linguistic structure, and in concert with counterpointing and nonprogressional pauses, contributes to the impression of stasis. We note in this citation from Albee's recent chamber play, *Listening*, that the continued reiteration of "Did you?" alternating with "Did you come?" and "Did you know?" reveals the Man's compulsiveness as well as the Woman's refusal to speak:

> The Man *(As the Woman hmmmmmmms and chuckles—closemouthed—throughout):*
>   Did you?
>   *Pause*
>   Did you know?
>   *(Pause)*
>   Did you come here with someone else, and did you know?
>   *(Pause)*
>   Was it full?
>   *(Pause)*

> Was it *full?*
>   *(Pause)*
> *Did you come here with someone else?*
>   *(Pause)*
> Did you know?
>   *(Pause)*
> *Did you?*[9]

Albee, like Beckett, employs repetitions to forestall the free flow of other thoughts and to exploit the only word that the character can think of at the moment. In *Who's Afraid of Virginia Woolf?* for instance, Martha, inebriated and disoriented by the fact that she is left alone, reveals her physical and emotional state in repetitions of "cry": "*(Pause)* I cry all the time too Daddy. I cry alllll the time; but deep inside, so no one can see me. I cry all the time. And George cries all the time, too" (*Virginia Woolf*, 185). Repetitions also serve, as they do in Maeterlinck's drama, to evoke mood, specifically one of anxiety. In *All Over* the Daughter, ostracized by her mother after she has allowed the newsmen to intrude upon the privacy of the family, repeatedly tries to gain her mother's attention. Her plaintive "Mother," "Mo-other," "Moooootherrrr!" "MOOOOTHERRRR!" reveals her steadily increasing anguish, which is ignored, and a steadily increasing psychic distance between mother and daughter. With each cry, the daughter's distress is exposed and the mother's stoic silence is underscored (*All Over*, 92–93).

Repetitions in Albee's dramas are employed, moreover, as an indication of evasion, of all that is intentionally left unexpressed. An excellent illustration of this technique is Peter's tripartite denial in *The Zoo Story*. With each repetition of "I don't understand" Jerry is more and more convinced that Peter is lying. By refusing to speak about the dog story, Peter indirectly reveals more than he explicitly expresses (*Zoo Story*, 36–37). Similarly, in *Listening* the Woman's repeated denials implicitly suggest that more is left unspoken than is intimated and implied:

The Man   *(Indicates the surrounding area):* Is any of this familiar?
The Woman   *(Laughs):* What! This!? Where we are!?
The Man: Well, as it was—as it may have been, back when it was . . . what? . . . personal, is that it? Back when it was clipped and trained and planned and . . . back *then.*
The Woman   *(Shakes her head):* No.
The Man: Did we leave the patio? Remember the sound the footfall made on the stone? even outdoors?
The Woman: No.
The Man: And the sudden silence of the grass after all that echoing, through a bower . . .
The Woman: A what?

The Man: A bower.
The Woman: No.

("Counting the Ways" and "Listening," 124–25)

The Man, hesitantly and unaided, gathers the threads of memory to fix a moment in time that they have shared. The Woman's denials, intended to short-circuit the line of conversation, combined with her refusal to speak about the memories he recalls, intensifies our awareness of her avoidance of subject and avoidance of speech.

Still another way in which Albee employs repetition is to "keep alive" by continual reference characters who are absent from the dialogue or dramatic action, but nonetheless integral. Thus in *All Over* the Wife and Mistress alternately inquire, "Is he dead?" "Is he dead?" "Has he . . . *died?*" "Will he die soon?" To rekindle interest in the dying man the Daughter comments, "He still is . . . Alive . . . Wondered; that's all" (*All Over*, 15–17, 108). Similarly, in *Who's Afraid of Virginia Woolf?* we learn that George and Martha's son is a "bean-bag," "a comfort," "a beautiful, beautiful boy," "baby-poo," and "the little bugger." These varying forms of endearment, while realistic in the situation, simultaneously evoke the presence of absence by repetition.

As we have noted in the studies of Chekhov, Beckett, and Pinter, repetitions are cumulatively effective. Therefore, reiteration of "bergin" in *Virginia Woolf*, "Move over" in *The Zoo Story*, and "adrift" in *A Delicate Balance* all illustrate the manner in which Albee employs repetitions to convey obliquely enlarging circles of meaning. Through an extensive reliance on echoing, this dramatist achieves nuanced variations of thought or reversals of meaning without direct statement. Peter's anguished response to Jerry's death—"Oh . . . my . . . God"—is echoed repeatedly by him before he tears himself away from the scene. Each repetition underscores his paralysis and traces spiralling hysteria as the reality impresses itself on his brain. Jerry's mocking supplication that concludes the drama offers a nuanced variation of the words (*Zoo Story*, 47–49). And in *A Delicate Balance* Albee achieves a reinforcement of terror of the void with each of Harry and Edna's nuanced and alternating repetitions:

Edna   (*Open weeping; loud*): WE GOT . . . FRIGHTENED.
        (*Open sobbing; no one moves*)
Harry   (*Quiet wonder, confusion*): We got scared.
Edna   (*Through her sobbing*): WE WERE . . . FRIGHTENED.
Harry: There was nothing . . . but we were very scared.
        (*Agnes comforts Edna, who is in free sobbing anguish. Claire lies slowly back on the floor*)
Edna: We . . . were . . . terrified.
Harry: We were scared.
        (*Silence*)

(Delicate Balance, 55)

Still another way in which Albee employs nuanced variations may be illustrated by Agnes's "if" speech in *A Delicate Balance* and Edna's "if" speech in the same play. Essentially, Albee employs the same phrase to imply, rather than directly state, differences in their ability to cope with psychological trauma. As employed by Agnes, "if" establishes her parental prerogative and position vis-à-vis behavior and punishment; later in the play, however, "if" orders a speech in which a frightened Edna explains the conditions under which she would take certain actions to acquire the parental benefits Agnes extends.

Although the static, nonprogressional pause is not the primary element of Albee's drama, as it is in Beckett's and Pinter's, pauses (noted earlier in relation to disjunctive speech) are employed variously to indicate a groping for words, an attempt to conceal information, and an unfinished thought. The following duologue between Nick and George in *Virginia Woolf* reveals many of these functions:

> *Nick:*   If you and your . . . wife . . . want to go at each other, like a couple
>   of . . . .
> *George:* *I!* Why *I* want to!
> *Nick:*   . . . animals, I don't see why you don't do it when there aren't any . . .
> *George* (*Laughing through his anger*): Why, you smug, self-righteous little . . .
> *Nick*   (*A genuine threat*): CAN . . . IT . . . MISTER!
>   (*Silence*)
> *Just* . . . *watch it!*
>
> (Virginia Woolf, 91–92)

In the citation above we observe that in addition to ellipses to indicate hesitation, Albee also employs the term *silence*. As this conversation illustrates, the term *silence* is generally utilized to indicate a moment of extreme tension in which there is a break in the conversation before either character is able to continue. Also notable in Albee's drama is the use of silence to frame dramatically and to emphasize the words that are between silences. Paralleling a technique employed by both Beckett and Pinter, this playwright freezes a moment in time so that words may reverberate and gain resonance in the silence. George's announcement of sonny-Jim's death, interrupted with pauses and ellipses, is accentuated by the silences that surround it:

> Martha . . . (*Long pause*) . . . our son is . . . dead.
>
> (*Silence*)
>
> He was . . . killed . . . late in the afternoon . . .
>
> (*Silence*)
>
> (Virginia Woolf, 231)

Unanswered questions provide Albee, as they do Pinter, with an authentic medium to expose evasions and avoidance. In *A Delicate Balance*, for example, Claire, leaving unstated her desire to stay up with Toby, provokes him with insistent questions: "Are you going to stay up, Tobias? Sort of a nightwatch, guarding?" He neither answers her questions nor invites her to join him. Rather, by a repetition of "Good night, Claire," he leaves unspoken any feelings he has about her or her companionship. Intuiting his "message" of rejection, and leaving unexpressed any other indication of hurt or disappointment, she concludes her inquiry with "Good night, Tobias" (*Delicate Balance*, 125–26). In the same drama, Agnes repeatedly asks Tobias, "What did you decide?" Avoiding the question, Toby speaks about what the house is like in the middle of the night, the state of disarray in the room, the quality of the help. Finally Tobias asks Agnes, "What are we going to do?" Avoiding his question, and subtly returning the decision to him, Agnes asks once again, "What did you decide?" After a pause Toby concedes, "Nothing" (*Delicate Balance*, 133–36). Unanswered questions are employed, moreover, to encourage the impression of indefiniteness and evoke the presence of the unexpressed. In *Listening*, for instance, the Girl's vague responses to and intentional avoidance of the Woman's questions contribute to the Woman's, and to our, bewilderment. Frustrated in her attempts at clarification, the mother endeavors to gain information from her disturbed daughter who has crawled into the water fountain. The Girl's provocative insinuations, however, succeed in disquieting her mother, whose monosyllabic "Oh" is itself suggestive and confusing.

The inarticulate or mute character, employed by Maeterlinck, Chekhov, Bernard, Beckett, and Pinter, figures importantly in Albee's theatre. Frequently this reticent character, who is linguistically withdrawn, functions as a silent observer. Claire, as her sister Agnes notes with biting sarcasm, is just such a character: "Claire, who watches from the sidelines, has seen so very much, has seen us all so clearly, have you not Claire. You were not named for nothing" (*Delicate Balance*, 110). Although Albee diminishes the impact of his taciturn character by having another announce her (as is the case with Claire), or by having him announce himself (as is the case with Peter in *The Zoo Story*), his or her silence is nonetheless striking in a drama characterized by its vital, vituperative dialogue and articulate characters. Albee typically provides his reticent characters with credible extenuating circumstances, such as emotional crises and excessive drinking, which realistically account for a change in linguistic behavior, specifically from silence and/or taciturnity to speech, and often loquacity. When the withdrawn character, be it Peter, Honey, Claire, Toby, or the Doctor, who has separated himself from the others in order to avoid participation, involvement, or judgment, speaks, the psychic distance between him and the others is underscored not necessarily by what he says, but by the fact that he speaks. Thus Toby, who typically defers to Agnes, surprises even himself when he demands that Harry and Edna stay. Similarly, Honey, Peter, and the Doctor all participate in the linguistic interaction as a result of stressful and disorienting circumstances.

The reticence of Albee's characters mirrors the silence of the playwright. When asked if *Tiny Alice* were intentionally confusing, Albee said, "I wonder if I meant it to be intentionally confusing. Maybe I meant it to be something a little different from confusing—provocative, perhaps, rather than confusing."[10] The playwright's thoughts and intentions with respect to *Tiny Alice* seem applicable to the dramas under discussion. Albee contributes to the impression of confusion and provokes response to the mysterious and the unexpressed by leaving thoughts unfinished, relationships undefined, situations unresolved. Through intimation and insinuation he conveys more than he directly states. One has the impression, however, that unlike Beckett, for whom confusion is fundamental to experience, Albee's use of confusion implies private knowledge. Like George in *Who's Afraid of Virginia Woolf?* the playwright teases, "That's for me to know and you to find out" (*Virginia Woolf*, 39).

Albee's first play, *The Zoo Story* (which premiered in Berlin on 28 September 1959 at the Schiller Theater Werkstatt), is an excellent example of Albee's treatment of the unexpressed. It is *The Zoo Story* that we will submit to exegesis in order to illuminate this playwright's distinctive use of the unspoken and the unspeakable as it evolves and develops within the text. In this one-act play, the tightness of which is responsible for its success, anxiety conducted along the lines of miniconversations electrifies the atmosphere and grips Peter in a terrified and escalating frenzy that dissipates only after Jerry's death. As textual analysis will support, these duologues are linked by motifs: interiority/exteriority, tranquility/anxiety, entrapment/free passage, and connection/separation. The unity of setting and the central symbol, the zoo, are integrating bonds between conversational units.

In the initial scene of *The Zoo Story* Peter sits contentedly reading a book on a bench in Central Park on a sunny summer Sunday afternoon. The heat, physical stasis, and solitary presence of Peter combine to evoke an impression of tranquility and fixity. Peter's stasis is broken only by the realistically credible, and symbolically significant, gesture of cleaning his glasses to clarify his vision. Jerry intrudes upon Peter's solitude, his personal space, and his territory in the park.

Engrossed in his book, Peter is aware of neither Jerry's presence nor his silent stare. After a silent moment in which Jerry hopes that his mere presence will initiate conversation, Jerry announces, "I've been to the zoo." Peter does not respond. Frustrated, Jerry more directly addresses Peter, "Mister," and shouts, "I'VE BEEN TO THE ZOO!" That Peter has been oblivious to Jerry's presence and his speech is evidenced by his hesitant, disjunctive response, "Hm? . . . What? . . . I'm sorry, were you talking to me?" Avoiding the rhetorical question, Jerry repeats for the third time that he has been to the zoo, and unwilling to lose Peter's attention now that he has finally gained it, poses a direct question: "Have I been walking north?" Peter, who has been figuratively lost in the world of his book, hesitates to reorient himself to his physical surroundings and determine where he is in relation to the zoo. Tentatively, he responds, "Why . . . I

. . . I think so." In their joint effort to establish the physical distance between this park bench and the zoo, Jerry and Peter establish a relationship that is not so clearly definable or measurable. In fact, Peter's reluctance to establish any verbal contact with Jerry is obvious from the first. He communicates only under duress, his hesitant, inconclusive comments indicative of his desire to return to his reading.[11]

The topic of direction exhausted, their communication breaks off. Peter silently fidgets with his pipe to conceal his uneasiness and annoyance and to avoid further conversation. Ignoring Peter's silence of rejection, Jerry finds the pipe a new source of inspiration and rhetorically remarks, "Well, boy, you're not going to get lung cancer, are you?" Reluctantly drawn back into the conversation, Peter responds, "No, sir." Jerry, repeating Peter's denial and twisting it into an affirmation, observes with shocking frankness, "No, sir. What you'll probably get is cancer of the mouth. . . ." The polite banter has rapidly become combative, progressing from allusions to the zoo to insinuations of disease. Characteristically, Jerry directs the chain of thoughts inward from impersonal to intimate subjects. Claiming not to recall the term *prosthesis*, Jerry again involves Peter in the conversation by direct inquiry. While this lapse of memory is realistically acceptable, and serves to indicate a disparity between educational background (a disparity in life-styles will continually inform their tenuous relationship), it is also a masterful ploy in the language game to draw the opponent out and catch him off balance with flattery. However, Jerry is unsuccessful in eliciting further information from Peter or in sustaining their conversation (*Zoo Story*, 11–14).

The initial conversational unit is characteristic of the manipulative and evasive nature of Albee's dialogue. We recall that in situations where the participants are unknown to each other, "sounding" or "brain battles" are typical verbal strategies employed to determine social strata and relative linguistic prowess.[12] Peter's evasive attitude, which is initially an avoidance of speech, rapidly becomes an avoidance of subject. His vague, noncommittal responses reveal his intention to short-circuit communication, whereas Jerry's direct, provocative, and opinionated remarks are designed to encourage conversation. Colloquial banter is distinguished by the use of repetition and echoing, both immediately apparent. Similarly obvious in the initial unit is Jerry's blunt and shocking use of the unspeakable.

Maintaining linguistic contact is a continual challenge to Jerry. Once again Jerry attempts to draw Peter into conversation and, as was the case in their initial interaction, Peter is lost in his book. In order to engage Peter in conversation, Jerry adopts a direct approach. "Do you mind if we talk?" he inquires. Although Peter denies minding, his hesitant "Why . . . no, no," reinforced by "No, really; I don't mind" and "No; I don't mind at all, really," counterpointed by Jerry's insistent "Yes you do, you do," support the fact that yes, Peter minds. His repetitive denials reveal that he protests too much. Putting away his book and his pipe as a tacit indication of his acquiescence to communication,

Peter leaves unspoken his feeling that this chat with Jerry is neither a welcome diversion nor an opportunity to begin a new friendship. Rather, it is the most expedient way of dealing with this disruptive intrusion.

Jerry initiates their conversation by eradicating linguistically what has been said before. Conversing casually as if they had just met and were exchanging salutory pleasantries, Jerry remarks, "It's . . . it's a nice day." Peter's response is similarly cordial: "Yes. Yes, it is; lovely." Another allusive comment about the zoo precipitates a discussion about Peter's family and we observe that the subject matter, as in the first conversational unit, begins as superficial, social chitchat and rapidly becomes probing and personal. Noting Peter's momentary hesitation about the sex of his children, and sensing intuitively from Peter's bearing and voice (this is neither explained nor expanded) that there will be no more children, Jerry impertinently asks, "Is it your wife?" Jerry insists on saying what is generally left unspoken in social, or even the most personal, conversations. Shocked by the invasion of his privacy, Peter does not respond to the question; rather, he recoils with an evasive "That's none of your business." The silence that follows Peter's outburst allows him a moment to regain his composure while simultaneously focusing attention on the fact that he has not answered the question. His evasive attitude is no longer one of evasion of speech, but rather an avoidance of subject. The motif of Peter's impotence, first intimated here and linked by innuendo to disease, will reiterate throughout the play. Peter finally overcomes his reserve and the awkwardness of the silent moment to concede, "We'll have no more children." Jerry intuitively senses a withdrawal and renewed reticence on the part of Peter, and endeavoring to maintain the line of communication suggests a new direction. "Well, now; what else?" he inquires. Peter, now actively involved in the language game and relieved at the opportunity to change the subject, finds inspiration by returning to an old topic: the zoo. Peter asks, "What were you saying about the zoo . . . that I'd read about it, or see . . . ?" His voice drifts off, the thought incomplete because he has nothing to say about the zoo, but Jerry, who does, chooses to avoid speaking about it. "I'll tell you about it soon," he promises, thereby both switching the topic and keeping it alive in the conversation. We note in the second conversational unit that the zoo, which links this unit to the preceding and succeeding ones, no longer seems to be a specific place. Rather, subjected to allusive reference, the zoo steadily assumes a symbolic significance. And Jerry, who on two occasions announced he had been to the zoo, progressively becomes more mysterious on the subject (*Zoo Story*, 14–19).

Jerry disassociates himself from Peter and the present moment in order to contemplate his strategy and predict the outcome of his plan. "Wait until you see the expression on his face," Jerry mutters to himself, but this fragment of interior monologue is overheard by Peter and it piques his interest. Peter's unanswered questions "What? Whose face?" indicate his confusion, Jerry's distraction, and the psychic distance separating them. In an effort to reorient himself and establish perimeters of discussion, Peter returns to the subject Jerry has raised repeatedly: the zoo. An extended pause allows Jerry a moment to return to the conversation and his reiteration "The zoo? Oh yes, the zoo" firmly fixes the topic on which both are apparently stuck.

In a tantalizing manner Jerry asks, "Do you know what I did before I went to the zoo today?" The question is not answered by Peter, who not only does not know what Jerry did earlier in the day, he does not know anything about this stranger who has intruded upon his privacy and remains an enigma. Peter's efforts to "place" Jerry in recognizable surroundings, as earlier the two had situated the zoo, elicit a disjunctive recitation on the sordid details of Jerry's life. Jerry's garrulity counterpoints Peter's taciturnity, as does his life, his room, and his earthly possessions. Silent and curious, Peter listens attentively as Jerry neatly catalogs his life. Hesitantly breaking his silence occasionally to ask a few questions, Peter's voice drifts off, embarrassed by his own probing. Jerry, sensing that Peter would be more comfortable with another subject, suggests that they talk about the zoo. Although Peter's disquietude has not been explicitly expressed, his excessively enthusiastic "Oh yes, the zoo" implicitly conveys his relief. The motif of the zoo plays a central role in this conversational unit, beginning, concluding, and echoing throughout. With each repetition of "zoo," Jerry is increasingly more evasive and obviously more distracted (*Zoo Story*, 19–27).

Jerry's allusive reference to the zoo is once again reiterated to keep the idea of the zoo alive in Peter's mind, but once again Jerry avoids speaking about the zoo. Typically, he diverts the conversation inward from the literal zoo in Central Park to the metaphoric zoo of the rooming house. As before, Jerry entices, disgusts, and surprises Peter with the directness and vividness of his description. He leaves nothing unspoken and invites response. An apparently articulate and educated man, Peter is reduced to muttering, "That's disgusting. That's . . . horrible." Groping for a more emphatic term to express his revulsion, Peter settles upon "It's so . . . unthinkable." In light of Jerry's description of his zookeeper/landlady and her black dog, Peter's understatement is striking.

Once again Jerry senses Peter's discomfort expressed in his silences. Addressing himself to a thought Peter has as yet left unspoken, Jerry insists, "Don't go," and follows immediately with a question, "You're not thinking of going, are you?" Peter's hesitant denial, "Well . . . no, I don't think so," confirms that yes, he has been thinking about it. First bribing Peter to stay, Jerry reverses his position to conceal his anxiety and fear that Peter would desert him: "You don't have to listen. Nobody is holding you here; remember that. Keep that in your mind." Jerry's comment underscores the motif of literal and figurative entrapment that has been alluded to since the beginning of the play through references to the zoo, caged birds, and cubbyhole rooms, but never explicitly stated.

Although Peter does not express his intention to remain, Jerry, assured of his continued presence by the fact that Peter has not acted on the challenge to leave freely, commences his recital of "The Story of Jerry and the Dog." We observe that hesitations reveal Jerry's effort to recall details and fix a portrait, and in concert with his agitated pacing, expose his increasing anxiety and fluctuating emotional state. The dog, as Jerry graphically describes him, is

> a black monster of a beast: an oversized head, tiny, tiny, ears, and eyes . . . bloodshot, infected, maybe; and a body you can see the ribs through the skin. The dog is black, all black; all black except the bloodshot eyes and . . . yes . . . and an open sore on its . . . *right* forepaw; that is red, too. And, oh yes; the poor monster, and I do believe it's an old dog . . . it's certainly a misused one . . .

Interrupting his speech repeatedly with "and" and "Oh, yes" and linking his disjunctive phrases with "so," Jerry recounts a story about his attempt to effect contact with the dog. Breaking the flow of the story, the narrator explains, "I hoped . . . and I don't really know why I expected the dog to understand anything, much less my motivations . . . I hoped that the dog would understand." Whereas earlier in his conversation with Peter, Jerry found it easy to bring order out of the chaos of his phenomenal reality, the chaos of psychological reality is more elusive and defies what Jerry terms "the old pigeon-hole bit." Starting to speak and breaking off his speech three times, "It's just . . . ," he finds it increasingly more difficult to delineate specifically what is essentially elusive and ambiguous. Jerry tests one image after another, and characteristically repeating a term or a phrase he is pleased with, he anticipates his summation with the rhetorical question, "Where better, where ever better in this humiliating excuse for a jail, where better to communicate one single, simpleminded idea than an entrance hall? Where?" Although it remains unspoken, Jerry's questions also imply, Who better to relate the story to than an intelligent, sensitive, attentive, and silent witness? In the beginning of the recitation, Peter's silence reflected well-mannered listening. However, in response to Jerry's story, the nature of the silence metamorphoses from a silence of contemplation to a silence of evasion, of confusion, of protest, of rejection. Peter's physical and linguistic rigidity belies the fluctuation of his emotions and sharply contrasts with Jerry's loquacity and agitated movement. His story concluded, the narrator is spent, and for the first time this afternoon, Jerry collapses on the bench next to the apparently hypnotized observer (*Zoo Story*, 27–36).

Recalling Pozzo in *En attendant Godot*, Jerry presses Peter for a review: "Well, Peter? . . . Well, Peter? . . . tell me what you think." Still stunned, Peter's disjunctive responses reflect his confused state: "I don't understand what . . . I don't think I . . ." Jerry's direct question "Why not?" goes unanswered as Peter evasively insists: "I DON'T UNDERSTAND!" Once again we observe that Peter intentionally leaves unspoken his true feelings on a subject. The repeated denials convince Jerry, as they did on several occasions earlier in the afternoon, that Peter is lying.

In "Tragic Vision in *The Zoo Story*," Bennett suggests that Jerry has risked a great deal in entrusting himself to Peter's understanding; failing to communicate with Peter confines Jerry to an even greater isolation.[13] Rather than admit the depth of his disappointment, Jerry assumes responsibility for Peter's failure to understand his story. "I don't know what I was thinking about," Jerry confesses. Significantly, it is now Jerry whose repeated denials cast doubt on the truthfulness of his statement. Noting that he did not know what he was thinking about, Jerry continues, "Of course you don't understand. *(In a monotone wearily)* I don't live on your block; I'm not married to two parakeets."

Having exhausted the topic of the dog, the roominghouse, and himself, Jerry once again initiates a new direction in the dialogue by direct inquiry: "Peter, do I annoy you, or confuse you?" Characteristically, Peter avoids the question and conceals his evasion of the subject by admitting that he had anticipated a different kind of afternoon. The mention of expectation raises for the first time the previously unspecified issue of concern with chronological progression. By continual repetitions, particularly of "zoo," and by nonprogressional pauses and incompleted statements, Albee has fashioned a fragment of time and entrapped Peter and Jerry in it. Consulting his watch, Peter concludes that having spent the afternoon with Jerry, it is time that he went home. Peter is once again coerced into remaining, but rather than employ verbal manipulation, Jerry establishes contact by the nonverbal technique of tickling. In an effort to prolong Peter's presence, Jerry returns to the topic of the zoo and admits that now, finally, he will tell Peter what happened at the zoo. His tension relaxed by the tickling, Peter is attentive, waiting for the recitation to begin, but he is singularly unprepared for Jerry's sudden verbal and physical abuse. Jerry's figurative victimization and entrapment of Peter metamorphose into a substantive reality. Repeatedly Jerry pokes Peter and commands, "Move over!" With each repetition, the punch is harder, the demand more emphatic. Finally, Jerry, who has been explicitly and implicitly monitoring and directing Peter's behavior throughout this long afternoon, directs the latter to remove himself to another bench. "I want this bench," he insists. Peter, ever logical, cannot understand Jerry's request. Clinging to a world of law and order and logical relationships, Peter rejects Jerry's demands. What ensues is a linguistic struggle for territory that descends into a physical struggle for survival.

In contrast with his former laconism, Peter begins to lecture Jerry in proper behavior, but Jerry typically counterpoints Peter's adult logic with infantile name-calling, labeling Peter "slow-witted" and a "vegetable." Peter's attempts to reason with Jerry are short-circuited by the latter's disjunctive outbursts, "Oh, what is the word I want to put justice to your . . . JESUS, you make me sick . . . get off here and give me my bench." He may not have found the word to "put justice" to Peter, but in employing the possessive pronoun "my," he has found the word to enrage Peter. The cause of Jerry's attack, suggests Bennett, may be traced to Peter's refusal to understand Jerry's confessional story.[14] Although not explicitly expressed at that time or since, Jerry's frustration has taken the form of nonverbal tickling and verbal aggression. Moreover, as Jerry provokes Peter into a physical confrontation, he simultaneously wears him down by twisting logic, Peter's principal defense, into a weapon against him:

> *Jerry:* Why? You have everything in the world you want; you told me about your home, and your family, and your *own* little zoo. You have every-thing, and now you want this bench. Are these the things men fight for? Tell me, Peter, is this bench, this iron and this wood, is this your honor? Is this the thing in the world you'd fight for? Can you think of anything more absurd?
>
> *Peter:* Absurd? Look, I'm not going to talk to you about honor, or even try to explain it to you. Besides, it isn't a question of honor; but even if it were, you wouldn't understand.

We observe that in this duologue, typical of their linguistic interaction through-out the play, Jerry provokes Peter by a series of direct questions. Peter, avoiding the questions, leaves them unanswered and raises other issues that camouflage the fact that he has not addressed himself to Jerry's questions. Close examination of Peter's response reveals that whereas he claims the "battle of the bench" is not "a question of honor," he does not specifically delineate what it *is* a question of. Their relationship is essentially defined by what they understand and are unwilling to admit, whether they speak of dogs and hamburger patties or benches and honor.

Pushed to his limits, Peter declares war: "THAT'S ENOUGH." His composure is displaced by hysteria, his methodical reasoning and thoughtful contemplation by stichomythic utterances. Faced with Jerry's switchblade, Peter shouts, "You *are* mad! You're stark raving mad!"—the qualification and repetition imbuing the repeated terms with new meaning. Peter struggles to break free of Jerry, whose physical and linguistic jabbing have him trapped, but Jerry, who has planned this Strindbergian "brain battle" down to the last skirmish, has saved his most devastating weapon for last. Spitting in Peter's face and employing the unspeakable, Jerry taunts his opponent, "You couldn't even get your wife with a male child." Enraged, Peter typically avoids both the statement and the implications and seeks refuge and support in logic. He begins to explain to Jerry that gender is a matter of genetics, but is suddenly cognizant of his audience and the fact that Jerry has not only dared to deprive him of his bench, but has also spoken the unspeakable. Brandishing the knife that Jerry has dropped, Peter offers Jerry escape, as earlier in the afternoon Jerry reminded Peter that he was free to leave. Jerry accepts the challenge by impaling himself on the knife. For a moment there is silence and stasis: Peter in paralyzed shock that Jerry has killed himself on the knife he holds; Jerry in paralyzed shock that he is dying. The silent moment is displaced by the screams of both. Peter's rhythmic repetitions of "Oh my God, oh my God, oh my God . . ." counterpoint Jerry's disjunctive conclusion to the story of Jerry and the "vegetable." The repetitions of "I think" and "You know" that similarly concluded "The Story of Jerry and the Dog" underscore the unreality of the incident and the certainty that it has occurred. Significantly, Jerry's actions and motivations remain undefined.

Repetitions, pauses, and echoing continue to reinforce the impression of stasis. In this apparently fixed moment in time, Jerry is acutely aware of the swift passage of time, whereas Peter, mute, frozen in time and space, exhibits no awareness of chronological progression. Repeatedly Jerry encourages Peter, "You'd better hurry now, Peter. Hurry, you'd better go." Peter neither moves nor speaks. Continually urged to flee, Peter hurries away with a howl: "OH MY GOD!" Ironically, Peter's final shriek is echoed disjointedly by the dying Jerry, whose "scornful mimicry and supplication" add a new dimension to "Oh . . . my . . . God." Peter has earned his "solitary free passage," but as Jerry had indicated in "The Story of Jerry and the Dog," such passage is gained at a loss greater than gain (*Zoo Story*, 36–49).

Unlike the story of the dog, the zoo story is not recited to a passive, silent witness, but rather dramatically presented with the active participation of the witness. The story conveyed elliptically through suggestion, innuendo, invective, groping speech, and silences is in fact a dramatization of what happened in the park. The fixity of the initial scene is recalled in the final tableau; Peter, who was seated comfortably on the park bench, is supplanted by Jerry's crumpled body. Death has concluded their struggle and precluded Peter's return.

In this drama, which relies so heavily on what is implied rather than specifically stated, what is suggested rather than what is comprehended, the final emphasis falls not to Jerry, but to Peter. Whereas Jerry's suffering terminates by suicide or by murder (a fact that Albee leaves ambiguous), the nature and duration of Peter's suffering is undefined. We surmise that the loss of the bench, the loss of tranquility, the loss of the protection and peace of this garden spot, will be a much greater loss than gain. Anne Paolucci observes that nowhere else in Albee's early work is "the existential vacuum drawn so boldly to resemble powerful affirmation."[15] Indeed, such critics as Rose Zimbardo have suggested that Jerry's death, comparable to that of Jesus, conveys the transference of awareness.[16] Rather than affirmation, the conclusion of this drama, supported by Jerry's mocking supplication and Peter's silence, gains resonance from all that Albee has chosen not to define and to delimit. Comparable to thoughts that typically drift off incompleted in Albee's drama, the end of this play is similarly incomplete and unresolved. Through insinuation rather than explicit statement this playwright implies that Peter, now a "permanent transient," will be isolated not only by the unspoken, but also by the unspeakable.

Richard Gilman suggests that "human reality can best be apprehended today by indirect, by 'inhuman' methods, which means a step beyond the literal, the behavioral, the natural."[17] In *The Zoo Story* and in the other plays under discussion in this study, we observe that Albee moves beyond the literal to the metaphoric, the behavioral to the psychological, the natural to the unreal in order to convey an authentic portrait of mysterious and confusing empirical and psychological experience.

NOTES

1. Edward Albee, *A Delicate Balance* (New York: Pocket Books, 1968), 83 (references hereafter will be to this edition).

2. Ruby Cohn, *Currents in Contemporary Drama* (Bloomington: University of Indiana Press, 1969), 4.

3. Anne Paolucci, *From Tension to Tonic: The Plays of Edward Albee*, Cross-Currents (Carbondale: Southern Illinois University Press, 1972), 65–66.

4. Foster Hirsch, *Who's Afraid of Edward Albee?* (Berkeley, Calif.: Creative Arts, 1978), 5.

5. Edward Albee, *All Over* (New York: Pocket Books, 1974), 17 (references hereafter will be to this edition).

6. Northrup Frye, *Anatomy of Criticism: Four Essays* (Princeton, N.J.: Princeton University Press, 1957), 156.

7. Albee, quoted in Michael Rutenberg, *Edward Albee: Playwright in Protest* (New York: DBS, 1969), 247.

8. Robert B. Bennett, "Tragic Vision in *The Zoo Story*," *Modern Drama* 20, no. 1 (March 1977): 55–56, makes this point in connection with Christian symbolism in *The Zoo Story*.

9. Edward Albee, *"Counting the Ways" and "Listening"* (New York: Atheneum, 1977), 99 (references hereafter will be to this edition).

10. R. S. Stuart, "John Gielgud and Edward Albee Talk about the Theatre," *Atlantic Monthly* 215, no. 4 (1965): 61–68, reprinted in *Edward Albee: A Collection of Critical Essays*, ed. C. W. E. Bigsby, 112–23, Twentieth Century Views (Englewood Cliffs, N.J.: Prentice-Hall, 1975), 121 (hereafter cited as *Edward Albee*).

11. One is reminded of the tension between Clov and Hamm in *Fin de partie*, and of Clov's efforts to break off communication and return to his kitchen.

12. See Chapter 1 in which I examine "sounding" and "brain battles" in greater depth.

13. Bennett, "Tragic Vision," 62.

14. Bennett, "Tragic Vision," 64, suggests that after Jerry's disappointment with Peter's reaction to the dog story, Jerry replaces words, in which he no longer has faith, with nonverbal, physical forms of contact.

15. Paolucci, *From Tension to Tonic*, 44.

16. Rose A. Zimbardo, "Symbolism and Naturalism in Edward Albee's *The Zoo Story*," in *Edward Albee*, 45–53.

17. Richard Gilman, *Common and Uncommon Masks: Writings on Theatre, 1961–1970* (New York: Random House, 1971), 136.

Conclusion

In this book I have tried to trace chronologically the tendency of the modern playwright to retreat from the word. Focusing on the nature and function of the unexpressed in the theatre of Maeterlinck, Chekhov, Bernard, Beckett, Pinter, and Albee, I suggest explanations for and provide illustrations of the elevated prestige of silence and its role as dramatic structure and statement.

Through language—structured, sequential, human—man seeks to humanize, define, and control the chaos of external and internal experience and with its essential correlative—time—to order and measure directional progression. Silence, on the other hand, is infinite. A nonverbal, nonanthropomorphic mode of communication, neither bound to nor fragmented by time, silence is a perfect medium for the multiplicity of human responses antithetic to place, time, and clarity. Historically, dramatists have rejected speech and employed silence to evaluate or censure an act, to indicate manipulative relationships, to increase or release tension, and to emphasize the significance of particular words. Since the end of the nineteenth century, however, silence has repeatedly been the chosen response of character and playwright.

Robert Brustein, describing drama of the Western world as a trajectory that arches from belief to uncertainty to unbelief, suggests that the movement is always in the direction of a greater skepticism in regard to temporal and spiritual laws.[1] Reflecting this skepticism and acknowledging human limitation, the playwright employs ellipses, pauses, and silences to authenticate the portrait of psychic and phenomenal reality, to emphasize the gap between comprehended experience and articulated experience, between one person and another and between each person and the world. For the artist for whom "art has nothing to do with clarity, does not dabble in the clear and does not make clear," silence is both medium and message.[2]

It is this artist who assumes the posture of the inarticulate or mute essentially to underscore his own uncertainty, his own inability to *speak* with certainty, who is the focus of our attention. The retreat from the word in the nineteenth century emphasized the untranslatability of inner experience. This rejection of verbal concordance is intensified when the twentieth-century dramatist does battle with the minotaur langauge and finds that he is trapped in a maze of possibilities, ambiguities, questions, and contradictions. Disbelief in ideas, in the mental virility that engenders them, in the meaning and importance they would convey, in the illumination they would hope to yield, and in the permanence they would attain, largely explains the contemporary playwright's reliance on silent communication. Torn from his religious, metaphysical, and transcendental roots, modern man discards the anthropomorphic assumption that the infinity of time and space can be limited and defined, that the chaos of interior and exterior reality can be understood and verbalized. The playwright refuses to play God with his characters, refuses to pull their strings and make them speak inexpressible doubt and anguish. Relinquishing the role of omniscient, the modern dramatist acknowledges that he can no more know the mind, motivations, and machinations of his characters then he can his own.

Striving for authenticity in an age when spiritual, empirical, and metaphysical certainty is conspicuous by its absence, illusion and reality, sleep and wakefulness, life and death, vision and blindness, interiority and exteriority, and speech and silence exist concomitantly. The coalescence of these variables and the silence of the playwright reinforces the sensation of disorientation and discontinuity. Indefiniteness is both subject and structure.

Pinter maintains that in a world characterized by doubt, we can only say with certainty that "the more acute the experience, the less articulate its expression."[3] Thus the playwright concerned with acute experience—isolation, bewilderment, terror—is faced with the awesome dilemma of how to speak about what must, by its nature, remain unspoken. Even more challenging to the postwar playwright is how to speak about the unspeakable—that which cannot be verbalized because the experience it would hope to illuminate exceeds the defining act of human consciousness—speech. Whereas the unspoken resists our ability to communicate subjective reality and abstract concepts through words, the unspeakable defies not only our articulation, but also our comprehension. Crying out from Picasso's *Guernica*, or from postwar drama, unspeakable silence communicates the personal and global disintegration that typifies our age, as transition and doubt characterized the late nineteenth century.

Samuel Beckett suggests that the essential inexplicability, the chaos, of experience, exerts increased demands on artistic form:

> What I am saying does not mean that there will henceforth be no more form in art. It only means that there will be new form, and that this form will be of such a type that it admits the chaos and does not try to say the chaos is really something else. The form and the chaos remain separate. The latter is not reduced to the former. That is why the form itself becomes a preoccupation, because it exists as a problem separate from the material it accommodates.[4]

The problem of a dramatic form to accommodate the ineffable, the inexplicable "chaos" of which Beckett speaks is one that has preoccupied modern dramatists for the last eighty years. Fin de siècle playwrights Maeterlinck and Chekhov found silence, which is characteristically ambiguous, mysterious, suggestive, and infinite, an excellent dramatic device to convey such undefined, abstract concepts as death and fear and to elicit interior states of being: contemplation, reverie, nostalgia, withdrawal, helplessness, and rejection. Increasingly in our century, notable for its scientific and psychological discoveries, global conflagration, and dehumanization, silence functions as a metaphor for solitary confinement. Entrapment, both within the world and within the self, both literal and figurative, informs the elevated status of silent reponse in postwar drama. The writer who attempts to communicate that which eludes language— isolation, evanescence, inhumanity—finds that language is inadequate to the task. Rejecting continuous, conceptual dialogue, he obliquely portrays personal and global disintegration through an elliptical, hesitant linguistic structure and evocative silences.

Although the elevated status of silence in modern drama characterizes distinctive artistic expression, we observe several obvious areas of compatibility in the theatre of these dramatists: disjunctive, colloquial, bivalent expression; the motif of waiting; the paradigm of arrival/departure; the exploitation of physical, emotional, and linguistic entrapment; apparently quiescent structure that belies psychological and cyclical fluctuation; the reliance on silent response; the use of symbols; the use of the inarticulate and/or mute; the use of pauses and silences that realistically indicate hesitation to find a word, recover a lost thought, qualify or modify a word, and allow time for response while simultaneously stalling the progression of thought, action, and time; the paradigm of substantial, insubstantial, and ephemeral intrusions; and the use of repetitions concomitantly with the technique of echoing to convey mood, expose distracted and compulsive behavior, and imply change between initial and successive use.

The compatibility of theme and technique in the work of these dramatists suggests a compatibility of attitude, a unity between otherwise disparate and distinctive playwrights. When viewed chronologically, the development and the refinement of a language of silence confirms a continuity of linguistic experimentation. It also confirms a continuing commitment to convey personal and political disjunction through disjunctive expression. For these playwrights silence is neither above, beneath, nor behind the text; it is an intrinsic and indispensable component of the text.

In the opinion of such esteemed critics as Robert Corrigan and Eric Bentley, the increased tendency of the drama to incorporate silence (and its concomitant stasis) as an integral element of the dramatic spectacle, bespeaks the demise of the genre.[5] Corrigan contends, moreover, that the "reticence, inarticulateness and homely idiom of our theatre," which was a healthy reaction to the hollow rhetoric of the romantic play (he refers specifically to Chekhov), is now a "lazy abdication, an inarticulateness which is not dramatically significant."[6] Rather than "lazy abdication," the drama of neonaturalist David Storey and of Marguerite Duras, to cite only two of the many dramatists currently experimenting with the unexpressed, would seem to contradict Corrigan's criticism.

An age plagued by disorder, disjunction, and dehumanization no longer finds credible the anthropocentric effort to hold the world together by human measurement, chronological progression, or human discursiveness, syntactical connection. Frank Kermode, whose *Sense of an Ending* poses the problem of time and its relationship to language in modern fiction, confirms that "ours is a world crying out for forms and stations and apocalypse"; in lieu of order and meaning and chronicity, all is "vain temporality, mad, multiform, antithetical influx."[7] Relying heavily on silence, the playwright synthesizes transitional states of simultaneity, stasis, and evanescence by the expansion and compression of time; past, present, and future coalesce in a world of silence to communicate perpetual crisis and illimitable chaos.

For the playwrights under discussion in this study, and for those currently experimenting with the unspoken and the unspeakable, silence is not merely an aesthetic technique; it is an intrinsic part of the writer's perspective on the viability of dramatic literature in his age.

NOTES

1. Robert Brustein, *The Theatre of Revolt: An Approach to Modern Drama* (Boston: Little, Brown, 1962), 5.

2. Beckett, quoted in John Fletcher, *Samuel Beckett's Art* (New York: Barnes and Noble, 1967), 17.

3. Harold Pinter, program of the Royal Court Theatre production of *The Room* and *The Dumb Waiter*, 8 March 1960, quoted in Martin Esslin, *The Peopled Wound: The Work of Harold Pinter* (Garden City, N.Y.: Anchor-Doubleday, 1970), 34.

4. Beckett, quoted in Tom F. Driver, "Beckett by the Madeleine," *Columbia University Forum* 4 (Summer 1961): 21–25, reprinted in *Drama in the Modern World*, ed. Samuel Weiss (Lexington, Mass.: D. C. Heath, 1974), 456.

5. See Robert W. Corrigan, "The Theatre in Search of a Fix," in *The Theatre in Search of a Fix*, (New York: Dell, 1973), 253–65; Eric Bentley, *The Playwright as Thinker: A Study of Modern Drama in Modern Times* (New York: Harcourt, Brace, 1946). It is Bentley's position that "*a drama not verbalized is a drama not dramatized.*"

6. Corrigan, *Theatre in Search of a Fix*, 263.

7. Frank Kermode, *The Sense of an Ending: Studies in the Theory of Fiction* (London: Oxford University Press, 1967), 115.

Works Consulted

Abel, Lionel. *Metatheatre: A New View of Dramatic Form*. New York: Hill and Wang, 1963.

Albee, Edward. *A Delicate Balance*. New York: Pocket Books, 1968.

———. *All Over*. New York: Pocket Books, 1974.

———. *"The American Dream" and "The Zoo Story."* New York: New American Library, 1961.

———. *"Counting the Ways" and "Listening."* New York: Atheneum, 1977.

———. *Who's Afraid of Virginia Woolf?* New York: Pocket Books, 1964.

Amacher, Richard E. *Edward Albee*. Twayne's United States Authors Series, no. 141. New York: Twayne, 1969.

Andrieu, Jean-Marie. *Maeterlinck*. Paris: Editions Universitaires, 1962.

Bair, Deirdre. *Samuel Beckett*. New York: Harcourt, Brace, 1978.

Baird, Jay W. *The Mythical World of Nazi Propaganda, 1939–45*. Minneapolis: University of Minnesota Press, 1974.

Balakian, Anna. *The Symbolist Movement: A Critical Appraisal*. New York: Random House, 1967.

Beckerman, Bernard. "Artifice of 'Reality' in Chekhov and Pinter." *Modern Drama* 21, no. 2 (June 1978): 153–61.

Beckett, Samuel. *Come and Go*. In *Modern Drama* 19, no. 3 (September 1976): 257–60.

———. *En attendant Godot*. Paris: Editions de Minuit, 1952.

———. *"Fin de partie" et "Actes sans paroles."* Paris: Editions de Minuit, 1957.

———. *Footfalls*. In *Ends and Odds*. New York: Grove Press, 1974.

———. *Happy Days*. New York: Grove Press, 1961.

———. *L'Innommable*. Paris: Editions de Minuit, 1953.

———. *"Krapp's Last Tape" and Other Dramatic Pieces*. New York: Grove Press, 1960.

———. *"Nouvelles" et "Textes pour rien."* Paris: Editions de Minuit, 1954.

———. *Proust*. New York: Grove Press, 1931.

Beckett at 60: A Festschrift. Edited by John Calder. London: Calder and Boyars, 1967.

Bennett, Robert B. "Tragic Vision in *The Zoo Story*." *Modern Drama* 20, no. 1 (March 1977): 55–56.

Bentley, Eric. *The Life of the Drama*. New York: Atheneum, 1964.

———. *The Playwright as Thinker: A Study of Drama in Modern Times*. New York: Harcourt, Brace, 1946.

Bergson, Henri. *Durée et simultanéité: A propos de la théorie d'Einstein*. Paris: Librairie Félix Alcan, 1926.

Bernard, Jean-Jacques. *Théâtre I: Le Feu qui reprend mal, Martine, Le Printemps des autres, L'Invitation au voyage.* Paris: Editions Albin Michel, 1925.

———. *Mon ami le théâtre.* Paris: Editions Albin Michel, 1958.

———. *Nationale 6.* Edited by Alexander Y. Kroff and Karl G. Bottke. New York: Appleton-Century-Crofts, 1950.

Bithel, Jethro. *Life and Writings of Maurice Maeterlinck.* London: Walter Scott, 1913.

Block, Haskell. *Mallarmé and the Symbolist Drama.* Detroit, Mich.: Wayne State University Press, 1963.

Bodart, Roger. *Maurice Maeterlinck.* Paris: Editions Pierre Seghers, 1962.

Bodkin, Maud. *Archetypal Patterns in Poetry.* 1934. Reprint. London: Oxford University Press, 1963.

Bonnerot, Sylviane. *Le Théâtre de 1920 à 1950.* Ensembles Littéraires. Paris: Masson, 1972.

Bradley, A. C. *Shakespearean Tragedy.* 1904. Reprint. Greenwich, Conn.: Fawcett, n.d.

Breuer, Rolf. "The Solution as Problem: Beckett's *Waiting for Godot.*" *Modern Drama* 19, no. 3 (September 1976): 225–36.

Brienza, Susan D. "Time in *How It Is:* 'Something Wrong There.'" Paper presented at the convention of the Modern Language Association, New York, 28 December 1978.

Brunel, Pierre. "Anton Tchekhov et Marguerite Duras: Le contrepoint du temps réel et du temps psychologique." In *La Mort de Godot: Attente et évanescence au théâtre,* edited by Pierre Brunel, 43–73. Situations, no. 23. Paris: Lettres Modernes Minard, 1970.

———. "Autour de Samuel Beckett: Devanciers, épigones et hérétiques." In *La Mort de Godot: Attente et évanescence au théâtre,* edited by Pierre Brunel, 11–39. Situations, no. 23. Paris: Lettres Modernes Minard, 1970.

Brustein, Robert. "Albee Decorates an Old House: *A Delicate Balance.*" In *Edward Albee: A Collection of Critical Essays,* edited by C. W. E. Bigsby, 135–37. Englewood Cliffs, N.J.: Prentice-Hall, 1975.

———. *The Theatre of Revolt: An Approach to Modern Drama.* Boston: Little, Brown, 1962.

Bucher, Bernadette. "Edward Albee ou la mort de Godot: Vers une dramaturgie structuraliste." In *La Mort de Godot: Attente et évanescence au théâtre,* edited by Pierre Brunel, 155–91. Situations, no. 23. Paris: Lettres Modernes Minard, 1970.

Bunin, Ivan A. "A. P. Tchekhov." In *Anton Tchekhov: Literary and Theatrical Reminiscences,* translated and edited by S. S. Koteliansky, 86–97. 1927. Reprint. London: Benjamin Blom, 1965.

Burkman, Katherine H. *The Dramatic World of Harold Pinter: Its Basis in Ritual.* Columbus: Ohio State University Press, 1971.

Case, Sue-Ellen. "Image and Godot." In *Casebook on "Waiting for Godot,"* edited by Ruby Cohn, 155–59. New York: Grove Press, 1967.

Chase, Stuart, with Marian Tyler Chase. *Power of Words.* New York: Harcourt, Brace, 1953.

Chekhov, Anton. *Four Great Plays: The Sea Gull, The Cherry Orchard, The Three Sisters, Uncle Vanya.* Translated by Constance Garnett. New York: Random House, 1930.

———. *The Selected Letters of Anton Chekhov.* Translated by Sidonie Lederer; edited by Lillian Hellman. New York: Farrar, Straus, 1955.

Chevigny, Bell Gale. Introduction. In *Twentieth Century Interpretations of "Endgame,"* edited by Bell Gale Chevigny, 1–13. Englewood Cliffs, N.J.: Prentice-Hall, 1969.

Chiari, Joseph. *Landmarks of Contemporary Drama*. London: Herbert Jenkins, 1965.

Cismaru, Alfred. *Marguerite Duras*. Twayne's World Authors Series, no. 147. New York: Twayne, 1971.

Coe, Richard. *Samuel Beckett*. Rev. ed. New York: Grove Press, 1968.

Cohn, Ruby, *Back to Beckett*. Princeton, N.J.: Princeton University Press, 1973.

————. *Currents in Contemporary Drama*. Bloomington: Indiana University Press, 1969.

————. *Samuel Beckett: The Comic Gamut*. New Brunswick, N.J.: Rutgers University Press, 1962.

————. "The World of Harold Pinter." *Tulane Drama Review* 6, no. 3 (March 1962): 55–68. Reprinted in *Pinter: A Collection of Critical Essays*, edited by Arthur Ganz, 78–92. Twentieth Century Views. Englewood Cliffs, N.J.: Prentice-Hall, 1972.

Corrigan, Robert W. *The Theatre in Search of a Fix*. New York: Dell, 1973.

Crémieux, Benjamin. *Inquiétude et reconstruction: Essai sur la littérature d'après-guerre*. Inventaires. Paris: R. A. Corrêa, 1931.

————. "Cronique dramatique: conclusions provisoires." *Nouvelle revue française* (1 October 1927): 529–33.

Daniels, May. *The French Drama of the Unspoken*. Language and Literature, no. 3. Edinburgh: Edinburgh University Press, 1953.

Davidowicz, Lucy S. *The War against the Jews, 1933–45*. New York: Bantam, 1976.

Debusscher, Gilbert. *Edward Albee: Tradition and Renewal*. Translated by Anne D. Williams. Brussels: American Studies Center, 1967.

Delpit, Louise. *Tableau de mouvement dramatique en France de 1925 à 1938: Deuxième partie*. Smith College Studies in Modern Languages. Northampton, Mass.: Smith College, n.d.

Doisy, Marcel. *Le Théâtre française contemporain*. Brussels: Editions "La Boitie," 1947.

Donneux, Guy. *Maurice Maeterlinck: Une poésie, une sagesse, un homme*. Brussels: Palais des Académies, 1961.

Driver, Tom F. "Beckett by the Madeleine." *Columbia University Forum* 4 (Summer 1961): 21–25. Reprinted in *Drama in the Modern World*, edited by Samuel Weiss, 455–58. Lexington, Mass.: D. C. Heath, 1974.

Duckworth, Colin. *Angels of Darkness: Dramatic Effect in Samuel Beckett with Special Reference to Eugène Ionesco*. New York: Barnes and Noble, 1972.

————. "The Making of *Godot*." In *Casebook on "Waiting for Godot,"* edited by Ruby Cohn, 89–100. New York: Grove Press, 1967.

Duras, Marguerite. *Théâtre I: Les Eaux et forêts, Le Square, La Musica*. Paris: Editions Gallimard, 1965.

————. *Théâtre II: Suzanne Andler; Des journées entières dans les arbres; Yes, peut-être; Le Shaga; Un Homme est venue me voir*. Paris: Editions Gallimard, 1968.

Ehrenburg, Ilya. "On Re-Reading Chekhov." In his *Chekhov, Stendhal and Other Essays*, translated by Anna Bostock in collaboration with Yvonne Kapp. London: MacGibbon and Kee, 1962, 11–77.

Eliot, T. S. "'Rhetoric'" and Poetic Drama." In his *Selected Essays*. 1932. Reprint. New York: Harcourt, Brace, 1950, 25–30.

Esslin, Martin. "*Godot* and His Children: The Theatre of Samuel Beckett and Harold Pinter." *Experimental Drama* 14 (1965): 128–46. Reprinted in *Modern British Dramatists:*

A Collection of Critical Essays, edited by John Russell Brown, 58–70. Twentieth Century Views. Englewood Cliffs, N.J.: Prentice-Hall, 1968.

———. Introduction. *Samuel Beckett: A Collection of Critical Essays*, edited by Martin Esslin, 1–15. Twentieth Century Views. Englewood Cliffs, N.J.: Prentice-Hall, 1965.

———. *The Peopled Wound: The Work of Harold Pinter*. Garden City, N.Y.: Anchor-Doubleday, 1970.

———. *The Theatre of the Absurd*. Rev. ed. Garden City, N.Y. Anchor-Doubleday, 1969.

Farb, Peter. *Word Play: What Happens When People Talk*. New York: Knopf, 1973.

Fergusson, Francis. *The Idea of a Theater*. Princeton, N.J.: Princeton University Press, 1949.

Fletcher, John. *Samuel Beckett's Art*. New York: Barnes and Noble, 1967.

Frye, Northrop. *Anatomy of Criticism: Four Essays*. Princeton, N.J.: Princeton University Press, 1957.

Gale, Steven H. *Butter's Going Up*. Durham, N.C.: Duke University Press, 1977.

Gallagher, Kent G. "Harold Pinter's Dramaturgy." *Quarterly Journal of Speech* 52, no. 3 (October 1966): 242–48.

Ganz, Arthur. Introduction. *Pinter: A Collection of Critical Essays*, edited Arthur Ganz, 1–18. Twentieth Century Views. Englewood Cliffs, N.J.: Prentice-Hall, 1972.

———. "Mixing Memory and Desire: Pinter's Vision in *Landscape, Silence* and *Old Times*." In *Pinter: A Collection of Critical Essays*, edited by Arthur Ganz, 161–78. Twentieth Century Views, Englewood Cliffs, N.J.: Prentice-Hall, 1972.

Gerhardi, William Alexander. *Anton Chekov: A Critical Study*. Rev. ed. 1923. Reprint. London: MacDonald, 1974.

Gilman, Richard. *Common and Uncommon Masks: Writings on Theatre, 1961–70*. New York: Random House, 1971.

———. "Out Goes Absurdism—In Comes the New Naturalism." *New York Times*, 19 March 1978.

Gorky, Maxim. "Fragmentary Reminiscences." In *Anton Tchekhov: Literary and Theatrical Reminiscences*, translated and edited by S. S. Koteliansky, 98–101. 1927. Reprint. London: Benjamin Blom, 1965.

Greene, Alice Borchard. *The Philosophy of Silence*. New York: Richard R. Smith, 1940.

Guichardnaud, Jacques, with June Beckerman. *Modern French Drama from Giraudoux to Beckett*. New Haven, Conn.: Yale University Press, 1961.

Gussow, Mel. "A Conversation (Pause) with Harold Pinter." *New York Times Magazine*, 5 December 1971, 42–43, 126–36.

Halls, W. D. *Maurice Maeterlinck: A Study of His Life and Thought*. Oxford: Clarendon Press, 1960.

Hanse, Joseph M. "La Genèse de *L'Intruse*." In *Le Centenaire de Maurice Maeterlinck, 1862–1962*, compiled by the Académie Royale de Langue et de Littérature Françaises, 177–202. Brussels: Palais des Académies, 1964.

Hassan, Ihab. *The Dismemberment of Orpheus: Toward a Post-Modern Literature*. New York: Oxford University Press, 1971.

———. *The Literature of Silence: Henry Miller and Samuel Beckett*. New York: Knopf, 1967.

Hatzfeld, Helmut. *Trends and Styles in Twentieth Century French Literature*. Rev. and enl. ed. Washington, D.C.: Catholic University of America Press, 1966.

Hayakawa, S. I. *Language in Action*. New York: Harcourt, Brace, 1939.

Helsa, David H. *The Shape of Chaos: An Interpretation of the Art of Samuel Beckett*. Minneapolis: University of Minnesota Press, 1971.

Hingley, Ronald. *Chekhov: A Biographical and Critical Study*. Rev. ed. 1950. London: George Allen & Unwin, 1966.

Hirsch, Foster. *Who's Afraid of Edward Albee?* Berkeley, Calif.: Creative Arts, 1978.

Hoffman, Frederick J. *Samuel Beckett: The Language of Self*. Carbondale: Southern Illinois University Press, 1962.

Hollis, James R. *Harold Pinter: The Poetics of Silence*. Carbondale: Southern Illinois University Press, 1970.

Hurêt, Jules. *Enquête sur l'évolution littéraire*. Paris: Fasquelle, 1891.

Ionesco, Eugène. *Journal en miettes*. Paris: Mercure de France, 1967.

Jackson, Robert Louis. Introduction. In *Chekhov: A Collection of Critical Essays*, edited by Robert Louis Jackson, 1–20. Twentieth Century Views. Englewood Cliffs, N.J.: Prentice-Hall, 1967.

Janvier, Ludovic. *Pour Samuel Beckett*. Arguments, no. 27. Paris: Editions de Minuit, 1966.

Jones, Robert Emmet. *The Alienated Hero in Modern French Drama*. University of Georgia Monographs. no. 9. Athens: University of Georgia Press, 1962.

Kahn, Beverly. *Chekhov: A Study of the Major Stories and Plays*. Major European Authors. Cambridge: Cambridge University Press, 1977.

Kermode, Frank. *The Sense of an Ending: Studies in the Theory of Fiction*. London: Oxford University Press, 1967.

Kerr, Walter. "A Majestic Joke from Harold Pinter." Review of *No Man's Land*, by Harold Pinter. *New York Times*, 21 November 1976.

Killinger, John. *World in Collapse*. New York: Dell, 1971.

Kitto, H. D. F. *Greek Tragedy*. 2d ed. 1939. Reprint. Garden City, N.Y.: Anchor-Doubleday, 1950.

Knapp, Bettina. *Maurice Maeterlinck*. Boston: Twayne, 1975.

Knowles, Dorothy. *French Drama of the Inter-War Years, 1918–1939*. New York: Barnes and Noble, 1968.

Kolb, James J. "Language, Sounds and Silence in Modern Theatre." Ph.D. diss., New York University, 1974.

Krutch, Joseph Wood. *"Modernism" in Modern Drama*. New York: Russell and Russell, 1953.

Lahr, John. "Pinter and Chekhov: The Bond of Naturalism." *Drama Review* 13, no. 2 (Winter 1968): 137–45. Reprinted in *Pinter: A Collection of Critical Essays*, edited by Arthur Ganz, 60–71. Twentieth Century Views. Englewood Cliffs, N.J.: Prentice-Hall, 1972.

———. "Pinter's Language." In *A Casebook on Harold Pinter's "The Homecoming,"* edited by John Lahr, 123–36. New York: Grove Press, 1971.

———. *Up against the Fourth Wall: Essays on Modern Theatre*. New York: Grove Press, 1968.

Lamont, Rosette. "Beckett's Metaphysics of Choiceless Awareness." In *Samuel Beckett Now*, edited by Melvin Friedman, 199–217. Chicago: Chicago University Press, 1970.

Langer, Lawrence L. *The Holocaust and the Literary Imagination*. New Haven, Conn.: Yale University Press, 1975.

Langer, Suzanne. *Feeling and Form*. New York: Charles Scribner's Sons, 1953.

———. *Philosophy in a New Key: A Study in the Symbolism of Reason, Rite and Art*. 3d ed. Cambridge, Mass.: Harvard University Press, 1942.

Lucas, F. L. *The Drama of Chekhov, Synge, Yeats and Pirandello*. London: Cassell, 1963.

Maeterlinck, Maurice. Preface. In his *Plays of Maurice Maeterlinck, 2d ser.*, translated by Richard Hovey, ix–xv. 1896. Reprint. Great Neck, N.Y.: Core Collection, 1977.

———. *Théâtre*. Vol. 1, *La Princesse Maleine, L'Intruse, Les Aveugles*. Brussels: P. Lacomblez, 1903.

———. *Théâtre*. Vol. 2, *Pelléas et Mélisande, Alladine et Palomides, Intérieur, La Mort de Tintagiles*. Paris: Bibliothèque Charpentier, 1929.

———. *Le Trésor des humbles*. Paris: Mercure de France, 1896.

Magarshack, David. *Chekhov the Dramatist*. New York: Hill and Wang, 1960.

Mallarmé, Stéphane. *Oeuvres complètes*. Edited by Henri Mondor and G. Jean-Aubry. Paris: Editions Gallimard, 1945.

Mauriac, Claude. *L'Alittérature contemporaine*. 2d ed. Paris: Editions Albin Michel, 1969.

Melchinger, Siegfried. *Anton Chekhov*. Translated by Edith Tarcov. World Dramatic Series. New York: Frederick Ungar, 1972.

Mercier, Vivian. *Beckett/Beckett*. New York: Oxford University Press, 1977.

Michaud, Guy. *Message poétique du symbolisme*. Paris: Nizet, 1947.

Minogue, Valerie. "Taking Care of the Caretaker." *Twentieth Century* 168 (September 1960): 243–48. Reprinted in *Pinter: A Collection of Critical Essays*, edited by Arthur Ganz, 72–77. Twentieth Century Views. Englewood Cliffs, N.J.: Prentice-Hall, 1972.

Mitchell, Breon. "Art in Microcosm: The Manuscript Stages of Beckett's *Come and Go*." *Modern Drama* 19, no. 3 (September 1976): 245–54.

Morse, Arthur D. *While Six Million Died: A Chronicle of American Apathy*. New York: Ace, 1967.

Moses, Montrose, J. *Maurice Maeterlinck: A Study*. New York: Duffield, 1911.

Mullen, Sammie Jo. "The Poetic Techniques of Maurice Maeterlinck." Ph.D. diss, New York University, 1974.

Nemirovitch-Dantchenko, Vladimir. *My Life in the Russian Theatre*. Translated by John Cournos. Boston: Little, Brown, 1936.

———. "Tchekhov and the Moscow Art Theatre." In *Anton Tchekhov: Literary and Theatrical Reminiscences*, translated and edited by S. S. Koteliansky, 135–38. 1927. Reprint. London: Benjamin Blom, 1965.

Oberg, A. K. "Edward Albee: His Language and Imagination." *Prairie Schooner* 40 (Summer 1966): 139–46.

Ortega y Gasset, José. *La deshumanización del arte e ideas sobre la novela*. Madrid: Revista de Occidente, 1925.

Palmer, John. *Studies in Contemporary Theatre*. 1927. Reprint. Freeport, N.Y.: Books for Libraries Press, 1969.

Paolucci, Anne. *From Tension to Tonic: The Plays of Edward Albee*. Cross-Currents. Carbondale: Southern Illinois University Press, 1972.

Pinter, Harold. "Between the Lines." Speech to the Seventh National Student Drama Festival in Bristol. *Sunday Times* (London), 4 March 1962, 25.

———. *"The Birthday Party" and "The Room."* New York: Grove Press, 1961.

———. *"The Caretaker" and "The Dumb Waiter."* New York: Grove Press, 1961.

———. *The Homecoming.* New York: Grove Press, 1965.

———. *"Landscape" and "Silence."* New York: Grove Press, 1970.

———. *No Man's Land.* New York: Grove Press, 1975.

———. *Old Times.* New York: Grove Press, 1971.

———. "Writing for Myself." *Twentieth Century* 168 (February 1961): 172–75.

Postic, Marcel. *Maeterlinck et le symbolisme.* Paris: Editions Nizet, 1970.

Pountney, Rosemary. "Samuel Beckett's Interest in Form: Structural Pattern in *Play.*" *Modern Drama* 19, no. 3 (September 1976): 237–44.

Quigley, Austin. *"The Dumb Waiter:* Undermining the Tacit Dimension." *Modern Drama* 21, no. 1 (March 1978): 1–11.

———. *The Pinter Problem.* Princeton, N.J.: Princeton University Press, 1975.

Radine, Serge. *Essais sur le théâtre, 1919–1939.* Geneva: Editions du Mont-Blanc, 1944.

Rhodes, D. A. *The Contemporary French Theatre.* New York: Appleton-Century-Crofts, 1942.

Robbe-Grillet, Alain. "Samuel Beckett ou le présence sur la scène." In his *Pour un nouveau roman.* Paris: Editions de Minuit, 1963, 95–107.

Robinson, Michael. *The Long Sonata of the Dead.* New York: Grove Press, 1969.

Rutenberg, Michael. *Edward Albee: Playwright in Protest.* New York: DBS, 1969.

Sartre, Jean-Paul. *Qu'est-ce que la littérature?* Paris: Editions Gallimard, 1948.

Schechner, Richard. "There's Lots of Time in *Godot.*" In *Casebook on "Waiting for Godot,"* edited by Ruby Cohn, 175–87. New York: Grove Press, 1967.

Sée, Edmond. *Le Théâtre français contemporain.* 2d ed. Paris: Librairie Armand Colin, 1933.

Simon, Pierre-Henri. *Histoire de la Littérature française au XXe siècle.* 2d ed. Paris: Librairie Armand Colin, 1963.

Skaftymov, A. "Principles of Structure in Chekhov's Plays." Translated by George McCracken Young. In *Chekhov: A Collection of Critical Essays,* edited by Robert Louis Jackson, 69–87. Twentieth Century Views. Englewood Cliffs, N.J.: Prentice-Hall, 1967.

States, Bert O. "Pinter's *Homecoming:* The Shock of Nonrecognition." *Hudson Review* 21, no. 3 (August 1968): 474–86. Reprinted in *Pinter: A Collection of Critical Essays,* edited by Arthur Ganz, 147–60. Twentieth Century Views. Englewood Cliffs, N.J.: Prentice-Hall, 1972.

Steiner, George. *After Babel: Aspects of Language and Translation.* New York: Oxford University Press, 1975.

———. *Language and Silence: Essays on Language, Literature and the Inhuman.* New York: Atheneum, 1976.

Stinson, John J. "Dualism and Paradox in the 'Puritan' Plays of David Storey." *Modern Drama* 20, no. 2 (June 1977): 131–43.

Storey, David. *"The Changing Room," "Home," "The Contractor."* New York: Bard-Avon, 1975.

Strindberg, August. *The Stronger.* In *Six Plays of Strindberg.* Translated by Elizabeth Sprigge. Garden City, N.Y.: Anchor-Doubleday, 1955.

Stuart, R. S. "John Gielgud and Edward Albee Talk about the Theatre." *Atlantic Monthly* 215, no. 4 (1965): 61–68. Reprinted in *Edward Albee: A Collection of Critical Essays*, edited by C. W. E. Bigsby, 112–23. Twentieth Century Views. Englewood Cliffs, N.J.: Prentice-Hall, 1975.

Styan, J. L. *Chekhov in Performance: A Commentary on the Major Plays*. Cambridge: Cambridge University Press, 1971.

Suzuki, D. T. *Zen Buddhism*. Edited by William Barrett. Garden City, N.Y.: Anchor-Doubleday, 1956.

Symons, Arthur. *The Symbolist Movement in Literature*. Rev. ed. 1913. New York: E. P. Dutton, 1958.

Taylor, Edmond. *The Strategy of Terror*. Rev. ed. Boston: Houghton Mifflin, 1942.

Taylor, John Russell. "Accident." *Sight and Sound* 35 (1966): 179–84.

———. "A Room and Some Views: Harold Pinter." In *Pinter: A Collection of Critical Essays*, edited by Arthur Ganz, 105–22. Twentieth Century Views. Englewood Cliffs, N.J.: Prentice-Hall, 1972.

———. "Pinter's Game of Happy Families." In *A Casebook on Harold Pinter's "The Homecoming,"* edited by John Lahr, 57–65. New York: Grove Press, 1971.

Valency, Maurice. *The Breaking String*. New York: Oxford University Press, 1966.

———. *The Flower and the Castle: An Introduction to Modern Drama*. New York: Macmillan, 1963.

Villiers de l'Isle-Adam, Jean-Marie. *Oeuvres complètes*. Vol. 4. Geneva: Slatkine Reprints, 1970.

Wagner, Richard. *On Music and Drama: A Compendium of Richard Wagner's Prose Works*. Translated by H. Ashton Ellis; edited by Albert Goldman and Evert Sprinchorn. New York: E. P. Dutton, 1964.

Wardle, Irving. "In a Land of Dreams and Actuality." Review of *No Man's Land*, by Harold Pinter. *Times* (London), 24 April 1975.

Way, Brian. "Albee and the Absurd: *The American Dream, The Zoo Story*." In *Edward Albee: A Collection of Critical Essays*, edited by C. W. E. Bigsby, 26–44. Twentieth Century Views. Englewood Cliffs, N.J.: Prentice-Hall, 1975.

Wellwarth, George. *The Theatre of Paradox and Protest*. Rev. ed. New York: New York University Press, 1971.

Wiesel, Elie. *One Generation After*. New York: Random House, 1965.

Wilson, Edmond. *Axel's Castle: A Study in the Imaginative Literature of 1870–1930*. New York: Charles Scribner's Sons, 1931.

Wittgenstein, Ludwig. *Philosophical Investigations*. Translated by G. E. M. Anscombe. New York: Macmillan, 1953.

———. *Tractatus logico-philosophicus*. Translated D. F. Pears and B. F. McGuiness. London: Routledge, 1961.

Wray, Phoebe. "Pinter's Dialogue: The Play on Words." *Modern Drama* 13, no. 4 (February 1971): 418–22.

Wysick, Max M. "Language and Silence in the Stage Plays of Samuel Beckett and Harold Pinter." Ph.D. diss., University of Colorado, 1972.

Yutang, Lin, editor. *The Wisdom of China and India*. New York: Modern Library, 1942.

Zimbardo, Rose A. "Symbolism and Naturalism in Edward Albee's *Zoo Story*." In *Edward Albee: A Collection of Critical Essays*, edited by C. W. E. Bigsby, 45–53. Twentieth Century Views. Englewood Cliffs, N.J.: Prentice-Hall, 1975.

Index

Adamov, Arthur, 103
Aeschylus, 23, 36
Albee, Edward: and Beckett, 156, 159, 166, 167, 168, 169, 170; and Bernard, 169; and Chekhov, 158, 159, 162, 165, 167, 169; and Maeterlinck, 166, 169; and Pinter, 156, 158, 160, 162, 165, 167, 168, 169; death, in plays of, 159, 160–61, 162; defamilarization (suprarealism), 159–62, 170; intrusions, 160; restricted surroundings, 159, 160; typifying techinques, 158–70; use of repetition, 166–68; use of silence, 12, 13, 33, 158–78, 179; use of symbols, 161; use of the unspeakable, 164; waiting, in plays of, 159, 160. Works: *All Over*, 158, 159, 160, 162, 163–64, 166, 167, 169; *A Delicate Balance*, 158–60, 162, 163, 164, 167–68, 169; *Listening*, 158, 160, 165–67, 169; *Tiny Alice*, 170; *Who's Afraid of Virginia Woolf?*, 20, 158, 159, 160, 161–62, 164, 165, 166, 167, 168, 169, 170; *The Zoo Story*, 19, 21, 158, 159, 160, 164, 165, 166, 167, 169, exegesis of, 170–77
Alladine et Palomides (Maeterlinck), 28, 29, 32, 33, 36, 38, 109
All Over (Albee), 158, 159, 160, 162, 163–64, 166, 167, 169
Âme en peine, L' (Bernard), 99
Andrieu, Jean-Marie, 34
Antoine, André, 78
Artifice of reality: definition of, 51. *See also* Chekhov; Pinter
Aveugles, Les (Maeterlinck), 21, 23, 28, 33, 36, 38, 39, 46, 108, 109

Balakian, Anna, 29–30, 38, 47, 48n.9
Baty, Gaston, 91, 101n.26. *See also* Bernard; Théâtre de l'inexprimé
Beckerman, Bernard, 51, 53, 82, 134, 154
Beckett, Samuel: and Albee, 100n.5, 156, 159, 166, 167, 168, 169, 170; and Bernard, 100n.5, 113, 117; and Chekhov, 110–12, 113, 114, 115, 117; and Maeterlinck, 108–10, 113, 114,

117; and Pinter, 100n.5, 130, 137–40, 146, 147; chaos, attitude toward and dramatization of, 113, 114, 117, 129, 170; colloquial language, 114–16; distinction between silences and Silence, 105–6, 116–17; influence on post-World War II drama, 104, 129–30, 131n.32; isolation, 105, 112, 113; language of cancellation, 106–8, 110, 129, 137; repetition, linguistic and structural, 106–7, 109, 110, 114–15, 118, 124, 130n.20; typifying techniques, 105–17; use of silence, 12, 13, 33, 104, 105–30, 179, 180; waiting, dramatization of, 108–10, 112, 118–29. Works: *En attendant Godot*, 18–19, 21, 24–25, 48n.22, 105, 106–7, 108–11, 112, 113–14, 115, 116–17, exegesis of, 118–29, 138, 159, 174; *Fin de partie*, 20, 105, 106, 108–9, 111–12, 113, 114, 115, 117, 138, 139–40, 157n.33, 159; *Footfalls*, 105, 116; *Happy Days*, 105, 106, 107–8, 109, 111, 112, 113, 115, 116, 117, 138; *L'Innommable*, 105; *Krapp's Last Tape*, 105, 110, 111, 112, 116, 117; *Nouvelles et textes pour rien*, 105
Bennett, Robert B., 175
Bentley, Eric, 129, 181
Bergson, Henri, 78–79, 80, 101n.26. *See also* Bernard
Bernard, Jean-Jacques: and Albee, 169; and Beckett, 100n.5, 113, 117; and Chekhov, 82–84, 88, 90, 98, 99; and Maeterlinck, 47, 81–82, 83, 86, 88, 90; and Pinter, 142, 146; Baty, relationship with, 91, 101n.26; confessions in the plays of, 84–87; distinction between silences and silence, 77; fairy tale in the plays of, 81, 92; evasion, 84, 85–86, 89; influence of Bergson on, 78–80, 82; influence of Freud on, 78–80, 82; influence of World War I on, 80–81, 82; silent scenes, 88, 90–91; suppression of speech, 77–78, 87–88, 89–91; typifying techniques, 78, 81–91; use of silence, 12, 13, 33, 77–100, 179. Works: *L'Âme en peine*, 99; *Les Enfants jouent*, 80; *L'Epicier*, 80; *Le Feu qui reprend mal*, 78, 80, 81, 82, 83, 84, 85, 90, 91;